The Christian Life:

Traditional Metaphors
and Contemporary Theologies

Harvard Dissertations in Religion

Editors

Margaret R. Miles
and
Bernadette J. Brooten

Number 29

The Christian Life:
Traditional Metaphors
and Contemporary Theologies

Harriet Crabtree

The Christian Life:

Traditional Metaphors
and Contemporary Theologies

Harriet Crabtree

Fortress Press   Minneapolis

THE CHRISTIAN LIFE:
TRADITIONAL METAPHORS
AND CONTEMPORARY THEOLOGIES
Copyright © 1991

The President and Fellows of Harvard College

Write to: Permissions, Augsburg Fortress, 426 S. Fifth St., Box 1209, Minneapolis, MN 55440.

Internal design: Chiron, Inc.
Cover design: Carol Evans-Smith

Library of Congress Cataloging-in-Publication Data

Crabtree, Harriet, 1958–
    The Christian life : the traditional metaphors and contemporary
theologies / Harriet Crabtree.
        p.   cm.—(Harvard dissertations in religion)
    Includes bibliographical references.
    ISBN 0-8006-7083-3 (alk. paper)
    1. Christian life—History. 2. Metaphor—Religious aspects.
I. Title. II. Series.
BV4490.C73 1991
248.4—dc20   91-27980
                                                                CIP

The paper used in this publication meets the minimum requirements of American National Standard for Information Sciences—Permanence of Paper for Printed Library Materials, ANSI Z329.48-1984.   ∞™

Manufactured in the U.S.A.   AF 1-7083
95   94   93   92   91   1   2   3   4   5   6   7   8   9   10

In Memory of

My Grandmother, Rhoda Keigwin Oliver
1904–1985

and

My Brother, Daniel Crabtree
1965–1983

Contents

Acknowledgments

I would like to thank my advisor Richard Niebuhr for his kindly and helpful guidance through the process of writing this thesis. I hope that something of his lightness of touch and eye for surprising detail have left their mark. I would also like to thank Margaret Miles for her guidance and beneficial suggestions, and Gordon Kaufman for his relentless efforts to get me to state the general with as much energy as I expend upon the particular. The bibliographic suggestions of Ralph Potter and Sharon Parks have also been of assistance to me, as has the extensive support (particularly the ordering of extensive inter-library loans and new purchases) provided by Charles Willard and his staff at Andover-Harvard Library.

Further back, stand others for whose teaching I am grateful, and whom I would like to thank retrospectively for encouraging me to pursue the studies that have resulted in this thesis: Leslie Houlden, Grace Jantzen, Graham Stanton, and Stewart Sutherland of the University of London, and Joyce Willcocks, Rosamund Pritchard, and "Alex" Alexander who taught me while I was at Lewes Priory.

This thesis is the final result of work conducted in the midst of three different Harvard communities: the Divinity School, the Committee on the Study of Religion, and the Center for the Study of World Religions. I would like to thank a number of people from each. I have been a member of the Center for the Study of World Religions since I first came to Harvard. Its community of people from different faiths and different countries has provided the best kind of study environment for which a scholar could hope. Thank you particularly to John Carman whose directorship fostered this atmosphere of collegiality, and who, together with Ineke Carman, has helped me clarify my thoughts about many issues.

The list of other friends in the three communities whom I should thank cannot be inclusive. Four fellow students have discussed the thesis all along the way and offered helpful criticisms and bibliography: Irit Averbuch, Ehud Ben-Or, Adina Davidovich, and Patricia Gleason. For their suggestions and for their good company, I have been most grateful. I would also like to thank Dianne Bazell, Susan Bruno, Steve Campagna-Pinto, Mary Condren, Deborah Finn, Deborah Haynes, Larry Kant, Mary McGee, Ken Rose, and Miranda Shaw. And on the bureaucratic front, I thank Maria Cedargren, Registrar of the Divinity School, for her friendly and energetic assistance on all matters, especially at the final stage.

None have helped me so much as my mother Cherry Baden-Powell, my father Jon Crabtree, and long time friend and fighter for the kingdom, Jim Stewart. Together with the other members of my family, and my friends Lenka Janiurek, Rosie Mestel, Phillipa Baker, and Iain Sankey, they have kept me going with kindly encouragement and useful criticism.

Some of my family have not lived to see me finish this thesis. My dear brother Dan, whose physical company on life's pilgrimage I miss keenly, but whose gentleness and composure in the face of death gave me a new vision of the depth and possibility of life. My grandmother, Rhoda Keigwin Oliver, who herself came to Radcliffe in the '20s, and encouraged me energetically in my studies to gain a doctorate—an opportunity that force of circumstance denied her fifty years ago. My grandfathers, Alan Oliver and Charles Crabtree. But the voices of the dead join with those of the living without discrimination in one's mind. It is in colloquy with them all that this thesis has been written.

Harriet Crabtree
June 1990

Short Titles

Information appears here for frequently used works which are cited by short title. A few short titles do not appear in this list, but in each instance full bibliography is given on the page(s) preceding such references. Abbreviations used in this volume for sources and literature from antiquity are the same as those used in *HTR* 80:2 (1987) 243–60. Some abbreviations from that list can be easily identified.

Austin-Sparks, *Our Warfare*
> T. Austin-Sparks, *Our Warfare* (London: Witness and Testimony, 1960).

Baggot, *Pilgrim*
> L. J. Baggott, *Pilgrim in the Modern World* (London: Allen and Unwin, 1963).

Barbour, *Myths, Models, and Paradigms*
> Ian G. Barbour, *Myths, Models, and Paradigms: A Comparative Study in Science and Religion* (1974; reprinted New York: Harper & Row, 1976).

Bartsch, *Kerygma and Myth*
> Hans Werner Bartsch, *Kerygma and Myth: A Theological Debate* (New York: Harper & Row, 1961).

Beachy, "Stewardship of Energy"
> Eleanor Beachy, "Stewardship of Energy," in Helen Alderfer, ed., *A Farthing in Her Hand: Stewardship for Women* (Scottdale, PA: Herald, 1964).

Besnard, "Le sens chrétien"
> A. M. Besnard, "Le sens chrétien du pèlerinage," *La Vie Spirituelle* 447 (February 1959) 147–84.

Billheimer, *Overcomers*
> Paul E. Billheimer, *Overcomers Through the Cross* (Wheaton, IL: Tyndale House, 1982).

Black, *Models and Metaphors*
> Max Black, *Models and Metaphors: Studies in Language and Philosophy* (Ithaca, NY: Cornell University Press, 1962).

Bloomfield, *Allegory*
> Morton W. Bloomfield, ed., *Allegory, Myth, and Symbol* (Harvard English Studies 9; Cambridge: Harvard University Press, 1981).

Boas, *Mind of Primitive Man*
> Franz Boas, *The Mind of Primitive Man* (New York: Macmillan, 1911).

Bregman, *Landscape of Faith*
> Lucy Bregman, *Through the Landscape of Faith* (Philadelphia: Westminster, 1986).

Briggs, *Theological Perspectives*
> E[dwin] A. Briggs, *Theological Perspectives of Stewardship* (Evanston, IL: The General Board of the Laity, Division of Stewardship and Finance of the United Methodist Church, 1969).

Briscoe, *Fullness*
> D. Stuart Briscoe, *The Fullness of Christ* (London: Marshall, Morgan & Scott, 1965).

Brown, *Image and Truth*
> Stephen J. Brown, *Image and Truth: Studies in the Imagery of the Bible* (Rome: Catholic Book Agency, 1955).

Bryant, *Heart in Pilgrimage*
> Christopher Bryant, *The Heart in Pilgrimage: Christian Guidelines for the Human Journey* (New York: Seabury, 1980).

Burkalow, "Call for Battle"
> Anastasia van Burkalow, "A Call for Battle Symbolism in Hymns," *The Hymn* 38 (April 1987) 14–17.

Burke, *Permanence and Change*
> Kenneth Burke, *Permanence and Change: An Anatomy of Purpose* (2d ed.; Los Altos, CA: Hermes, 1954).

Bushnell, *Women's Suffrage*
> Horace Bushnell, *Women's Suffrage: The Reform Against Nature* (New York: Scribner, 1870).

Bushnell, *God in Christ*
> Horace Bushnell, *God in Christ* (1849; reprinted New York: Garland, 1987).

Calver and Copley, *Fight of Your Life*
> Clive Calver and Derek Copley, *The Fight of Your Life* (Eastbourne, E. Sussex: Kingsway, 1986).

Cupitt, *Crisis of Moral Authority*
Don Cupitt, *Crisis of Moral Authority* (Philadelphia: Westminster, 1972).

Doherty, *Strannik*
Catherine de Hueck Doherty, *Strannik: The Call to Pilgrimage for Western Man* (Notre Dame, IN: Ave Maria, 1978).

Durkheim, *Elementary Forms*
Emile Durkheim, *The Elementary Forms of the Religious Life* (1915; reprinted New York: Free Press, 1965).

Edwards, *Images*
Jonathan Edwards, *Images or Shadows of Divine Things* (ed. Perry Miller; New Haven: Yale University Press, 1948).

Epp, *Joshua*
Theodore H. Epp, *Joshua Victorious by Faith* (Lincoln, NE: Back to the Bible, 1968).

Farley, *Requiem*
Edward Farley, *Requiem for a Lost Piety: The Contemporary Search for the Christian Life* (Philadelphia: Westminster, 1966).

Gammons, *Battle Stations*
Peter Gammons, *Battle Stations* (Eastbourne, E. Sussex: Kingsway, 1984).

Geertz, *Interpretation of Cultures*
Clifford Geertz, *The Interpretation of Cultures* (New York: Basic Books, 1973).

Getz, *Serving*
Gene A. Getz, *Serving One Another* (Wheaton, IL: Victor Books, 1984).

Hall, *Steward*
Douglas John Hall, *The Steward: A Biblical Symbol Come of Age* (New York: Friendship Press, for the Commission on Stewardship of the National Council of the Churches of Christ in the U.S.A., 1982).

Hall, "Mission as a Function"
Douglas John Hall, "Mission as a Function of Stewardship," in W. Donald Goodger, ed., *Spotlighting Stewardship* (Ontario: United Church of Canada, 1981).

Holifield, *History of Pastoral Care*
E. Brooks Holifield, *A History of Pastoral Care in America: From Salvation to Self-Realization* (Nashville: Abingdon, 1983).

James, *Pragmatism*
William James, *Pragmatism* (ed. Bruce Kuklick; Indianapolis: Hackett, 1981).

James, *Varieties*
William James, *The Varieties of Religious Experience: A Study in Human Nature* (New York: Macmillan, 1961).

5

John of Taizé, *Pilgrim of God*
  Brother John of Taizé, *The Pilgrim of God: A Biblical Journey* (Washington, DC: Pastoral, 1985).

Kauffman, *Challenge of Christian Stewardship*
  Milo Kauffman, *The Challenge of Christian Stewardship* (Scottdale, PA: Herald, 1955).

Kauffman, *Stewards of God*
  Milo Kauffman, *Stewards of God* (Scottdale, PA: Herald, 1975).

Kaufman, *Theological Imagination*
  Gordon D. Kaufman, *The Theological Imagination: Constructing the Concept of God* (Philadelphia: Westminster, 1981).

Lakoff and Johnson, *Metaphors*
  George Lakoff and Mark Johnson, *Metaphors We Live By* (Chicago: University of Chicago Press, 1980).

McFague, *Metaphorical Theology*
  Sallie McFague, *Metaphorical Theology: Models of God in Religious Language* (Philadelphia: Fortress, 1982).

McFague, *Models*
  Sallie McFague, *Models of God: Theology for an Ecological, Nuclear Age* (Philadelphia: Fortress, 1987).

Mc Kay, *Servants and Stewards*
  Arthur R. Mc Kay, *Servants and Stewards: The Teaching and Practice of Stewardship* (Philadelphia: Geneva, 1963).

Miles, *Practicing Christianity*
  Margaret R. Miles, *Practicing Christianity: Critical Perspectives for an Embodied Spirituality* (New York: Crossroad, 1988).

Niebuhr, *Responsible Self*
  H. Richard Niebuhr, *The Responsible Self: An Essay in Christian Moral Philosophy* (1963; reprinted San Francisco: Harper & Row, 1978).

Nietzsche, "Truth and Falsity"
  Friedrich Nietzsche, "On Truth and Falsity in Their Extramoral Sense" in Shibles, *Essays.*

Peace, *Pilgrimage*
  Richard Peace, *Pilgrimage: A Handbook on Christian Growth* (Grand Rapids, MI: Baker Book House, 1976).

Penn-Lewis, *Spiritual Warfare*
  Jessie Penn-Lewis, *The Spiritual Warfare* (Poole, Dorset: Overcomer, n.d.).

Pentecost, *Design*
  J. Dwight Pentecost, *Design for Discipleship* (Grand Rapids, MI: Zondervan, 1971).

Powell, *Complete Disciple*
  Paul W. Powell, *The Complete Disciple* (Wheaton, IL: Victor Books, 1982).

Price, *Victory*
> Roger Price, *Victory in Jesus* (Basingstoke, Hants.: Marshall, Morgan & Scott, 1982).

Saiving, "Human Situation"
> Valerie Saiving, "The Human Situation: A Feminine View," in Carol P. Christ and Judith Plaskow, eds., *Womanspirit Rising: A Feminist Reader in Religion* (San Francisco: Harper & Row, 1979).

Schaeffer, *Pollution*
> Francis Schaeffer, *Pollution and the Death of Man: The Christian View of Ecology* (1970; reprinted Wheaton, IL: Tyndale House, 1981).

Scupoli, *Spiritual Combat*
> Lawrence [Lorenzo] Scupoli, *The Spiritual Combat and a Treatise on Peace of the Soul* (rev. William Laster and Robert Mohan; New York: Paulist, 1978).

Segovia, *Discipleship*
> Fernando F. Segovia, ed., *Discipleship in the New Testament* (Philadelphia: Fortress, 1985).

Shibles, *Essays*
> Warren Shibles, ed., *Essays on Metaphor* (White Water, WI: Language, 1972).

Sobosan, "Pilgrimage Theology"
> Jeffrey G. Sobosan, "Pilgrimage Theology: A Scriptural Basis," *The Bible Today* (December 1973) 1400–1405.

Spring, *Ecology and Religion*
> David and Eileen Spring, eds., *Ecology and Religion in History* (San Francisco: Harper & Row, 1974).

Stedman, *Spiritual Warfare*
> Ray C. Stedman, *Spiritual Warfare* (Waco, TX: Word Books, 1975).

Swindoll, *Improving Your Serve*
> Charles R. Swindoll, *Improving Your Serve: The Art of Unselfish Living* (Waco, TX: Word Books, 1981).

Taylor, *Poems*
> Edward Taylor, *The Poems of Edward Taylor* (ed. Donald E. Stanford; New Haven: Yale University Press, 1960).

Timmerman, *Way*
> John H. Timmerman, *The Way of Christian Living* (Grand Rapids, MI: Eerdmans, 1987).

Wallis, *Into Battle*
> Arthur Wallis, *Into Battle: A Manual of the Christian Life* (Eastbourne, E. Sussex: Kingsway, 1973).

Wallis, *Agenda for Biblical People*
> Jim Wallis, *Agenda for Biblical People* (New York: Harper & Row, 1976).

White, *Fight*
>   John White, *The Fight* (Downers Grove, IL: InterVarsity, 1976).

Wiles, *Faith and the Mystery*
>   Maurice Wiles, *Faith and the Mystery of God* (Philadelphia: Fortress, 1982).

Wyon, *On the Way*
>   Olive Wyon, *On the Way: Some Reflections on the Christian Life* (London: SCM, 1958).

Preface

When I arrived at Harvard Divinity School eight years ago, I found myself in classes where I was requested to reflect upon "God" as a construct of the human imagination, to consider how we shape the divine in our own image (or desired image), and how this picture of the divine then affects us. The teaching and writings of the instructor in question amount to a sustained summons to appraise our inherited symbolism; to winnow out those symbols which provide no insight and guidance for our situation today,[1] and to espouse only those aspects of our own (and others') traditions which promote greater humanization and human flourishing.[2] This stance is a radical one and few Christian theologians have shown themselves so unequivocal in their identification of religious language as imaginative construct or in their willingness to invoke overtly a criterion of "humanization" in the process of symbol evaluation. The general call to evaluate inherited Christian symbols is, however, widespread. It is perhaps the keynote of much liberal theology of the last twenty years.

In one respect, the call is as old as Christianity itself. Insofar as the evaluation of our symbolization of God means asking what may "truly" be said or predicated of the divine by finite beings, the current discussion of how we may discuss God appropriately retraces and complements hundreds of years of discussions about the difficulties of applying human language to

---

[1] Gordon D. Kaufman, *Theology for a Nuclear Age* (Philadelphia: Westminster, 1985) 28.

[2] Ibid., 56; idem, *The Theological Imagination: Constructing the Concept of God* (Philadelphia: Westminster, 1981) 197–200.

God.[3] Now, as then, a multiplicity of different positions exists upon the matter of how our words for God relate to the "reality" of God. The core of observation remains the same: all language used of God and God's actions both describes and fails to describe.

The evaluation of inherited Christian symbols also involves assessment of the relative truth or merit of particular symbolizations of God, God's saving action, and the appropriate human response, which are found in the Bible and the various traditions of Christianity. One part of this process of assessment is the historical-critical task of establishing the priority of particular symbols or images on the basis of their greater historical authenticity. Like the discussion of the nature of language about God, this is not a new enterprise. There has always been the desire to establish what were the actual words and deeds of Jesus (or for that matter of Moses or other key figures) and to determine which doctrines were the earliest.[4] Regardless of their ideas of Scripture as inspired, infallible, etc., theologians have invariably made decisions about what constitutes the heart or "essence" of the canon, and interpreted the rest accordingly. The rival canons themselves emerged in the context of protracted disagreement about what constituted the authentic tradition, and the decisions about what should be included have been second guessed ever since. Thus Martin Luther, for example, was to suggest that the Epistle of James was "unapostolic" or out of keeping with the Gospel as he construed it. In the last hundred years, awareness of the findings of the various disciplines of biblical criticism has led to increased selectivity on the part of many Christians in their use of traditions about and sayings of Jesus. This, in turn, has led them to pick and choose accordingly among the ideas and doctrines that grew out of these traditions.

At another level, the process of evaluation involves the sifting of symbols according to perceived degree of importance. This kind of evaluation arises from a conviction that certain symbols of the tradition are more foundational than others—that they speak more directly or truly of the way things are, and that other symbols are less important (or even inaccurate) either because they

---

[3] "God" is the foundational symbol of the monotheistic traditions. The symbol is, in turn, interpreted and revised by means of subsidiary symbolizations. Beyond the question of the validity of particular ways of symbolizing the deity lies, necessarily, the question of the adequacy of "God" itself as a symbol of all that it is of ultimate worth.

[4] The assumption being that the earlier in the Christian tradition an idea appears, the more worthy it is—hence the extended discussions among New Testament scholars about, e.g., which titles for Jesus of Nazareth and which understandings of his nature and mission go back to his own self-understanding. A helpful overview of the criteria employed in assessing "authenticity" in the biblical context can be found in Norman Perrin and Dennis C. Duling, *The New Testament: An Introduction* (2d ed.; New York: Harcourt Brace Jovanovich, 1982).

are purely figurative or because they are time bound and replacable by a better contemporary alternative. Again, this kind of evaluation is not an entirely modern phenomenon. Contemporary Christians are not the first to notice that biblical writers such as Paul drew upon activities and ideas of the social world of their day in their attempts to convey the Christian message and that these figures do not exhaust or fully convey the message. Nor are they the first to note that the biblical writers do not seem to intend all language to be interpreted with the same level of literalness. The rise of allegorical exegesis was in part a recognition of the fact that many things exist in the biblical texts which cannot be taken at their face value. What *has* changed, however, is that the extent of the materials that many consider to need such exegesis has grown. For the kind of generic modern mind that Rudolf Bultmann, for example, describes in his various writings on myth, the entire cosmological (mythic in his terms) framework of the Bible has to be demythologized and reunderstood in terms of *Existenz*.[5]

The kinds of evaluation or theological prioritizing discussed thus far tend to be carried out with at least the assumption that there is some remaining authoritative high ground within the tradition from which other aspects can be adjudged authentic or inauthentic, foundational or ephemeral. But some modern theology moves beyond this internal discussion in its attempt to evaluate and reshape the symbols of the tradition. In recent years liberal and radical theologians and lay people have been subjecting the key images of God, Christ, human and world that they have inherited to increasingly sharp scrutiny. They have noted the human element in their creation and they have also been asking of the images how they may also, in turn, shape the consciousness of individual and society; how they may function to encourage a particular outlook on the world, and even lead us to act in certain ways. Convinced that the images do have this formative power, many have underlined the importance of rejecting those images which are believed to reflect and foster dangerous attitudes, and encouraging those which it is believed will have positive effects. They are the more motivated to do this by a sense of the extreme danger in which they believe society to be as a result of its apparent move toward ecological breakdown and nuclear destruction. The times are seen to provide an especially strong mandate for a reshaping of our vision of the divine. Although the criteria according to which the images are judged may have their roots in the Christian tradition, they may not be solely or explicitly Christian. Insofar as they reflect a humanist ethic which draws

---

[5] See, e.g., the essays by Rudolf Bultmann in Hans Werner Bartsch, ed., *Kerygma and Myth: A Theological Debate* (rev. ed.; New York: Harper & Row, 1961).

upon a number of different sources of ethical evaluation, there is a departure
from specifically internal Christian judgments.[6]

Most theologians engaged in this kind of project are aware that it is, at
least in its self-consciousness and thoroughgoingness, alien to the spirit of
Christianity as it has been manifested in most of its forms throughout history.
They realize that in the eyes of more conservative believers it may appear
that they are setting themselves up as glorified symbol brokers, claiming an
overview that belongs only to the divine. Somewhere God laughs at the
cosmic presumption of it all. The whole enterprise may perhaps be seen to
be the product of a rejection of any notion of revelation as a given and as the
fruit of a faith in the rights and powers of human reason which a good part of
the Christian tradition has devoted much attention to ruling impossible.

Sometimes an uncomfortable suspicion is voiced that if one lays bare the
constructed nature of the divine image, it may seem as though God is nothing
but a fiction. By drawing attention to the element of the human imagination,
one may undermine the very belief in God that would lead other people to be
interested in the reshaping project that one holds so dear; God will appear as
no more than a culturally potent symbol for the motivation and sanctioning of
certain behaviors, and the moment God is perceived as such God will lose all
power.[7] Few theologians, of course, intend to go to quite such heights or
depths of reductionism. They have no wish to say that God is merely the sum
total of certain human concepts and desires. With some vigor they claim a
part of the great heritage of analogical thinking, or of the via negativa, and
continue to express belief in a divinity that somehow transcends our human
constructions, yet has some real continuity with them. Like Ian Barbour they
are insistent that they are maintaining a "critical realism" that affirms the
creative dimension of symbol while also affirming that it has some real ontological basis.[8] Whether this position is convincing to others, particularly to
the laity, and whether it can coexist with a lively faith remains to be seen.
Wayne Proudfoot is typical of those writers who feel this may not be the
case, arguing that the experience of the religious person (theist) is one in

---

[6] Some might argue that Christians have never exercised a "purely Christian" criticism of
their tradition—they have always supplemented their biblical and ecclesiastical teachings with
ethical reflection which owes much to the culture in which they find themselves. There may be a
good deal of accuracy to this assessment. Nevertheless, it remains true to say that this drawing
upon diverse sources for ethical evaluation appears to be on the increase.

[7] Upon which paradox, H. Richard Niebuhr commented: "The instrumental value of faith for
society is dependent upon faith's conviction that it has more than instrumental value" (*The Kingdom of God in America* [Chicago: Willett, Clark & Co., 1937] 12).

[8] Barbour, *Myths, Models and Paradigms: A Comparative Study in Science and Religion* (New
York: Harper & Row, 1974) 37–38; 172–81.

which God is apprehended in a way that approximates to the process of perception, rather than that of appreciating fiction;[9] a naive realism is at work which resists mightily the metaphorizing attitudes of the theologian. The worry is that this trusting naivety may turn out to be the backbone of religion, and in seeking to "educate" it, the theologian may destroy the religious impulse itself. At this point the theologian must surely ask herself what she is up to in proposing a resymbolizing of the divine and of the symbolic structures that cluster around the central symbol of God. Who is she proposing should follow this project through? Is it only for the intellectual elite—for those who have "passed through" the more literal stages of faith and emerged as the gnostics of the modern day?

This dissertation is intended as a contribution to the study of the ways that we use certain symbolic structures to organize our religious thinking and our lives in general, and to the overall debate concerning what it means to speak of appraising and renewing these structures. In broad terms it follows the lines outlined so optimistically in the prospectus in 1985. It remains an exploration of the ways that contemporary writers of popular theologies of the Christian life use the guiding images or ideas of servanthood, stewardship, fruitbearing, warfare, athletic contest, and pilgrimage, to convey their picture of the theological cosmos, to highlight certain aspects of human existence in the world, to explore the different moments of the Christian life, and to encourage certain dispositions and virtues. It looks at some of the historical and personal factors that contribute to the favor or disfavor with which the images are viewed at a particular time. It also addresses the question of precisely what it means for Christians to evaluate inherited images and to propose changes and additions to their language about God and about their lives in relation to God. What shall the criteria for evaluation be? Is it even realistic to expect people to accept the kind of changes in religious symbolization that have been discussed above?

In a number of respects, however, the direction of the dissertation has shifted since the prospectus. It was originally intended to show how each of the models chosen entailed clear theological and moral implications and could be judged good or bad accordingly, either across the board or according to circumstance. Fresh from classroom discussions where broad statements were often made by students (including myself) about the goodness and badness of particular symbols because of their effects on the individual and society—King bad, Mother good; Christus Victor triumphalist, Christ the suffering servant correct—I was inclined to look for straightforward, one-

[9] Wayne Proudfoot, *Religious Experience* (Berkeley: University of California Press, 1985) 215.

on-one correlations between images and world views and to make broad assumptions about how a given model might, for example, lead to specific psychological or social problems for particular groups within the church. I expected to find, for example, that "pilgrimage" always was set in a dualistic world view, necessarily entailed a low estimation of the physical world, and would lead people to think and behave accordingly. There is no doubt that the images and ideas do affect people, but perhaps the implications of particular images are not as clear as one might initially think. Up to a point, each model does produce certain constant theological traits and emphases. For example, wherever one has the model of the Christian as servant/subject of the master/king, one does tend to find a stress on transcendent power as the chief characteristic of God, and grateful obedience as the prized disposition of the human. However, it is apparent that while there are constants, the models produce radically different theologies when understood in different contexts. They alter shape according to the biblical passages and other external influences which inform the writer's development of the theme. It makes a terrific difference whether you see yourself battling against evil in the world to establish the kingdom, or whether your focus is the conquest of your own passions.[10] This phenomenon of multiple developments of the same basic metaphor will be given particular attention in the chapter on pilgrimage. We will see, for example, that pilgrimage understood in terms of the Exodus journey or of Abraham's travels, goes in a very different direction from pilgrimage developed with the dualistic cosmology of Hebrews or the Epistle to Diognetus as its informing philosophy. The metaphor does not simply give rise to the cosmology, nor become taken over by it, it is developed with its aid. The resulting virtues or dispositions stressed are also different. The highlighting of variations as well as general similarities in the use of the images has become, therefore, one of the tasks of the primary material chapters.

A related observation is that, in the hortatory context, the models can be made to lead to pedagogical and ethical conclusions that seem surprisingly unallied to the cosmological or theological pictures that are simultaneously spun out with their aid. The mythic picture of principalities and powers need not appear in discussions of soldierly discipline of the self; the writer may harken back to the older idea of *aretē* involving a fight with one's own pas-

---

[10] The difference here is well pointed by Kenneth E. Kirk's remark about the monks of Basil's time: "The monk's warfare is more a fighting to God than a fighting for God; his interest is not so much in rescuing and conserving a fallen world, as in achieving for himself the fullness of spiritual experience" (*The Vision of God: The Christian Doctrine of the Summum Bonum* [Cambridge: James Clarke, 1934] 120).

sions. Paul drew upon a figure of his day and it is not surprising that writers should find it relatively easy to revert to the rhetoric of that model, leaving aside such cumbersome Christian notions as grace with relative ease.[11] Similarly, stewardship can be developed with a full theological context or it can devolve into the kind of discussion of being a steward of one's own potentialities or gifts which would fit easily into a context of humanistic psychology, or indeed into the broad category of what H. Richard Niebuhr referred to as the "man-the-maker" image.[12] In the chapter on stewardship, special attention will be paid to this phenomenon of decontextualized usage, particularly as it applies to women. One might well want to put forward the argument that what one is dealing with in Christian life literature that uses these models are in fact perennial ethical models developed to differing degrees with appropriate theological frameworks and "transformed" in the Christian context. The transformation is, however, sometimes awkward; we shall see again and again how difficult it is for the writers to tailor the models to make room for grace and for love and sacrifice of a spontaneous kind. In a number of cases the transformation is barely attempted. The kind of optimism about the human will and reason which informs contemporary secular humanistic psychologies has made deep inroads into Christian thinking about the religious life and has lessened the need to transform non-Christian ethical models (which assume the ability to strive for the good) to make room for the fact of weakness of the will vitiated by radical evil. This phenomenon is well documented in such works as E. Brooks Holifield's *A History of Pastoral Care in America: From Salvation to Self-Realization* (Nashville: Abingdon, 1983). The literature I have studied provides an extensive attestation of the degree to which there has been a "triumph of the therapeutic" in liberal Christianity—and even in more conservative quarters.[13]

The other point that impressed itself strongly upon me as I continued to read through the materials is that in almost no case do ethical injunctions of any specificity arise directly from the images. Stewardship, for example, may well inculcate a disposition of care and carefulness for self, others and earth, but the precise ramifications of this are far from clear. In the chapter on this image, I go beyond the confines of the main genre under considera-

[11] It is interesting to compare his use of the language of warfare with that, e.g., of his contemporary Seneca. Seneca used the metaphor of the philosopher as soldier extensively. See Gerard B. Lavery, "Metaphors of War and Travel in Seneca's Prose Works," *Greece and Rome* 27 (1980) 147–57.

[12] H. Richard Niebuhr, *The Responsible Self: An Essay in Christian Moral Philosophy* (1963; reprinted San Francisco: Harper & Row, 1978) 49.

[13] The term is that of Philip Rieff, *The Triumph of the Therapeutic: Uses of Faith after Freud* (2d ed.; Chicago: University of Chicago Press, 1987).

tion to point up this fact—to show that the lack of connection between model and moral code is not simply a result of the brevity of treatment that popular theologies provide—rather, this problem becomes clearer and clearer as one moves in the direction of more carefully formulated ethical treatises. James Gustafson has in the past emphasized that Christ is not all-sufficient as a source of moral guidance for the Christian, nor is the Bible an exhaustive repository of moral guidelines.[14] The same cautions need to be sounded with regard to the images under discussion in this thesis. They may well act, as Clifford Geertz says do all religious symbols, "to establish powerful, pervasive, and long-lasting moods and motivations,"[15] but we need to mark the difference between the establishment of disposition and motivation and that of specific ethical decisions and injunctions.

I had originally set about the study and evaluation of each image as an independent block; however, their interconnectedness rapidly became apparent. One model inevitably shades into others when a particular aspect or context is stressed. Servanthood, for example, passes easily into soldiery when the service is construed to be service to a King at war. On the other hand, it passes over into stewardship if the King is felt to be at peace and desiring the tilling of the lands. Pilgrimage can develop seamlessly into warfare when battling the trials on the journey is the key theme, or into a form of nomadic stewardship if it is developed with the aid of the image of the sojourner.

Even insofar as each image is homogenous or has a constant theme, its evaluation still cannot take place in isolation. This is because the images interlock to a high degree—standing in judgment upon each other's limitations and together forming what appears to be a well-rounded whole.[16] This partial quality of each image is well underlined by the way that authors using only or mainly one image have to torture it to spin out a whole theology and to address every dimension of the Christian life within its Procrustean confines. Bathos frequently results in the case of the more limited models. The books themselves may be seen as an eloquent testimony both to the fruitfulness of a given image and its shortcomings or limits. The phenomenon of structural limitation will be given special attention in the chapters on horticultural and athletic imagery.

It will be argued in the final chapter that one of the dangers of piecemeal

---

[14] Gustafson, *Christ and the Moral Life* (1979; reprinted Chicago: University of Chicago Press, 1968) 187.

[15] Geertz, *The Interpretation of Cultures* (New York: Basic Books, 1973) 90.

[16] My choice to focus on works where one model was dominant obscured this fact for me initially. It becomes far clearer in the more general books on living the Christian life.

evaluation and substitution of symbols is an unbalancing of the whole that together they have traditionally provided, without the providing of a new balance. In the primary material chapters I offer some preliminary evaluative comments on each image. The evaluations draw upon the criticisms offered by contemporary theologians but represent primarily my own perspective; namely, that the world was created by a God (force/spirit/being) that intends and supports the development of all beings to the fullest extent of their potential. This potential I understand in terms drawn from the Christian tradition (in particular from such pictures of Christ as the New Testament provides) and from the secular humanist tradition. I understand the fullest form of human life to be one in which one's freedom, dignity, compassion, wisdom, and ability to live amicably with others are brought to fruition. In the preliminary chapters, the images of the religious life are discussed in terms of their possibilities for fostering these. They will also be examined in their capacity to speak truly to the dimension of evil in the world and within the individual, and to assist the Christian in standing firm against these. Obviously this provisional sketch of the criteria of evaluation begs a number of questions. It is entirely preliminary. The task of evaluation, and of establishing the criteria for evaluation, is taken up and discussed at length in the final chapter.

In most chapters, attention is paid to any distinctive features that may appear in texts written by women. The potential possibilities and dangers for women of particular modes of developing the models are also considered. This reflection on women and the use of the images is not without its problems. It is debatable whether the texts by women authors have anything particularly distinctive about them. For the most part, they are written by women who feel themselves in perfect continuity with the worldview and outlook of their male counterparts. They are not conscious of having a separate vision. Only in quite recent times do we find many women writers of popular Christian theologies incorporating explicit reflection on their femaleness and on the possibility that they might contribute to a different vision of Christianity (indeed, of the world). Nevertheless, there are aspects of the texts written by women that seem to call for special comment. For example, as we shall see in the chapter on warfare, only one of the authors thinks of the *militia Christi* as a peaceful army of occupation—that author is a woman.[17] And in the writings on stewardship, the domestic situation of some of the women authors leads them to develop the idea of stewardship in a highly distinctive way to give meaning to all aspects of their lives as homemakers. Not only that, but we see a number of the women authors also

---

[17] JoAnne Sekowsky, *Spiritual Warfare: Strategy for Winning* (Lynwood, WA: Aglow Publications, 1983) 9.

developing the idea of their stewardship in new and radical ways to sanction the nurture and furtherance of their own "talents" of intellect and ability. Responsible stewardship is invoked as a mandate for their entry into the previously male world of the public workplace.

In discussing these texts by women one needs, therefore, to be sensitive to a number of issues: the way that the writings may reflect the authors' absorption of the dominant patriarchal values of their day; the way that—by contrast—the texts may reveal the use of traditional images for untraditional and even radical purposes; and the way that the texts may bear the imprint of a different (generally domestic) experience of reality and offer insights which (while still within the patriarchal sphere) complement those of male writers of the same era and social context.

Discussing the issue of the potential dangers and possibilities of particular images for women, one is confronted by yet another set of difficulties. For example, What is the vantage point from which one evaluates? I evaluate from the perspective of liberal feminism with its rejection of all aspects of culture which appear to support the picture of woman as subordinate to man or as less capable than him in any respect. Anita Bryant would be unlikely to share my resultant idea of what is helpful to women. Also, it needs to be noted that a given image may have been consoling and encouraging to women at particular times, but may not be at all helpful in the present. For example, for women whose culture restricted them to a subordinate role, it may have been helpful to think of themselves as epitomizing the glorious servanthood exemplified by Christ. If you have no chance of escape from servitude, its glorification may perhaps offer you a temporary consolation. However, to continue to glorify the spiritual posture of servanthood may be to help perpetuate its physical actuality. The image may become dangerous.[18] Given this fact, one needs to be sensitive to the ever changing relationship between metaphor and culture.

The Focus, Materials, and Scope of the Project

The Focus

Much of the literature currently being produced on metaphor, image, and symbol in theology is theoretical in bent. It examines the nature of religious language and attempts to appropriate relevant contemporary developments in

---

[18] Joseph Vogt (*Ancient Slavery and the Ideal of Man* [2d ed.; Oxford: Blackwell, 1974]) devotes a chapter, "*Ecce Ancilla Domini*," to illustrating how the religious metaphors of *ancilla* and *servus dei* may have affected people's perception of the human institution of slavery, lending it an air of acceptability.

linguistics and philosophy.[19] In such works, necessarily, scant attention is paid to the details of the actual use of the images by individual writers. It would seem that the time is ripe for some more detailed studies which test theory upon specific cases.

As already stated, this thesis arose from an initial interest in the general topic of the role of particular images in theological literature, and a desire to examine just how they were actually used by specific writers in specific contexts. The decision that had to be made was in *what* context to study the topic. One possibility would have been to have taken a single image and looked at the ways in which it had been treated in a broad spectrum of theological writings over the centuries. However, this would have precluded any comparative analysis of the way that such images are used. The study of a number of different images throughout Christian history could have resulted, by contrast, in shallow analysis and unfounded generalizations. Instead, I have opted to study a number of images or metaphors as used in a specific type of text from the modern period. I have tried to give enough historical information to put these in some context, but no claims to completeness are made.

The Choice of Period

The primary materials examined in this thesis are, except for those used to provide historical context, from the period since 1956. There are two reasons for this. The first is that this period of time is particularly interesting because of the spectrum of different treatments of similar themes produced by its writers. Its literature reveals that many Christians have been engaged in a process of reassessing the models for the religious life with which their tradition has provided them, consciously rejecting certain traditional models as restrictive or oppressive and looking to see which others may be most appropriate for them. By contrast, other works from the same period attest to a continued faithfulness on the part of many to traditional images, and often to a belligerent reassertion of them in response to the kind of appraisal and change just described. In short, the period provides us with a wide array of divergent treatments for study.

The second reason for this choice of the period since the mid-1950s is practical. The first year of the current National Union Catalogue is 1956, and materials dating from this year tend to be better catalogued. Since I was aware that many of my materials would not be available through Harvard, being able to locate and obtain them easily was an important consideration.

[19] See, e.g., the recent study by Garrett Green, *Imagining God: Theology and the Religious Imagination* (San Francisco: Harper & Row, 1989).

The Choice of Genre

Metaphors and models are present in all forms of religious writing. One could profitably study their contemporary use in the liturgy, in sermons, in hymns, in Christian fiction and poetry, and in systematic theology. Yet the place where they seem to appear in the most thoroughgoing way is in the more theological sector of the kinds of books and popular magazine articles traditionally classified under such headings as "The Christian Life," "Religious and Inspirational Literature," or "Devotional Literature." Authors of such works will frequently construct an entire theology in *nuce* around the kernel of one image or theme such as stewardship. For this reason alone, such literature provides an extremely interesting case study. Within their pages the strengths and limitations of certain images or approaches to an image become rapidly apparent.

There is perhaps another reason for focusing on this type of text—especially on the books. Together with the pulpit and church study group, they provide the theological school of the majority of middle-class, practicing Christians in America.[20]

---

[20] Also of sections of the middle and working class in Britain. "Middle class" in the American context includes what in a British context is sometimes referred to with delicately graded snobbery as the "upper working class." In their old—but still valuable—study, Louis Schneider and Sanford M. Dornbusch (*Popular Religion: Inspirational Books in America* (1958; reprinted Midway Reprint, 1973]) had the following to say concerning the readership of texts similar to many of those under discussion in this thesis: "[T]he readership studies make it clear that book readers are people of education and income above minimal level. Internal evidence reinforces the belief that the readers have middle-class backgrounds or aspirations. Thus, throughout the pages of Peale and Blanton's *The Art of Real Happiness* appear such persons as overstrained business executives, chemical engineers afflicted with great anxiety, and doctors suffering from gastric ulcers . . ." (pp. 10–11). I would want to modify their conclusions slightly based on the internal evidence of some of the texts that I have used. In the years since 1958, the working class audience for book length popular theological literature would appear to have grown, presumably due to rising literacy rates. The same audience to whom tract literature was once (and is still) largely addressed, also purchases such works as Hal Lindsey's *Combat Faith* (New York: Bantam Books, 1986). On the intended audience for the evangelical popular theologies, James Davison Hunter (*American Evangelicalism: Conservative Religion and the Quandry of Modernity* [New Brunswick, NJ: Rutgers University Press, 1983] 93) remarks that it is only since the second world war that so much has been directed toward the person on the street. Although the works may be geared to particular audiences, they often have in common with the devotional texts that Margaret Miles (*Practicing Christianity: Critical Perspectives for an Embodied Spirituality* [New York: Crossroad, 1988] 9) has studied, the tendency to "claim implicitly or explicitly to be universally valid," to exhibit a "universalizing rhetoric [which] . . . operates to steer the reader away from questions about the gender, social location, education, and state of health of the manual's ideal reader."

The Choice of Images

The images were selected according to a number of different criteria. The first was empirical. I compiled a provisional list of biblical images of the Christian life and worked through the *Catholic Periodical and Literature Index*, and the *Christian Periodical Index*, noting all relevant articles whose titles included the terms or looked as though they might deal with the image in a substantial way.[21] I then went through *Religious Books 1872–1982*, the most recent volumes of *Religious Books in Print* and *Religious and Inspirational Books and Serials in Print*, and the catalogue of the British Library for the years from 1956 to the present—again combing the titles for the images.[22] The books and articles from which the selections were made were those by North American and British authors working within the Christian tradition.

The majority of titles did not indicate the use of any key image. The present vogue, apparently in both Protestant and Catholic circles, is to choose titles that speak softly of maturity, wholeness, wholisticness, joy, etc. The psychotherapist is not far away.[23] Still other works had highly idiosyncratic titles, such as *Clowning in Rome*.[24] Popular theological writers often seem to opt for whimsical titles. Nevertheless, a very high proportion of the works and articles listed declared clearly in their titles or descriptions that they dealt with a given image. Warfare in its various forms topped the list in conservative Protestant quarters.[25] Stewardship ran it a close second among

---

[21] Nancy A. Logan, ed., *The Catholic Periodical and Literature Index* (Haverford, PA: Catholic Library Association, 1967–); *Christian Periodical Index* (Buffalo: Christian Librarians' Fellowship, 1956–). I also consulted G. Fay Dickerson and Steven W. Cole, eds., *Religion Index One: Periodicals* (Evanston, IL: American Theological Library Association, 1977–), however this publication lists mainly articles in scholarly journals, and was of limited assistance.

[22] *Religious Books in Print: A Reference Catalogue* (London: Whitaker & Sons, 1985); *Religious and Inspirational Books and Serials in Print* (New York: Bowker, 1987); *Religious Books 1876–1982* (New York: Bowker, 1983).

[23] I ordered up a representative sample of these generic offerings and discovered that quite frequently they turned out, on inspection, to take the journey or pilgrimage as their central image. On the phenomenon of the "psychologization" of guides to the Christian life, and the psychological subjectivism that tends to accompany it; see, e.g., Hunter, *Evangelism*, 93–101, and Rieff, *Triumph of the Therapeutic*, 232–61.

[24] Henri J. M. Nouwen, *Clowning in Rome: Reflections on Solitude, Celibacy, Prayer, and Contemplation* (Garden City, NY: Doubleday, 1979).

[25] The meaning of labels such as "conservative," "liberal," and "radical," is to some extent relative to the writer's own position. These terms are notoriously difficult to define, although the reader generally has a perfectly good idea what is meant. In this thesis, the term "radical" is applied to those such as Rosemary Radford Ruether who, in the author's view, sit on the borderline betwixt a prophetic Christianity and a secular socialism or perhaps a new religion. "Liberal" is applied to writers such as Letty Russell who take on board many of the insights of the political left and are strongly informed by the presuppositions of Protestant modernism. On

mainstream Protestant writers, but appeared very rarely in Catholic materials. Pilgrimage was noticeably more popular among Catholics and liberal Protestants than it was in conservative Protestant circles.[26] Athletic metaphor abounded among both liberal and conservative Protestants but appeared to have made little inroad into Catholic literature. Servanthood was a common theme, as was discipleship, although curiously few books have discipleship in their titles. Oddest in its absence was the image of the "citizen." Even in works on the Kingdom, the writers tended to leave aside the imagery of citizenship, using instead language of servanthood.[27] Likewise, the less overtly pictorial notion of "vocation," did not feature largely.[28]

As a result of this research, I decided to focus on the prevalent models of servanthood, stewardship, warfare, athletic contest, and pilgrimage, prefacing them with a general discussion of the foundational concepts of discipleship and imitation. I also selected one less prominent metaphorical domain, that of horticultural imagery. In the latter case, the criterion was a concern to examine some of the reasons that can militate against an image being developed beyond a certain point. In the context of discipleship, membership of the Family of God and the Body of Christ are also discussed, since discipleship is rarely considered out of this communal context. Since they are there to give context, they are not as fully discussed as other images. The short chapter on discipleship and imitation is, itself, primarily intended to provide context for the more overtly metaphorical conceptions of the Christian life which are treated in the chapters that follow.

I found that at the end of the day, I was operating almost entirely with Protestant literature, except in the case of the pilgrimage chapter. It would

---

liberals, see William R. Hutchinson, *The Modernist Impulse in American Protestantism* (1976; reprinted Oxford: Oxford University Press, 1982) 1–11. The term "conservative" is applied to all groups or individuals who continue to affirm the articles of the creed with a minimum of explanatory caveats, and for whom the Bible (and in the Catholic case, tradition) takes precedence over the claims of experience in the hermeneutical circle. Except where an author has called himself or herself "evangelical," I tend to avoid that term. I have also avoided use of the term "fundamentalist."

[26] Pilgrimage and journey are key metaphors in much writing by those interested in faith development and the psychological dimensions of religious experience. In the chapter on pilgrimage I have stretched the category of primary materials to illustrate this fact.

[27] One major exception is John Driver, *Kingdom Citizens* (Scottdale, PA: Herald, 1980). "Building" also appears in passing, but again, is rarely a key idea. It appears to lack possibilities for development.

[28] Vocation, "calling," is perhaps a subsidiary concept. It follows upon the initial commitment to discipleship and service, and clarifies the issue of to what service the servant is called. Works dealing with the issue of vocation are generally somewhat specialized, assuming the basic theological groundwork has already been given.

appear that Catholic devotional or popular theologies have a tendency to focus to a greater degree upon the persons of the saints or Holy Family, while Protestants (esp. American Protestants) are as fond of tropes as ever their pilgrim ancestors were. Perhaps the initial choice of thesis topic reflected an unwitting Protestant bias on the author's own part which led necessarily to selecting a preponderance of Protestant materials.

Characteristics of the Literature

One of the effects of the recent resurgence of evangelical Christianity in America has been the appearance in bookstores of popular theologies in increasingly large numbers. Sometimes they rest next to Catholic texts on the Christian life. Often they sit side by side with the devotional literature of the New Age: an array of assorted wisdoms on living wisely and well. Dipping into the books on the stand, the theologian may recollect with mixed emotion the youthful piety that first led her or him to study theology. The books have a vigor and purposefulness alien to much contemporary high theology. They have the satisfying quality of the manual: the world in a book that fits in your hand; theology and advice mingled in a most appealing and integrated way. At the same time, they can depress—ridiculous, perhaps, in their attempts to encapsulate all of life into a small swatch of pages. At their worst they can breath a narrow piety that reminds one of the worst and driest of one's tradition.[29]

The texts studied in this thesis all address the one who seeks assistance in understanding and living the Christian life. Their authors assume a lay readership without theological training and so they tend to spell out their theologies very clearly with extensive biblical references, and to eschew the finer and more controversial points of theology where possible.[30] Chuck

[29] Oswald Sanders, *The Servant as His Lord* (1957; reprinted Fort Washington, PA: Christian Literature Crusade, 1972) is an example of the kind of book that had this effect on me. The edition itself is produced on cheap, already discoloring, paper with cramped print. The admirable reason for this is no doubt to make it available cheaply to souls in need, but the effect is depressing. The dismal effect is compounded by the fact that the author has a didactic and somewhat dry style, unrelieved by image and example. His text is also peppered with such terse statements as: "If we are self-willed when God tries to break us and will do anything rather than submit, we shall never be of any use to nourish other souls; we shall only be centres of craving self-pity, discrediting the character of God" (p. 122).

[30] On the rise of theological materials offering the laity interpretations of the Christian life and assistance in how to live it, see Helen C. White, *The Tudor Books of Private Devotion* (1951; reprinted Westport, CT: Greenwood, 1979) esp. the "Introduction" (pp. 3–10), "The Medieval Inheritance," (pp. 11–30), and "Guides to the Devout Life," (pp. 149–72).

Swindoll, for example, tackles the issue of what it means to say that God is committed to conforming us to the image of His son. He writes,

> Exactly what does our heavenly Father want to develop within us? What is the "image of His Son"? Well, rather than get neck deep in tricky theological waters, I believe the simple answer is to be found in Christ's own words . . . the Son of Man did not come to be served, but to serve, and to give His life as a ransom for many (Mark 10.45).
> No mumbo jumbo. Just a straight-from-the-shoulder admission. He came to serve and to give.[31]

However, despite the tendency to resolve some of the finer theological points by ignoring them, it would not be true to characterize the texts as theologically simplistic. It is remarkable how much the authors are often able to convey in clearly understandable form. This is true particularly of writers usually defined as "evangelical." From the earliest times, American evangelical preachers and writers have tried to ensure that the faith was intellectually open to all. Men such as Charles Finney and Dwight L. Moody pioneered ways of preaching and writing intended to make the basics of evangelical theology easily appropriable by even the least educated. Nathan Hatch notes that

> evangelical scholars are far more likely to speak and write to a popular evangelical audience than to pursue serious scholarship. This pattern is quite evident in the extraordinary contingent of evangelicals who first did graduate work in theology at Harvard in the 1940s and 1950s. The collective experience of Merrill Tenney, Samuel Schultz, Roger Nicole, Kenneth Kantzer, John Gerstner, Harold Kuhn, Paul Jewett, Glenn Barker, and E.J. Carnell demonstrates a much greater concern with instructing the evangelical rank and file than in engaging in serious theological scholarship. . . . Evangelicals characteristically subordinate the task of first-order thinking to tasks that seem to affect more tangibly the lives of people at large.
> Even when facing the most serious and complex intellectual issues, the instinct of evangelicals is to play them out before a popular audience. . . .[32]

---

[31] Charles R. Swindoll, *Improving Your Serve: The Art of Unselfish Living* (Waco, TX: Word Books, 1981) 18. Chuck Swindoll is a pastor in the Evangelical Free Church. Based in California, he has an international "radio ministry" and writes prolifically. If sales are anything to go by, he is one of the most popular authors in the mainstream evangelical community.

[32] Hatch, "Evangelicalism as a Democratic Movement," in George Marsden, ed., *Evangelicalism and Modern America* (Grand Rapids, MI: Eerdmans, 1984) 79. This is, from the laity's point of view, an advantage. Hatch, however, argues that as a result of this concentration on the immediate needs of the evangelical populace, evangelicals have failed notably in sustaining serious intellectual life. "They have nourished millions of believers in the simple verities of the gospel, but have abandoned the universities, the arts, and other realms of 'high' culture. Even in

The theological content of many of the books is made more easily accessible by frequent use of homey example or analogy. Here is Wally Drotts explaining the total corruption of the unredeemed human being:

> When our son was a child, one day he found on our front lawn pieces of ice.
> The warm weather tempted him to quench his thirst by licking them. As he
> began to do so, he noticed they were dirty. It was at the kitchen sink, where he
> was trying to wash them, that we, his parents, met his problem. However much
> he would drench the cubes under the faucet, they refused to come clean. We
> quickly discovered the reason. The ice was frozen from dirty water. No
> amount of external rinsing would cleanse that ice. It needed to be completely
> purified and refrozen. Here is a modern parable, for such is man. So
> thoroughly polluted is the ungiven [sic] self that no amount of human effort can
> recreate us.[33]

There is frequent reference to personal experience, particularly to key encounters with other people who have exemplified what it means to be, for example, a faithful steward or pilgrim. Stories are woven together neatly with biblical reference and theological point. Discussing stewardship, Arthur R. Mc Kay writes:

> True stewardship is always touched with glee, mirth, gaiety, joyousness, and
> exhilaration. It has to do with the spirit in which we give ourselves in response
> to the love of God.
>   The heart of it is caught up in the wonderful story of an old woman who
> came up to the great evangelist Charles Spurgeon after one of his meetings and

---

its more progressive wing, evangelicalism has little intellectual muscle. . . . Evangelicals spend enormous sums of money on higher education. But the diffusion of resources among hundreds of colleges and seminaries means that almost none can begin to afford a research faculty, theological or otherwise. The problem is compounded by the syndrome of the reinvented wheel . . . figures such as Bill Bright, Oral Roberts, Jerry Falwell, and Jim Bakker all assume that no education that has gone before is capable of meeting the demands of the hour. Despite the absence of any formal educational credentials, each man presumes to establish a genuinely Christian university. Small wonder that evangelical thinking, which once was razor-sharp and genuinely profound, now seems dull, rusty, even banal" (pp. 81–82). I quote Hatch at length because I think his observations help one understand the reasons for the massive volume of conservative popular theologies of the Christian life at the moment. His analysis also helps explain the high quality of these: the considerable intellectual acumen of many evangelicals has been channeled into the production of popular texts instead of into more academic theologies. In liberal Protestant quarters, the reverse phenomenon is often the problem. Liberal theologians often work in contexts where the writing of popularly oriented books may be viewed as a worthy but unfortunate blot on an academic resumé.

[33] Drotts, in Mary L. Johnson, ed., *Take up Your Cross: An Invitation to Abundant Life* (New York: Paulist, 1985) 12. Drotts is minister of parish life at a Presbyterian church in California.

exclaimed, "Ah, Mr. Spurgeon, if Jesus Christ does save me, he will never hear the end of it!" It is to be found in the life of Paul, whose astonishment that God could love such a one as he never ceased. Once smitten by a divine love on that Damascus road, this man who had taken such sinful pride in the power of his position, the range of his intellect, the correctness of his religious practice, was never the same again. His life was lost in wonder, love, and praise![34]

Where Scripture is quoted, it is frequently the King James Version that is used by conservative Protestant authors.[35] The exegetical approach varies. There is a tendency in some of the writings toward what Richard Mouw has called the "pietistic" use of Scripture:[36] encouraging the reading of the Bible to foster a personal sense of divine presence and applying scripture sayings like poultices to the subjective needs and emotional states of the Christian. More common, however, is what Mouw terms the "moralistic" mode of exegesis which views the Bible as a sourcebook for moral principles or rules.[37] A certain brand of biblical moralism, says Mouw, stresses the development of good character and views the Bible as a repository of stories of persons of good character who should be imitated.[38] We certainly see this kind of approach in works such as Theodore H. Epp's *Joshua Victorious by Faith*, which draw out lessons for the contemporary Christian from the stories of past heroes of the faith.[39]

The texts do not fit easily into any one genre as usually defined. Some exhibit certain characteristics that one usually associates with "devotional manuals,"[40] in that although they offer a coherent theology, they place more emphasis on the practical implications of this for life, and give guidelines for life of prayer and meditation, as well as for the day-to-day life of the religious person. Other texts resemble more the modern bastard offshoot of the devotional manual, namely, the "self-help" manual. They focus strongly on *success*, sketching out a kind of plan of campaign for a more visibly success-

---

[34] Mc Kay, *God's People in God's World* (Philadelphia: Westminster, 1961) 40. Mc Kay was a Presbyterian writer who was president of McCormick Theological Seminary, at the time he wrote this book.

[35] In this thesis, however, quotations are from the Revised Standard Version unless otherwise noted.

[36] Richard J. Mouw, "The Bible in Twentieth Century Protestantism: A Preliminary Taxonomy," in Nathan O. Hatch and Mark A. Noll, eds., *The Bible in America: Essays in Cultural History* (New York: Oxford University Press, 1982) 144–45.

[37] Ibid., 146.

[38] Ibid.

[39] Epp, *Joshua Victorious by Faith* (Lincoln, NE: Back to the Bible, 1968).

[40] For a discussion of the genre of the "devotional manual" see Miles, *Practicing Christianity*, 1–15.

ful Christian life, and offering extensive suggestions for ways to implement
to effect their ideas.[41]
Still others of the texts are more undilutedly theological. They do discuss
the ethical implications of their theology, but do not suggest helps for putting
them into action. These kind of texts, such as Douglas John Hall's *The Steward: A Biblical Symbol Come of Age*, are closer in form to what is perhaps
more usually thought of as "academic" or "high" theology.[42] It is difficult
to draw sharp lines between "popular" and "academic" treatments. It is
often far from clear exactly for whom an author is writing. Among the hardest books to classify are those written by university or seminary theologians
for a popular audience. Although geared to this audience, they are frequently
footnoted almost to the level of a scholarly text. Hall's book is a good example of this.

Because the texts under consideration cut across the genres as traditionally
defined, I have chosen to designate them as "popular theologies of the Christian life." This terminology reflects both their topic of concern and their
common feature of popular presentation of theological tenets. It intentionally
cuts across the traditional division between "theology" and "devotional
literature" or "inspirational literature." This division simply does not seem
helpful when considering the kind of books examined in this thesis. It is
perhaps a carryover from the days when there were "theologies" for those
with the necessary training and inclination, and tracts or devotional works for
other persons. An intermediate audience would now appear to exist, and it is
to this audience that the literature examined in this thesis would appear to be
addressed. The use of the term "theologies" also serves to underline the fact
that this thesis does not take into consideration works in which the theological import of a given image is not developed with some degree of completeness.[43]

Background information

Where information was forthcoming, I have tried to footnote basic details
about the author's denominational affiliation and position at the time of

---

[41] Schneider and Dornbusch (*Popular Religion*, 58–77) discuss at some length the predilection of writers of such texts for offering "technologies" for improving one's religious life. On
the genre of "self-help" literature and its relation to the all-American idea of the "self-made
man," see John G. Cawelti, *Apostles of the Self-Made Man* (Chicago: University of Chicago
Press, 1965). See esp. 77–98 and 167–99.

[42] Hall, *The Steward: A Biblical Symbol Come of Age* (New York: Friendship, 1982). Hall is
Professor of Christian Theology at McGill University in Montreal.

[43] For example, Frances J. Roberts's loosely strung series of reflections, *Progress of Another
Pilgrim* (Ojai, CA: Kings Farspan, 1970).

writing. Who published a work often tells you a great deal about the political and theological views of the author. Unfortunately, it was not possible to provide a complete appendix of religious book publishers. Complete information is curiously hard to come by. A certain amount of information on some of the presses can be found in the *Associated Church Press Directory*. The only other source of information available is the now defunct *Directory of Religious Publishers*, a serial not available at Harvard.

Limitations to the Project

A number of objections could be made to the project. Firstly, it focuses on English and North American texts. For reasons discussed earlier, they are also predominantly Protestant. Works by Catholic authors are drawn upon as counterpoints rather than with the sustained attention that one might desire. Works by authors from other traditions are rarely used. It would have been instructive to look at a number of different areas of the genre, say, at Latin American liberation spiritualities with their strong anti-individualist, kingdom-centered emphasis. It would also have been instructive to look more closely at post-Christian feminist texts on the goddess image. I might even have stepped beyond the written word and examined the visual expressions of these symbols. Numerous other possibilities present themselves. This would be a life's work. As Roger Sessions once remarked, "It is not sufficient to have the whole world at one's disposal—the very infinitude of possibilities cancels out possibilities, as it were, until limitations are discovered."[44] I have opted to try and work thoroughly with a small slice of the tradition which has been formative in my own life, and with the materials with which I am most familiar. Unavoidably, what I write will speak most clearly to those of a similar background.

A second objection is equally cogent: if one is going to talk about the effect of images on the individual or community, one must surely carry out some kind of field study to establish the facts.[45] How can we really talk about the effects of the image of warfare if we do not examine in detail its effects in the community at large? This is a criticism that is well taken. We are

[44] Sessions, "Problems and Issues Facing the Composer Today," in P. H. Lang, ed., *Problems of Modern Music* (New York: Norton, 1962) 31; cited by Nelson Goodman, *Languages of Art: An Approach to the Theory of Symbols* (2d ed.; Indianapolis: Hackett, 1976) 127.

[45] For an example of an extended study of a metaphor in its social context, see Darrand and Shupe's study of the image of the "tabernacle" in the Latter Rain sect. Tom Craig Darrand and Anson Shupe, *Metaphors of Social Control in a Pentecostal Sect* (Studies in Religion and Society, 6; New York: Mellen, 1983). The authors call for more such studies, and criticize the broad generalizations of many contemporary writers on metaphor in religious contexts (p. 201).

much inclined in theology to make very broad statements about the interrelation of religion and culture. Nevertheless, it is hard to see how it can be otherwise. We cannot all be simultaneously sociologists, psychologists, and experts on religion. The rise of interdisciplinary studies has led to a feeling that one has to delve into every connection, but one cannot in a thesis make a systematic study of the theological use of images and a sociological study of their specific effects. Let each do what they can.

1

Introduction: Points of Departure

Before beginning discussion of the individual images, it is important to lay out in more detail the reasons for taking them with such seriousness as shapers of human life, and to provide some preliminary theoretical groundwork for the discussion of religious language which runs through the chapters that follow.

Preliminary Observations on Language and Culture

Humans are both creators and products of their cultural systems, and in particular of their linguistic systems. In the dawn of time, perhaps, our ancestors ventured forth unencumbered or unaided by existent frameworks of interpretation, differentiating themselves by degree from the world around them, and gradually coming to order the flux of reality in accordance with their needs, their mental capacities or forms, and—perhaps—in accordance with how the manifold of being presented itself to them.[1] To a certain degree, each of us even today continues to encounter the world with a freshness of vision; its

---

[1] The insights of Vico, Cassirer, Kant, James, and others are clearly behind this composite description and the point will be discussed in greater detail later. It should be said, however, that we will probably never know the exact origins of language, and that all descriptions of its early phases are necessarily speculative and tend to have a highly mythic flavour.

sheer existence always overflows the categories that we have received to interpret it. And throughout our lives we perceive fresh points of connection between events in the world or anomalies in interpretations that have been inherited. We continue the human process of reshaping our language, manipulating our inherited language texture to formulate still other relationships.[2] However, to a high degree, we are more acted upon than acting so far as our frameworks of interpretation are concerned. We learn to construe the world in terms of the categories of the culture and of its language that we have grown up speaking. Logically, for creatures who speak, our categories precede the experiences to which we apply them. And in actuality, the work of anthropologists such as Franz Boas has shown, for example, that "The difference in the mode of thought of primitive man and that of civilized man seems to consist largely in the difference of character of the traditional material with which the new perception associates itself."[3] Our modes of interpreting reality, are highly dependent on the categories or classifications with which we have been provided.[4]

Of particular interest is the way that the extended metaphors or models that we use to interpret the world appear especially important in this shaping process. Where they are widely held as valid by all or part of a community, they are treated as if they were precise pictures of reality. It is this process Emile Durkheim had in mind when he described the whole notion of "impersonal truth" in terms of the individual's apprehension of society's categories of interpretation.[5] And with clearer reference to the dimension of language, Nietzsche's perception of the same phenomenon led him to describe truth as no more than an unrecognized "mobile army of metaphors."[6]

Particular metaphors dictate to a high degree the way that we understand the world. They may operate on a metaphysical scale, as for example does the metaphorical construal of the world as a giant machine.[7] Or they may

---

[2] The expression is that of Kenneth Burke, *Permanence and Change: An Anatomy of Purpose* (2d ed.; Los Altos, CA: Hermes, 1954) 36.

[3] Boas, *The Mind of Primitive Man* (New York: Macmillan, 1911) 203.

[4] Two linguists have been particularly associated with theories of the shaping power of language: Benjamin Lee Whorf and Edward Sapir. See Whorf, *Language, Thought and Reality: Selected Writings of Benjamin Lee Whorf* (ed. John B. Carroll; 1956; reprinted Cambridge: MIT Press, 1964); and Sapir, *Culture, Language and Personality* (ed. David G. Mandelbaum; Berkeley: University of California Press, 1960) esp. 68–69. I focus here on the effects of language. Other symbol systems—visual, political, etc.—also perform this function.

[5] Durkheim, *The Elementary Forms of the Religious Life* (1915; reprinted New York: The Free Press, 1965) 485.

[6] Friedrich Nietzsche, "On Truth and Falsity in their Extramoral Sense," in Warren Shibles, ed., *Essays on Metaphor* (Whitewater, WI: Language, 1972) 5.

[7] The history of this particular image has, of course, been extensively documented, together with its negative consequences. See, e.g., Elizabeth Sewell, *The Human Metaphor* (Notre Dame,

operate on the more limited but equally important political level with definite consequences. Robert A. Nisbet writes:

> Metaphor allies itself well with proposals for social action. Most of the millennialist visions of revolution that we find in the Western tradition spring from diagnoses of society that are at bottom metaphoric. If one believes that the society around him is a "sick" society, dying of poisons generated in its own being, or ridden with "cancers", "tumors", "gangrenous" substances . . . what else but total action can remove the alien bodies or poisons?[8]

As Nisbet's remarks suggest, we are likely to *act* upon our understandings of reality. They locate us like maps in the world and impel us to assess situations and act in particular ways. The anthropologist James W. Fernandez observes that, "the metaphoric assertions men make about themselves or about others influence their behavior. Such assertions make manageable objects of the self or of others and facilitate performance. In respect to behavior such assertions . . . provide images in relation to which the organization of behavior can take place."[9] With their aid we appraise situations, draw inferences, set goals, judge other people's motives, treat them accordingly, and so on.[10]

Religious metaphors are particularly powerful shapers because of their blend of cognitive, affective, and motivational elements. The idea of God as Creator and Lord of the earth and man and woman as the stewards of God's great estate makes a statement about the way that the cosmos actually is, and by implication how we should act in it: "The powerfully coercive 'ought' is felt to grow out of a comprehensive factual 'is,' and in such a way religion grounds the most specific requirements of human action in the most general contexts of human existence."[11] And in the case of religious concepts and

---

IN: University of Notre Dame Press, 1964) 69–75.

[8] Nisbet, *Social Change and History: Aspects of the Western Theory of Development* (New York: Oxford University Press, 1969) 6.

[9] Fernandez, *Persuasions and Performances: The Play of Tropes in Culture* (Bloomington: Indiana University Press, 1986) 6–7.

[10] On these points see, e.g., George Lakoff and Mark Johnson, *Metaphors We Live By* (Chicago: University of Chicago Press, 1980) 142; Burke, *Permanence and Change*, 35. It is important to realize that it is not simply unsophisticated people who are thus swayed. A recent study of the effect of metaphor on political attitudes indicates that if anything the reverse is true: "We had originally expected that the more politically sophisticated, whose thinking would presumably be anchored in the context of a more fully developed political philosophy, would exhibit greater resistance to influence by the fleeting images of metaphors. The results instead support the opposite conclusion . . . for the more politically sophisticated actually displayed far greater susceptibility to the effect of figures of speech" (Joel T. Johnson and Shelley E. Taylor, "The Effect of Metaphor on Political Attitudes," *Basic and Applied Social Psychology* 2 [1981] 313).

[11] Geertz, *Interpretation of Cultures*, 126.

images, their power is continually strengthened by their presence in the language of ritual, private devotion, and the rhetoric of civil religion. The result is, as Geertz puts it, that religion offers

> a system of symbols which acts to establish powerful, pervasive, and long- lasting moods and motivations in men by formulating conceptions of a general order of existence and clothing these conceptions with such an aura of factuality that the moods and motivations seem uniquely realistic. . . .
>
> The concrete symbols involved . . . both express the world's climate and shape it. They shape it by inducing in the worshipper a certain distinctive set of dispositions (tendencies, capacities, propensities, skills, habits, liabilities, pronenesses) which lend a chronic character to the flow of his activity and the quality of his experience. . . .
>
> For those able to embrace them, and for so long as they are able to embrace them, religious symbols provide a cosmic guarantee not only for their ability to comprehend the world, but also, comprehending it, to give a precision to their feeling, a definition to their emotions which enables them, morosely or joyfully, grimly or cavalierly, to endure it.[12]

Religious language, perhaps more than any other kind, also affects the lives of its users because those earthly phenomena upon which it draws in speaking of divine matters receive a reflected glory and power from the object upon which they are projected. In the monotheistic traditions, as Tillich put it, "Religious symbols are double-edged. They are directed toward the infinite which they symbolize and toward the finite through which they symbolize it. They force the infinite down to finitude and the finite up to infinity."[13] To take the example of the symbol of divine kingship, what this means is that,

> if a segment of reality is used as a symbol for God, the realm of reality from which it is taken is, so to speak, elevated into the realm of the holy. It no

[12] Ibid., 90; 95; 104. Here, as in much of Geertz's book, the voice of William James may be heard echoing through the anthropological observations. James, perhaps more than any other individual observer, has drawn the connections between religious patterns of interpretation and particular modes of existing in the world. However, it is important to note that he believed that the individual temperament plays a role in determining precisely what picture of the world we find convincing; our culture offers us a variety of religious pictures and our choice is, in part, dictated by our needs and our leanings. If there is a determinism at work, it is as much temperamental or genetic, as cultural. See, e.g., James, *The Varieties of Religious Experience: A Study in Human Nature* (New York: Collier Books, 1961) 266. The same, in James's opinion, holds true for one's tendency to be convinced by particular philosophical outlooks (idem, "The Present Dilemma in Philosophy," in Bruce Kuklick, ed., *Pragmatism* (Indianapolis: Hackett, 1981) 8–11.

[13] Paul Tillich, *Systematic Theology*, vol. 1: *Reason and Revelation; Being and God* (Chicago: University of Chicago Press, 1951) 240.

longer is secular. It is theonomous. If God is called the "king," something is said not only about God but also about the holy character of kinghood.[14]

The office of king is glorified.[15] And this works for everything, says Tillich:

> For instance, if God is symbolized as "Father," he is brought down to the human relationship of father and child. But at the same time this human relationship is consecrated into a pattern of the divine-human relationship. If "Father" is employed as a symbol for God, fatherhood is seen in its theonomous, sacramental depth.[16]

This dangerous dynamic is one of which feminist theologians are particularly aware. Mary Daly's early work *Beyond God the Father* contains an extended and angry analysis of the many ways in which if God be male, the male will be god; how "If God in 'his' heaven is a father ruling 'his' people, then it is in the 'nature' of things and according to divine plan and the order of the universe that society be male-dominated."[17] A shaping of deity has taken place which she believes has the long term potential to, in turn, misshape the human. When looking at the images under consideration in this thesis it will be important to consider what might be the reciprocal effects of discussing life as, for example, warfare. Does one automatically glorify physical warfare when drawing upon it to elaborate the meaning of the religious life?

Religious symbols exert great power, but they are themselves to a high degree the product of the human imagination. In the realm of religious discourse, the human role in the shaping of ideas has frequently been obscured—at least in traditions where a supernatural revelation has traditionally provided the basis for life and belief. This has made the interpretative images and ideas doubly powerful in that they have been seen as true in the strongest sense of "God-given." The language of and about God in, for example, the Tanakh is true because God has guaranteed it to be so.[18] Even so, it has become a commonplace of the last hundred years that we have

---

[14] Ibid., 241.

[15] If one wants a specific example of this phenomenon in action, Dante's *De Monarchia* provides a good example. He argues that it is obvious that the world should be an empire under a monarch or single princedom, because this is how heaven is ordered. Dante, *Monarchy and Three Political Letters* (ed. Donald Nicholl; 1947; reprinted Westport, CT: Hyperion, 1979) book 1.

[16] Tillich, *Systematic Theology*, 1. 240–41.

[17] Daly, *Beyond God the Father: Toward a Philosophy of Women's Liberation* (Boston: Beacon Press, 1973) 13. On her discussion of the general point, see esp. 13–43.

[18] In the context of general discussions of the nature of religion, the Tanakh will be referred to as such. In the context of the traditional Christian exegesis in the primary materials, the name Old Testament will be used.

created God much in our own image, whether this be understood in terms of a reified contemplation of selfhood as by Feuerbach,[19] or as a projection of psychological mechanisms as Freud believed,[20] or as a kind of picture of external personification of the forces binding society together, as Durkheim was convinced.[21] Often the writer will draw quite specific connections between particular characteristics of God's behavior and wishes and those of society and the individual:

> The faith of Chrysostom and Luther is entangled with, and supported upon, the assumption that the universe was created and is governed by a father and king. They had projected upon the universe an imaginary picture which reflected their own daily experience of government among men. These pictures of how the universe is governed change with men's political experience. . . . The God of medieval Christianity . . . is . . . like a great feudal lord, supreme and yet bound by covenants to treat his vassals on earth according to a well-established system of reciprocal rights and duties. The God of the Enlightenment in the Eighteenth Century is a constitutional monarch who reigns but does not govern. And the God of Modernism, who is variously pictured as the *élan vital* within the evolutionary process, or as the sum total of the laws of nature, is really a kind of constitutionalism deified.[22]

It is clear, then, that humans have to some degree created their religious concepts and structured the language with which their import is elaborated. The ways in which they have done this, and also the ways that they have been affected by their own creations, can be illuminated further by some discussion of specific aspects of religious discourse.

Metaphors, Images, and So On

The question of what one may and may not designate a "symbol" a "metaphor" an "analogy," etc., has become the ground of endless clarification and obfuscation in recent years. One of the major problems is that within

---

[19] "The divine being is nothing else than the human being, or, rather, the human nature purified, freed from the limits of the individual man, made objective—i.e., contemplated and revered as another, a distinct being" (Ludwig Feuerbach, *The Essence of Christianity* [New York: Harper & Row, 1957] 14).

[20] See, e.g., Sigmund Freud, *Totem and Taboo* (ed. A. A. Brill; 1913; reprinted New York; Random House, n.d.) 190–91. A useful overview of the different aspects of Freud's thought on the psychological bases of religion may be found in Ana-Maria Rizzuto, *The Birth of the Living God: A Psychoanalytic Study* (Chicago: University of Chicago Press, 1979) 13–36.

[21] Durkheim, *Elementary Forms*, 236; 239–40; 323–32; 459.

[22] Walter Lippmann, *Preface to Morals* (New York: Macmillan, 1929) 54–55.

each field the terms have different histories and are used with differing levels of appreciation of their histories. Theologians have participated in both the clarification and obfuscation. On the topic of "symbol," for example, Swiatecka takes the theologian to task (amusingly and convincingly) for sloppy and unhelpful uses of the term. Swiatecka underlines the need for each writer to be precise about exactly what they intend by the term and Swiatecka stresses that this involves a careful explanation of how the term is understood in relation to other key concepts such as "analogy," "history," and "knowledge."[23] Individual precision is about as much as one can hope for. The problem, if such it is, is that one person's symbol is another person's metaphor, and one person's analogy another person's model, and so on. Thus, Sallie McFague can insist that "one critical difference between symbolic and metaphorical statements is that the latter always contain the whisper, "it is *and* it is not," and remark that "the tension of metaphor is absorbed by the harmony of symbol."[24] Philip Wheelwright, by contrast, can speak cheerfully of "expressive symbols" which are marked by their plurisignation and their "soft focus" and their "assertorial lightness," stressing precisely the same qualities that incline McFague to speak rather of metaphor.[25]

Appeal to historical usage of the various relevant terms results in the finding of no convenient consensus. Usage shifts over the centuries. The sixteenth-century writer George Puttenham can speak of allegory, for example, with a meaning that would not now usually be given to the term:

> Properly and in his principall vertue Allegoria is when we do speake in sense translative and wrested from the owne signification, neverthelesse applied to another not altogether contrary, but having much conveniencie with it as before we said of the metaphore: as for example if we should call the common wealth a shippe; the Prince a Pilot, the Counsellours mariners, the stormes warres, the calme and [haven] peace, this is spoken all in allegorie: and because such inversion of sense in one single worde is by the figure Metaphore, of whom we spake before, and this manner of inversion extending to whole and large speaches, it maketh the figure allegorie to be called a long and perpetuall Metaphore.[26]

[23] M. Jadwiga Swiatecka, *The Idea of the Symbol: Some Nineteenth Century Comparisons with Coleridge* (Cambridge: Cambridge University Press, 1980) 7–30; 177.

[24] McFague, *Metaphorical Theology: Models of God in Religious Language* (Philadelphia: Fortress, 1982) 13; 16.

[25] Wheelwright, *The Burning Fountain: A Study in the Language of Symbolism* (rev. ed.; 1968; reprinted Gloucester, MA: Peter Smith, 1982) 81; 91–92.

[26] Puttenham, *The Arte of English Poesie* (1589; reprinted Constable, 1906; facsimile reprint Kent, OH: Kent State University Press, 1970) 197.

Most contemporary writers would not limit "metaphor" to the juxtaposition of individual words and senses, and they would tend to think of allegory as an extended narrative exposition of a theme where specific ideas are personified or embodied by others on a one-to-one basis. "Allegory", in fact, provides us with a good example of how pitched battles are fought over rhetorical terms and how the results of a battle can shape usage over the following centuries. The still prevalent Romantic idea of symbol was formed in part by showing its superiority to allegory, and belaboring the shortcomings and contrivedness of the latter. Tzvetan Todorov writes that for the Romantics, symbol

> is productive, intransitive, motivated; it achieves the fusion of contraries; it is and it signifies at the same time; its content eludes reason: it expresses the inexpressible. In contrast, allegory . . . is already made, transitive, arbitrary, pure signification, an expression of reason. . . . [T]he symbol is produced unconsciously, and it provokes an unending task of interpretation; the allegory is intentional, and can be understood without remainder.[27]

The writings of Coleridge, which have been extremely influential in the theological sphere, provide us with one of the foundational texts on this topic:

> [A]n Allegory is but a translation of abstract notions into a picture language which is itself nothing but an abstraction from objects of the senses; the principal being more worthless even than its phantom proxy, both alike unsubstantial, and the former shapeless to boot. On the other hand a Symbol (ὃ estin aei tauĕtgorikon) is characterized by a translucence of the Special in the Individual or of the General in the Especial or of the Universal in the General. Above all by the translucence of the Eternal through and in the Temporal. It always partakes of the Reality which it renders intelligible; and while it enunciates the whole, abides itself as a living part in that Unity, of which it is the representative. The other are but empty echoes which the fancy arbitrarily associates with the apparitions of matter. . . .[28]

What Coleridge, and those of like mind, are attempting to do is to anchor certain disclosive structures as revelatory. For the Romantics, "symbol" is the operative name for these structures. We see the same kind of usage in the theological writings of authors such as Paul Tillich.

The same dynamic or desire has led others to employ different terms in

---

[27] Todorov, *Theories of the Symbol* (1982; reprinted Ithaca, NY: Cornell Paperbacks, 1984) 206–7.

[28] Samuel Taylor Coleridge, "The Statesman's Manual," in Kathleen Coburn, ed., *The Collected Works of Samuel Taylor Coleridge*, vol. 6: *Lay Sermons* (ed. R. J. White; Bollingen Series 75; Princeton: Princeton University Press, 1972) 30.

search of precisely the same anchoring or mooring of perceptions in eternal verity. Thus, for example, Jonathan Edwards strove to differentiate divinely established type from freewheeling trope, arguing that "it is God's way in the natural world to make inferiour things in conformity and analogy to the superiour, so as to be the images of them,"[29] so that, with the Scripture as our interpreter, "Wherever we are, and whatever we are about, we may see divine things excellently represented and held forth."[30] The same dilemma of how to differentiate between the fanciful—and therefore at best ornamental, at worst misleading—and the true, is behind the discussion.

Rather than dwell at further length on the way that different writers in different eras have attempted to root our ideas in ontological reality via the use of different sets of terminology, I shall respond to Swiatecka's injunction to authors at least to define the use of their own terms. I shall give working definitions, and also introduce selected theoretical observations on the use of language which appear relevant and illuminating in the context of the material discussed in this dissertation.[31]

Image

"Image," is used in this thesis as a catchall word, as both a generic term for figures of speech and a designation of mental events and visual representations.[32] In the English language, the term "image" originally meant a copy, imitation or picture. The dimension of "figure" was absent. Thomas Hobbes used the term "image" to refer to the prints or impressions that perceived objects made upon the mind and Dryden picked up this notion and developed the idea that the poet's imagination operated like a spaniel beating through the field of memory in search of its quarry of images. During the eighteenth century, epistemology and aesthetics merged in the development of a vision of art—especially poetry—as fundamentally descriptive or imitative of reality. "Image" gained a place of primacy in the literary vocabulary. At the same time, insofar as a poet's descriptions appeared to exceed or alter the reality that their reader personally perceived, the term "image" came to carry the connotation of "figure" or "creation."[33]

[29] Jonathan Edwards, *Images or Shadows or Divine Things* (ed. Perry Miller; New Haven: Yale University Press, 1948) 46.

[30] Ibid., 69.

[31] The selective aspect of what follows must be underlined strongly. Given the breadth of the field of philosophy of language in the last ten years, all attempts to present this kind of working overview are bound to have lacunae.

[32] This is the definition given by Janet Martin Soskice, *Metaphor and Religious Language* (1985; reprinted Oxford: Oxford University Press, 1987) 55.

[33] This description of the development of the term is drawn from Ray Frazer, "The Origin of the Term 'Image,'" *ELH* 27 (1960) 149–61. For a more extended treatment, see P. N. Furbank,

This double dimension of picturing representation and figurative quality is picked up by Wallace Mitchell when he writes, "We speak of verbal imagery as, on the one hand, metaphoric, figurative, or ornamented language. . . . But we also speak of it in Wittgenstein's manner, as the way a proposition 'like a tableau vivant . . . presents a state of affairs.' "[34] It is not my presumption that any of the images under study in this thesis necessarily do represent actual states of affairs in this way, but the visual component is present and important and the term "image" preserves this. One of the reasons that the images discussed may be so effective is that they are markedly pictorial and in this lies, to a high degree, their convincingness. "[M]etaphysical systems, for the most part, become popular not for their truth but in proportion as they attribute to causes a susceptibility of being seen, if only our visual organs were sufficiently powerful," writes Coleridge as he speaks of the "despotism of the eye" under whose "strong sensual influence we are restless because invisible things are not objects of vision."[35] This is no less true of religious descriptions. Good models in science may not have to be picturable,[36] but picturability certainly seems important in the realm of metaphysics and religion; descriptions in this arena would appear to follow Marcus Hester's dictum that at least one of the two components of a metaphor must be "image-exciting."[37] They catch the imagination and lodge more firmly in the memory.[38] It should be noted, however, that some people do not seem to

---

Reflections on the Word 'Image' (London: Secker and Warburg, 1970).

[34] Wallace Mitchell, *Iconology: Image, Text, Ideology* (Chicago: University of Chicago Press, 1986) 21.

[35] Samuel Taylor Coleridge, *Biographia Literaria* (ed. George Watson; rev. ed.; 1965; reprinted London: Dent, 1975) 62.

[36] Max Black, *Models and Metaphors: Studies in Language and Philosophy* (Ithaca, NY: Cornell University Press, 1963) 232–33.

[37] Hester, "Metaphor and Aspect Seeing," in Shibles, *Essays*, 114.

[38] The precise degree to which we think and remember in visual rather than verbal terms is, of course, at the heart of some of the most protracted arguments in the field of cognitive psychology. On this topic see, e.g., Ned Block, ed., *Imagery* (Cambridge: MIT Press, 1981) where various dimensions of the role of imagery in human thought and behavior are addressed. See also Allan Paivio, "Psychological Processes in the Comprehension of Metaphor," in Andrew Ortony, ed., *Metaphor and Thought* (Cambridge: Cambridge University Press, 1979) 150–71, where the interconnection of the verbal and visual dimensions of metaphorical interpretation are considered. For an overview of the relevant literature of cognitive psychology and a particular construction of it, see Earl R. Mac Cormac, *A Cognitive Theory of Metaphor* (Cambridge: MIT Press, 1985) esp. 127–57. For a discussion of visual imagery and the relation of visual and verbal imagery in the Christian context, see Margaret Miles, *Image as Insight: Visual Understanding in Western Christianity and Secular Culture* (Boston: Beacon, 1985) esp. 139–54. Here, as elsewhere, Miles draws particular attention to "visual training" in the development of the devotional life.

depend very strongly on the visual dimension in their thinking. In C. S. Lewis's view this might make them good theologians. He argues that the visual element of "image" can actually be a positive hindrance in theological thinking. He writes that all religious language tends toward the poetic and imaginative, but cautions against becoming hung up on individual images saying that a too lively visual imagination is a bane, it works against us "as toys too elaborate and realistic, spoil children's play."[39] We will see that in the development of, for example, the image of soldiery, the mental picture of a Roman legionary decked out in the armor of Ephesians, does indeed seem to obsess certain writers, leading them by the nose into the mire of conceit.

Symbol

In its broadest sense, I take symbol to be "any device whereby we make an abstraction."[40] The abstraction involves the expression of meaning by the use of a sign to designate something other than itself. Thus a symbol is at one level simply a designatory sign with an agreed significance. Sign develops into symbol only in its cultural context. Symbols of the most powerful kind are those words, objects, persons etc. which have been invested by history, shared experience, or common consensus with multiple dimensions of meaning which elude easy paraphrase. Helpful on this score is Norman Friedman's definition of symbol as "an image alive with an idea; a fact saturated in value ... either by virtue of its history, its relation to certain archetypal patterns appearing in myths and dreams, or by virtue of its context, its frequency of recurrence, and its relation to other images in the same work and to the author's intentions."[41]

Metaphor and Model

I use the term "metaphor" to refer to instances of the writing or speaking about one area of experience in terms commonly ascribed to another.[42] No

[39] Lewis, "The Language of Reflection," in idem, *Christian Reflections* (London: Bles, 1967) 139. Lewis, in fact, goes so far as to say that visual images are simply the slag from the furnace of the imagination. "Imagining," he says, "is something other than having mental images ... [the latter] come and go rapidly and assist what I regard as the real imagining only if I take them all as provisional makeshifts, each to be dropped as soon as it has served its (instantaneous) turn" (pp. 138–39).

[40] Susanne K. Langer, "On a New Definition of Symbol," in *Philosophical Sketches* (1962; reprinted New York: Arno, 1979) 63.

[41] Friedman, "Imagery: From Sensation to Symbol," in Shibles, *Essays*, 49.

[42] This definition is similar to that given by Martin Soskice, *Metaphor*, 15. I stress the verbal or written aspect because I would also agree with her that metaphor is a figure of speech and not

initial presupposition is made about the truth value of metaphors, nor about which of the two domains involved is primary. As we shall see, some argue that to call the Christian life a fight is no metaphor; Christians are in the midst of a cosmic battle, and earthly fights are mere echoes of this.

Metaphor seems currently to be the leading candidate for the naming of almost every symbolic structure in theology. A trip through the ever bur- geoning literature on the topic finds such a plethora of definitions of "meta- phor" available that a wide array of phenomena could be brought within its embrace. The extremes of definition are those of metaphor as a sort of ellipt- ical simile ("this is like that" with the "like" knocked out) to metaphor as a tensive conflation or juxtaposition of two words or sets of terminology in such a way that an entirely new piece of knowledge is produced in the mind that is obliged to hold together the improbable partners.[43] Advocates of the second, tensive, theory put great stress on the "novelty" and compelling oddness of the metaphor—the way its revelation bursts upon the mind as it offers its tantalizing bundle of "is" and "is not," shocking the hearer by the simultaneous aptness and inappropriateness of the use of terms drawn from one area of life to describe another.[44]

If one takes this "novelty" or even "absurdity" to be the primary hall- mark of a "live" metaphor, it must be said that the symbolic structures that we will be examining do not always fit the definition well. Like the images of God which they accompany, each must once have had this startling

---

a mental act or an object. Whatever the mental process may be, it is the words or expression that is metaphorical (p. 16), and calling objects metaphors seems purely inappropriate: "He who points to daffodils in the garden and says they are metaphors of rebirth speaks carelessly and indeed metaphorically" (p. 17).

[43] I bypass at this point the issue of the semantic status of the new knowledge. An enormous body of literature concerns itself with the location of meaning, transfer of meaning, deviation of meaning, etc., involved in metaphorical statements. For an excellent discussion of these issues, see Mogens Stiller Kjärgaard, *Metaphor and Parable: A Systematic Analysis of the Specific Structure and Cognitive Function of the Synoptic Similes and Parables qua Metaphors* (Leiden: Brill, 1986).

[44] One becomes quite dizzy after reading some of the more breathless descriptions of the pro- duction of creative metaphor, e.g., those of Paul Ricouer, *The Role of Metaphor: Multidisci- plinary Studies of the Creation of Meaning in Language* (1975; reprinted Toronto: University of Toronto Press, 1981). When I read extensive passages about the tensive interaction of words and their exciting offspring I am reminded of nothing so much as my first attempts as a child to pro- duce a flame by rubbing two grubby bits of cherry twig together. No doubt the scientist working on atomic energy or fusion has the same prospect of rapture. It is an interesting question whether Protestant theologians are inclined to be drawn to these theories of metaphors which focus on "shock," "tension," etc., because there is an affinity between this kind of energy-burst picture of language and the way that such men as Luther, Barth, and Bultmann have felt themselves con- stantly and unexpectedly apprehended and grasped by the ever new Word.

quality—indeed for differing periods in the life of each individual they continue to do so—but once they take hold in the tradition in the way that we have examined, their novelty is not what is foremost or at a premium.[45] One might even say that they had taken on instead a consoling familiarity and a new role as extended structurers of thought and action. They have solidified because of their convincingness and their great potential for point by point reflection on the nature of the Christian life. This is a sign of their productiveness. As McFague puts it: "The most fruitful metaphors are the ones with sufficiently complex grids to allow for extension of thought, structural expansion, suggestions beyond immediate linkages. . . . It is because some metaphors have structural possibilities that . . . models can develop from them, for models are dominant metaphors with comprehensive organizational potential."[46]

This last quotation highlights the organizational aspect of metaphor which permits a new realm to be construed in terms of imported characteristics of another realm. What is being pointed to here is our interpretation of one whole field of experience in the light of another whole field of experience; in Nelson Goodman's language "a label along with others constituting a schema is in effect detached from the home realm of that schema and applied for the sorting and organizing of an alien realm."[47] A similar point is made from a different angle by Lakoff and Johnson in their description of systematic metaphors:

[U]nderstanding takes place in terms of entire domains of experience and not in terms of isolated concepts. The fact that we have been led to hypothesize metaphors like LOVE IS A JOURNEY, TIME IS MONEY, and ARGUMENT IS WAR suggests to us that the focus of definition is at the level of basic domains of experience like love, time, and argument. . . .

Each such domain is a structured whole within our experience that is conceptualized as what we have called an *experiential gestalt.*[48]

---

[45] Ina Loewenberg draws a helpful distinction between "live," "dead," and "novel" metaphors, arguing that a "dead" metaphor should be understood as one used without any sense of its metaphorical origins or status, a novel metaphor is one that is new for the speaker or hearer, and live metaphors are ones that are "neither clearly novel, or obviously dead . . . [which] stand out as metaphors, although familiar ones, for some speakers and hearers, while for others they are already moribund" ("Truth and Consequences of Metaphors," *Philosophy and Rhetoric* 6 [1973] 31). No metaphor's death or conventionalization is necessarily permanent.

[46] McFague, *Metaphorical Theology*, 39.

[47] Goodman, *Languages of Art: An Approach to a Theory of Symbols* (2d ed.; Indianapolis: Hackett, 1976) 72.

[48] Lakoff and Johnson, *Metaphors*, 117.

This might appear to be a fair characterization of what is going on in our use of such images as pilgrimage or stewardship. The lesser known domain of our life in relation to God, or in the cosmos as a whole, is interpreted with the aid of schema drawn from our daily lives. H. Richard Niebuhr characterized this process thus, referring to the process in terms of synechdoche, a subcategory of metaphor where the whole is spoken of in terms of the part:

> [M]en in isolating, defining, understanding, directing, explaining their life as agents, their moral existence, have made a manifold use of simile, metaphor and symbol. They have, in general, used synecdoche, that is, they have apprehended their total activity and their total existence as agents or with the aid of some one of their many activities as representative of all. They have said the whole is like one of its parts; they have then analyzed the part and have interpreted the whole in the light of that analysis.
>
> Many partial activities have been used to interpret the whole. The active life of man has been understood as being like warfare, and then indeed been symbolized by, and even identified with, a warfare in which the enemies are not physical.[49]

This kind of synechdochic extrapolation is akin to the process that William James observes at work among philosophers: "All philosophers...have conceived of the whole world after the analogy of some part of it."[50] To the extent that one realm is consistently explored by means of understandings drawn from another, we may want to adopt the terminology of "model" as used by such writers as Black, Barbour and McFague to designate an "extended metaphor" of an exploratory variety.[51] How exactly do the imported schema function to organize the new or less accessible realm of experience? At one level, what happens is that the schema drawn from the realm of the known operate to *highlight* certain believed aspects of the less well known and to *suppress* others. This aspect is explored at length by Max Black and by Lakoff and Johnson. Black discusses what has now become the most hackneyed example in the metaphor specialist's book, namely "man is

[49] Niebuhr, *Responsible Self*, 159. On Niebuhr's understanding of symbol and image, see the dissertation by Gay House Welch, "Symbol, Metaphor and the Affections: The Legacy of H. Richard Niebuhr's Responsible Self" (Ph.D. diss., Vanderbilt University, 1980).

[50] James, *A Pluralistic Universe* (Cambridge: Harvard University Press, 1977) 9. And philosophers are obliged to work ever thus, since "the only material we have at our disposal for making a picture of the whole world is supplied by the various portions of that world of which we have already had experience" (ibid.). Stephen Pepper was later to develop this insight in his *World Hypotheses: A Study in Evidence* (Berkeley: University of California Press, 1942).

[51] Barbour (*Myths, Models, and Paradigms*, 16) writes: "Metaphors are employed only momentarily and symbols only in a limited range of contexts, but models are more fully elaborated and serve as wider interpretive schemes in many contexts."

a wolf'' and explains how this points up certain characteristics of both wolves and men (males?) and suppresses others.

Precisely how one realm is understood in terms of another is not a straightforward matter. Contemporary writers on metaphor disagree widely about what kind of a transfer is involved and how the uprooted terms are understood by user and hearer. To continue with the example used by Black, what does it mean to speak of a man as a wolf? Obviously you are not evoking some of the wolf-like characteristics when you speak thus. You are not drawing attention, perhaps, to carnivorousness or bushy coat. You are probably highlighting viciousness and predatoriness. In which case, Black believes you are evoking a "wolf-system of related commonplaces." "What is needed," he says, "is not so much that the reader shall know the standard dictionary meaning of 'wolf'—or be able to use that word in literal senses— as that he shall know what I will call the system of associated commonplaces."[52] In somewhat similar fashion, Monroe C. Beardsley attempts to distinguish between primary, "denotative" uses of terms and secondary "connotative" uses. The former he sees as more literal (the "sea" refers to a large body of water) and public; the latter he sees as more private or perhaps restricted to a certain community's use. In metaphorical usage the literal references are thwarted while certain of the connotations are evoked.[53]

These and similar theories have been subjected to much criticism because of their attempt to draw a line between characteristics that are "dictionary" characteristics, and those that are somehow less "literal" yet sufficiently objective or generally understood to allow the hearer to appreciate the metaphor. There is indeed a problem here, but the problem has a constructive dimension in that it arises from and points to the difficulty of ever being certain precisely what elements of the vehicle are being evoked in the description of the tenor (to use the language of I. A. Richards).[54] Both the historical context and the personal histories of speaker and hearer enter into the equation.[55] One of the classic mistakes made by devotional writers is trying to give equal weight to features the source did not intend to be primary, or simply misinterpreting its very point. The point being made is not always as

---

[52] Black, *Models and Metaphors*, 40.

[53] Beardsley, *Aesthetics: Problems in the Philosophy of Criticism* (2d ed.; Indianapolis: Hackett, 1981) 123–33. Beardsley ("The Metaphorical Twist," in Shibles, *Essays*, 79–82) later comes to speak of words as having a total set of properties which are "potential." Of these, those the most readily evoked are "staple," or "defining" while those drawn out by metaphor are "marginal" and still potential, although they may themselves become staple.

[54] Richards, *The Philosophy of Rhetoric* (New York: Oxford University Press, 1936).

[55] And of course there is the additional twist that the author does not always use the same image in the same way. This is a helpful caution to bear in mind in the case of St. Paul.

obvious as one might think approaching a metaphor from a different perspective from that of its initiators. For example, Nathalie Bruyère-Demoulin says that one might think that the image of life as a race is intended to highlight speed or winning; in fact in the classical Greek texts she is studying, the metaphor was more generally employed to indicate the idea of steady progress.[56]

Sometimes, when a metaphor is in frequent use, the connotations understood to be drawn upon become relatively stable. Christian use of the idea of kingship as a metaphor for divine activity or role exemplifies this kind of conventionally established usage. A traditional Christian using this language would not expect earthly connotations of despotism or sexual prerogative to intrude. Nor, speaking of God as Father, would a maternal counterpart be a necessary corollary according to the traditional context of usage. However, one of the important points that Beardsley makes is that the connotations of a word are rarely if ever fully known.[57] And, he might have added, they change according to historical circumstance. When looking at the images under consideration in this thesis it will be interesting to consider whether strict conventions govern the properties and connotations drawn upon and how much leeway there is for idiosyncratic interpretation. It will also be interesting to note whether there are lurking inappropriate connotations which have a habit of intruding regardless.

A second important aspect of the interaction theory as proposed by Black and others is that there is a two-way process in operation. We change our picture of the wolf as well as of the man. Or perhaps let us change now to a more irenic image and say a child is a spaniel. If you read this unexpected metaphor, presumably your mind will set to work trying to figure out what is meant. You will think probably of a spaniel and child together and your mind will shuttle to and fro between what you think of both and you will pull out sets of characteristics of both which have some approximation to each other and remold them accordingly. Of course you may be a person who thinks of your pet as a child to begin with and this may speed up the process. But the point of the exercise is to realize that one is probably now thinking of the childish characteristics of spaniels as well as vice versa.

We are back, of course, to precisely the dynamic that Tillich noted when speaking of the effects of talking of God as King. The work of Black and others serves to explain further why it is that symbols are "double-edged," and to remind us that when looking, for instance, at the image of life as

---

[56] Bruyère-Demoulin, "La vie est une course: comparaisons et métaphores dans la littérature grecque ancienne," *L'Antiquité Classique* 45 (1976) 447.

[57] Beardsley, *Aesthetics*, 143.

warfare it is important to consider whether, in the process of drawing upon the language of war, the phenomenon of physical warfare inevitably accrues a patina of honorableness and respectability from its juxtaposition with the idea of the religious life, and whether indeed it becomes glorified as a way of existence insofar as it is seen as a "type" (in Edwards's sense) of the true religious life.

Analogy

Analogy involves an explicit setting out of the precise ways in which one thing may be understood in relation to or with the help of another. It is possible that both analogy and metaphor begin with the same kind of moment of sudden vision of similarity between things, but as Loewenberg puts it, "an analogy is not used for the sake of the vision of two-in-one but because of the conclusions that can be drawn from seeing A as B, in terms of further B traits."[58] She also points out that one of the differences between a metaphor and an analogy is that you can reject an analogy by citing a disanalogy; the same process cannot be carried out with a metaphor.[59] Obscure metaphor is turned into express analogy as cognizance of similarities and differences increases.[60] One metaphor can only be countered with another when both have been developed to a degree.

Although I am not convinced that an extended metaphor must necessarily be described as an analogy rather than as metaphor or model, Loewenberg's definition makes clear that Christian life as pilgrimage may indeed be spoken of as analogy since the writers do work methodically through the similarities between the two dimensions of physical and spiritual journey. Stephen J. Brown says that he believes that in fact the working out of comparisons and parallels between the physical and spiritual worlds is generally the work of deliberate reflection, not the spontaneous flash of the imagination which commonly creates metaphors.[61]

In the more specific context of language about God—and these images as correlates of such language—analogy will be used to designate the predication of terms by attribution or proportion where univocity or equivocity is impossible.

---

[58] Loewenberg, "Truth and Consequences," 43.

[59] Ibid.

[60] Harvey Nash, "The Role of Metaphor in Psychological Theory," *Behavioral Science* 8 (1963) 339.

[61] Brown, *Image and Truth: Studies in the Imagery of the Bible* (Rome: Catholic Book Agency, 1955) 155.

Ideas, Notions and Concepts

Insofar as the images have a developed cognitive dimension they also qualify to be referred to by this terminology.

Root Metaphors and Paradigms

These will be avoided where possible. Stephen Pepper appears to have given us the term "root-metaphor," and we find him remarking that in recent years "paradigm" has moved far from the sense that Wittgenstein intended and, at the hands of Thomas Kuhn, has metamorphosed into something remarkably like his own notion of "root metaphor"—which, in turn, has been adopted by the philosophical world and changed from meaning the source of categories of world hypotheses to mean "any central idea about which any complex problem can be organized."[62] Because of the problems involved with the terminology, I shall try to avoid both where possible. When "paradigm" is used it will be with the older meaning of "pattern, exemplar, example" (OED).

Myth

One other key term—or perhaps, rather, its absence—calls for explanation. Those familiar with myth theory will surely have recognized in the functional descriptions of metaphor much that has also been said about mythic constructions. There is much overlap. Lauri Honko writes that "myths have, of course, numerous specific functions, but we may generalize and say that they offer both a cognitive basis for and practical models of behaviour."[63] And Bronislaw Malinowski observed that the special class of stories which constitute myth "are to the natives a statement of a primeval, greater, and more relevant reality, by which the present life, fates, and activities of mankind are determined, the knowledge of which supplies man with the motive for ritual and moral actions, as well as with indications as to how to perform them."[64] In other words, myths locate one in what is believed to be cosmic reality and provide the matrix and the impetus for all aspects of human life. While writers on myth differ widely in their discussions of specifics, they seem inclined to agree upon this much, and numerous studies in the field bear witness to the

[62] Pepper, "Metaphor in Philosophy," *The Journal of Mind and Behavior* 3 (1982) 202–4. He first put forward the idea of "root metaphors" in idem, *World Hypotheses*.

[63] Honko, "The Problem of Defining Myth," in Alan Dundes, ed., *Sacred Narrative: Readings in the Theory of Myth* (Berkeley: University of California Press, 1984) 51.

[64] Malinowski, *Magic, Science and Religion and Other Essays* (Glencoe, IL: The Free Press, 1948) 86.

orienting and shaping power of myth, and also to its flexibility and retailoring in the light of anomalous experience.

The images discussed in this thesis clearly serve these orientational functions: they provide a cognitive orientation to the cosmos and a framework for the interpretation of human life and for the development of one's own life. They have, therefore, much in common with myths. If one sees such ideas as stewardship as the crystallizations of biblical mythic stories about the nature of God and the universe, one might well call them mythic images. Insofar as they remain firmly embedded in their story context, this may be helpful. Ian Barbour has asserted that the difference between "myth" and "model" (or extended metaphor) in the religious context lies in the fact that myth is necessarily in narrative or story form. By contrast, a model, he says, "represents the enduring structural components which myths dramatize in narrative form . . . like myths models offer ways of ordering experience and of interpreting the world."[65] If we take this point of view, we would see models as picking out the metaphoric structure of the myth and drawing out their logical possibilities and we would not wish to use the terms "mythic" or "mythical." I find this distinction dubious. The restriction of "myth" to narrative seems appropriate, but it is an impossible task to figure out whether metaphor of a non-story variety somehow "precedes" myth, or can be extricated from it in the way suggested. We are unlikely ever to find, for example, the metaphoric structures of the myths of Genesis existing *simpliciter*. And what would it mean to say that they did? Could one even speak of God the Creator without narrative, without story? The primary materials at which we will look display varying levels of use of story, but none remove themselves from it entirely. In so far as we acknowledge that we are dealing with stories which attempt to explain the cosmos and locate us within it, giving us guidelines for behavior etc., we may say that we are dealing with myths: extended narrative metaphors. An insistence on avoiding the term can only have to do with a dislike of its negative connotations of "untruth" or "unscientificness." Unfortunately, this latter dislike does need to be taken seriously. In certain quarters "myth" most definitely has these negative connotations. Hence you find a contemporary writer like Earl MacCormac describing myth in terms of the mistaken attribution of reality to root-metaphors.[66] Here he of course perpetuates a particular strand of late eighteenth- and nineteenth-century myth theory which used the word myth to designate "the savage's charming but wrongheaded ascription of reality to

[65] Barbour, *Myths, Models, and Paradigms*, 27.

[66] MacCormac, *Metaphor and Myth in Science and Religion* (Durham, NC: Duke University Press, 1976) 102.

poetic fancies.''[67] What is clearly at issue is the ''truth'' of the construct, or the lack of consciousness of its hypothetical nature. But if this be the case, as we shall see, ''metaphor'' represents no safe alternative higher ground for the theologian to escape to. There are Christians who take their metaphors literally, just as their are so-called savages who live in the worlds spun by their myths. We reject the term ''myth'' because some recent usage carries with it the connotation of untruth, but we should not suppose that by using the terminology of metaphor and symbol we escape precisely the same problems of the relation of our constructs to reality.[68]

With this brief overview of potentially helpful theory, let us turn to an examination of the images under discussion in this thesis.

---

[67] This is the kind of view still appearing as late as the works of James Frazer: ''Myths are mistaken understandings of human and natural phenomena, founded on ignorance and misapprehension they are always false, for were they true they would cease to be myths'' (''Introduction'' to *Apollodorus* [ed. James George Frazer; LCL; London: Heinemann, 1921] xxvii – xxxi).

[68] It is interesting to note, however, that in her latest book McFague—who in earlier works assiduously avoided such terms—is talking of the importance of ''remythologizing'' (*Models of God: Theology for an Ecological, Nuclear Age* (Philadelphia: Fortress, 1987) 32.

2

Disciples and Imitators

It is tempting, perhaps, to jump to the more picturesque elaborations of the Christian life and to ignore the most common; tropological instincts may draw one toward expositions of the nature of Christian warfare or pilgrimage, and lead one to bypass discussions of the Christian life as, for example, discipleship or imitation—concepts which appear less overtly metaphorical in that they have their root in the ethical and religious domain as much as in any other domain.[1] Only when discipleship and imitation begin to be elaborated with the aid of other concepts such as being a "child of God" or "member of the body," does the element of live metaphor enter in with clarity.[2] Nevertheless, a discussion of symbolizations of the Christian life cannot begin without some preliminary examination of discipleship and the accompanying concept of imitation of Jesus Christ. The use of the more particular images can only be understood properly in relation to these more foundational ones.

The exact way in which Christians relate to the divine through Christ and the Spirit is, of course, the subject of innumerable doctrinal controversies and refinements. Such ideas as "union with Christ" are articles of faith for some denominations, subsidiary images for others. The study of what it means to

---

[1] See discussion in K. H. Rengstorf, "μαθητής," *TDNT* 4 (1967) 415–26; and W. Michaelis, "μίμησις," *TDNT* 4 (1967) 661–63.

[2] Here it is helpful to remember the distinction discussed earlier between "live" and "dead" metaphor. All terms are metaphorical in their origin, but only where there is consciousness on the part of the user that he or she is speaking of one thing in language primarily associated with another can one meaningfully speak of live metaphor.

be in relation to Christ and how one's life as a redeemed person continues to develop in the Spirit is at the heart of pastoral theology and writings on Christian ethics. Any treatment of them in short compass is bound to be over-simplificatory. Likewise, the issue of the extent to which Christ's importance lies in his exemplary conduct and the extent to which it is situated in his redemptive action is at the heart of almost every soteriological discussion and disagreement. However, despite the many denominational and doctrinal currents that eddy through the various works that I have studied, certain clear patterns of discussion emerge. The genre has a tendency to resolve some of the finer issues by overlooking them.

Disciples

The New Testament offers a number of concepts for comprehending the nature of the Christian life. The variety and complexity increase when the terms are translated into other languages. "Disciple," for example, carries overtones of "discipline" which are absent from the Greek term *mathētēs*. And during the course of Christian history, the various terms such as "discipleship," "imitation," "witness," have come to be identified with specific doctrines and practices; authors embrace reject, or reclaim them in specific contexts. Thus for example, under the influence of Thomas à Kempis, the idea of "imitation of Christ" became immensely popular but understood in a highly specific way.[3]

If one were asked what was the fundamental concept through which contemporary Christians understood their existence in relation to Christ, one might perhaps answer "discipleship." Discipleship certainly appears to be a broadly used category among Protestants.

---

[3] Imitation is understood in terms of an asceticism which can only find its fullest fruition in the monastic context. For a discussion of the place of Thomas's text in the history of reflection on *imitatio*, see Miles, *Practicing Christianity*, 22–26. For an extensive discussion of the ethical implications of the categories of "discipleship" and "imitation" see James Gustafson, *Christ and the Moral Life* (Chicago: The University of Chicago Press, 1968). He is most informative on the concepts as employed in the Reformation and Modern periods by Protestant German and American writers. On the biblical and pre-biblical contexts of the terminology, see E. J. Tinsley, *The Imitation of God in Christ: An Essay on the Biblical Basis of Christian Spirituality* (London: SCM, 1960) and, more recently, the volume of essays edited by Fernando Segovia which include essays on discipleship in each of the gospels and on "kenotic" or "self-emptying" imitation of Paul and Christ in Philippians and on the injunction in Ephesians to be "imitators of God"; Fernando Segovia, *Discipleship in the New Testament* (Philadelphia: Fortress, 1985).

Discipleship as Obedient Learning and Witness

In its narrowest sense, as Fernando Segovia explains, discipleship "is to be understood technically and exclusively in terms of the 'teacher/disciple' relationship with . . . its accompanying terminology (for example, 'following,' or 'on the way')."[4] It is a relatively empty concept insofar as the content of the teaching and its consequences are not specified and the focus is on the teacher-disciple relationship itself. For most contemporary writers, this dimension of Christian life has only a preliminary descriptive status. It is a way of speaking of Christian response to Christ as an authoritative teacher:

> *Disciple (mathētēs)* says we are people who spend our lives apprenticed to our master, Jesus Christ. We are in a growing-learning relationship, always. A disciple is a learner, but not in the academic setting of a schoolroom, rather at the worksite of a craftsman. We do not acquire information about God but skills in faith.[5]

But the response is more than that to a teacher—it is a response to Christ as Son of God and Lord, for contemporary Christians have a clear knowledge of Christ's status that was denied the original disciples and hence their initial discipleship is of a variety that responds to his divine status as much as to his general teaching.[6]

"Discipleship" as learning from the teacher or hearing the word of the master becomes the key theme of the Christian life for those who see Jesus' disciple-making function as that aspect of his work that he demanded be imitated and perpetuated; the Christian life is a life of continuing the process of making disciples by bearing witness to Christ as he bore witness to the Father:

> The ministry of a disciple is the ministry of imparting to others the truth concerning the Father and the Son that has been revealed to us by the Holy Spirit. . . .
> Men are not disciples because of what they give or what they do. They are disciples because of what they communicate to others about Jesus Christ.[7]

---

[4] Segovia, *Discipleship*, 2. This stock exegesis or etymology is recognized by most of the authors. See, e.g., J. Dwight Pentecost, *Design for Discipleship* (Grand Rapids, MI: Zondervan, 1971) 14.

[5] Eugene H. Peterson, *A Long Obedience in the Same Direction: Discipleship in an Instant Society* (Downers Grove, IL: InterVarsity, 1980) 13. Peterson is pastor of a Presbyterian church in Bel Air, Maryland.

[6] So J. Christopher Grannis, Arthur J. Laffin, and Elin Schade, *The Risk of the Cross: Christian Discipleship in the Nuclear Age* (New York: Seabury, 1981) 4–5.

[7] Pentecost, *Design*, 104.

This is a mode of discussion which focuses heavily on the conversion point in people's lives. It is not a model of self-understanding which illuminates the meaning of the whole Christian life. This much is evident from the constant reminders by evangelical writers to "disciplers" and "soul-winners" to pay some attention to people that they have converted. It reflects a belief of a do-or-die variety in the need to make people repent and confess Christ as their Savior. It may also be rooted in a broader picture of a universe ruled by a God who desires that all created beings constantly praise him and spread the word of his great doings.

The other corollary to focusing exclusively on the Master-disciple relationship is a high emphasis on the knowledge and authority of the Master and on the ignorance, weakness and necessary obedience of the disciple. We are here in the world of the depraved will and perverted reason with all that this entails. The Master-disciple relationship resembles everyday learning relationships in that the less knowledgeable are taught by the more knowledgeable, but now the gap in knowledge is infinite and the pupil can in fact only learn by total submission to the Master, letting the Master mold him or her completely: "Christian discipleship is unique because it requires a radical obedience. Christ sets the agenda and he makes the rules."[8] Up to a point, this kind of discipleship is conceived of as a direct process involving the individual and Christ; however, it is just as frequently understood in terms of obedient submission to the teaching and leading of Christ's deputies: either the Church or, in certain evangelical circles the "discipler," "shepherd," or "leader."

The moment that the meaning of the content of Jesus' message starts to be discussed, the concept of discipleship has to be broadened to speak to the issue of what particular kind of life God is calling the person to, above and beyond continuing to spread the message.

The Communal Context of Discipleship

Children of God: Sons and Daughters in Christ

The idea of the Family of God (or Christ) tends to be more prominent in ecclesiological works than it is in those focusing on the nature of the life of the Christian individual. Although the latter presuppose and allude to the idea of Christians being children of God, they tend to do so only in the contexts of assuring the person of their redeemed status (now you are a "son"

---

[8] Kenneth C. Kinghorn, *Dynamic Discipleship* (Old Tappan, NJ: Revell, 1973) 16. At the time of writing, Kinghorn was a Professor of Church History at Asbury Theological Seminary. He describes himself as "defending no particular denominational tradition" (p. 11).

not a "slave"), discussing of prayer to the Father (the privilege of saying "Abba") and accepting the Father's will and acts, or in the context of reminding the reader that the ecclesiastical setting for their faith is to be understood in terms of a family. In the first two cases it is rare to find extended discussion carried out in the language of father and child. The image is usually drawn upon in passing to highlight trust, obedience, and wonder, the Christian being supposed to construe the happenings of the universe as to some high degree mysterious yet for the best, as a child (in this picture of things) trusts the loving, wise and powerful *pater familias*:

> Our Lord gave us the picture of the child as a model for Christian faith (Mk 10:14–16) not because of the child's helplessness but because of the child's willingness to be led, to be taught, to be blessed.[9]

The longest treatment I came across was a chapter entitled "Called to Childlikeness," in Paul Powell's *The Complete Disciple*. Powell enumerates such childlike virtues as being quick to forgive (is this really true?), responsiveness, and living by faith. "What does it mean," he asks, "to become as a little child?" It means "to be open and honest with God and ourselves. It means to forgive so that we can be forgiven. It means to respond to the call of God. It means to trust in God fully and completely."[10]

Jung's avowed discovery of the child archetype has prompted some to pay more attention to this construal of life in terms of living as a child, but for most authors the idea has its limits. We are, after all, as Stuart Briscoe points out in manly tones, exhorted elsewhere in the Scriptures to grow to fullness and maturity: "God's desire is that His enemies should become His children, and that His children should become men, and that His men should be mature!"[11]

In the second case, the focus is on the sisterhood and brotherhood of those in the family rather than their vertical relationship to the Father.[12] Robert A. Raines writes:

---

[9] Peterson, *Long Obedience*, 150.

[10] Powell, *The Complete Disciple* (Wheaton, IL: Victor Books, 1984) 31. Powell is a Baptist pastor from Texas who is an evangelical campaign preacher and has written a number of books on the Christian life.

[11] Briscoe, *The Fullness of Christ* (London: Marshall, Morgan & Scott, 1965) 15. Presumably, though, Briscoe would agree that true maturity retains those dimensions of childlikeness that are good.

[12] "[A] new relationship in Christ and with Christ is more than *vertical*. It is also *horizontal*. We become members of Christ's body, the church" (Gene A. Getz, *Serving One Another* [Wheaton, IL: Victor Books, 1984] 13). Getz describes himself as a pastor who spent most of his life as a full-time professor. He taught at the Moody Bible Institute (p. 115).

The church is the family of Christ. Jesus spoke of His disciples as His brothers and sisters (Mk 3:35), called them to an allegiance higher than blood-tie loyalty (Lk 14:26) and promised them new brothers and sisters in the fellowship of His followers (Mk 10:30).[13]

Their privileged relationship to Christ must needs be complemented by a new relationship with fellow Christians:

> Because we belong to Christ, we also belong to each other. He who has chosen us also chooses those who are our brothers and sisters. We have no choice in the matter. Some of our brothers we may like; others we may dislike. . . . We cannot be loyal to Him without being loyal to them. We cannot deny them without denying Him. We might wish to avoid this horizontal belonging and cling only to Him. But we cannot do so. We belong to Christ only by belonging to each other.[14]

And they are not supposed to relate in the kind of curmudgeonly way that this last paragraph perhaps implies. The family of God is like a human family in that its members have to struggle to love one another.[15] However, there is a general understanding that the paradigm of the human family has its limits for understanding life in community. When reflecting upon the manner in which the sisters and brothers manifest their love for each other, it is necessary for Raines to introduce the language of ministering and servanthood. One earthly analogy breaks down; another must be sought to supplement it.

Members of the Body

Like the metaphor of family, that of the Body of Christ is intended to speak primarily to the issue of the nature of the Christian community as a whole, pointing to the need for the church to be one in which "all have different functions, but in which all play an equally important role."[16] It is invoked in treatments of discipleship to underline the general context in which discipleship takes place and to emphasize that Christians are (or should be) distinguished by the harmony among them. But, although it is always presupposed, and periodically alluded to, the image of the Body has limited potential for extended development in the particular context that we are considering. It is not one, in Max Black's words, "with implications rich enough to

---

[13] Raines, *Reshaping the Christian Life* (New York: Harper & Row, 1964) 17.

[14] Ibid.

[15] Ibid., 19.

[16] Susan Brooks Thistlethwaite, *Metaphors for the Contemporary Church* (New York: Pilgrim, 1983) 61.

suggest novel hypotheses and speculations in the primary field of investigation.''[17] In the present context, this means that it cannot be drawn out to discuss in full what it means to live the Christian life. How far can one get using the language of limbs? What does it mean for me to decide I should be an arm? I learn from the image overall that the virtues of living in harmony (and possibly being obedient to the head) are of importance, but it is hard to get much further. The development of the image is stymied by the fact that there is no room within it for the idea of independent action. It is there to stress ideas of participation in the united community which has Christ as its head. It is intended to downplay individualistic aspects of the religious life and therefore, hardly surprisingly, does not lend itself well to a genre that focuses on the individual's development (albeit within a community setting). Other images have to be brought in to supplement it.

Imitators of Christ

> We cannot honour God more nor express our advancing of his name better for his honouring us so highly, than by imitating Christs Living in our Nature. This will be a Cleaving to him in our practice. It will be a living as he lived: and better we cannot Live. . . . No example like this. . . . He is all Example, and examplary. Save onely in Such things in which he is above Examplariness: as in all his life taken as a Mediator. . . . Christs life is peculiarly Imitable by us; because it is accomplished in our Nature . . . the most Naturall Imitableness and Imitation are in things of the Same kinde. Birds of a kinde imitate one another. Beasts of the same kinde do follow one another. So men imitate one another. . . . We were made, and formed with an Imitating Principle in our Nature, which cannot be Suffocated, or Stifled, but will act in imitating Some Example; God to prevent us from taking wrong Patterns to follow, hath presented us with a perfect Pattern of right practice in our own nature in Christ, which is most Examplary, being a most Exact Coppy, written by the Deity of the Son of God, with the Pen of the Humanity, on the milk white Sheet of an Holy Life.[18]

What it means to be reconciled to God and to develop further in christlikeness has been interpreted from the earliest times in terms of the wiping away or covering of sin and the restoration of the imago in the fallen human by a process beginning with repentance and baptism. The extent to which this is

---

[17] Black, *Models and Metaphors*, 233.

[18] Edward Taylor, "The Human Nature," in idem, *Christographia* (ed. Norman S. Grabo; New Haven: Yale University Press, 1962) 32–34. Edward Taylor was born in England but came early to America. He was a minister (in Westfield, Massachusetts), theologian, and poet who lived and wrote during the late seventeenth and early eighteenth centuries.

seen as having been accomplished by Christ's initial work of salvation and the extent to which it is a process drawn out in the life of the Christian, and the degree to which it is a matter of the Christian's own effort or a matter entirely of the Spirit in accordance with predestination might be seen as the heart of every major soteriological and pastoral disagreement in history. Whenever we seek to discuss the nature of the Christian life, it is necessary to speak of it in relation to Jesus as both Saviour and Pattern. Insofar as discipleship involves acting according to the content of Christ's teaching and his life, this cannot be avoided. However, contemporary writers differ as sharply as ever did Augustine and Pelagius over the extent to which our wills enter into this proceeding and as bitterly as ever did Luther and his various opponents over the extent to which the post-conversion acts of the Christian have "value" in God's eyes.

Mimēsis (imitation) as the means of ethical development, and its accompanying goal of *homoiōsis theō* (conformation to God) were central concepts in the teachings of the Middle Platonic tradition.[19] Philo speaks of both rulers and parents as imitators of God and invites all humans to become imitators of God through their imitation of the logos in the image of which they were made and which is also God's image.[20] Within the earthly realm, the Greco-Roman pedagogy stressed particularly the exemplary role of the teacher and the *pater familias*.

For Paul, the imitation is of Christ through the imitation of himself, Paul, who is the imitator of Christ (1 Cor 11.1; 4:15–16). What this imitation means is spelt out throughout his letters, but particularly in Philippians 2–3 where the self-emptying of Christ and his adoption of the form of a slave or servant is made the paradigm for the Christian. In this context, the language of the 'image' is not directly invoked; however, Paul elsewhere defines sonship of God in terms of conformation to the image of the Son (Rom 8:29; 2 Cor 3:18).[21] The composite picture, therefore, is one of the Christian being

---

[19] The idea of *homoiōsis* of course goes back beyond this, Plato's *Theaetetus* being one of the classic references.

[20] F. H. Colson, *The Works of Philo* (LCL; Cambridge, MA: Harvard University Press). On kings and rulers, see *On the Special Laws* 4.187–88 (*Works*, vol. 8); on parents, see, e.g., *On the Decalogue* 51 (*Works*, vol. 7); on the invitation to all to imitate God, see, e.g., *Special Laws* 4.73 (*Works*, vol. 8); *On the Virtues*, 168 (*Works*, vol. 8). A helpful overview of Philo's view of imitation is found in Robert Wild, " 'Be Imitators of God': Discipleship in the Letter to the Ephesians"; in Segovia, *Discipleship*, 128–33.

[21] The letter to the Ephesians drops the idea of Christ as the image or *eikōn*, seeing Christ and the Church together as the new humanity, the writer's injunction to imitate God as children do their father being an invitation to a direct form of imitation. The concept of the imitation of God persists during the patristic period. "And do not wonder that it is possible for man to be the imitator of God [*mimētēs theou*]; it is possible if he will," says the writer of the "Epistle to Diog-

consistently conformed to the likeness of Christ through imitation of his pattern of suffering servanthood: dying and rising with him in baptism and suffering persecution and possible death in this life with the sure hope of entering the resurrected life of which Christ was the first fruits. This connection of image and imitation holds together through most of Christian history—for as long as the picture of God as Creator of creatures in the divine image holds good.

Precisely what the imitation involves depends upon the person's understanding of the relative roles of human will and divine grace and upon their understanding of what it is about Christ that should be imitated. If we turn to contemporary authors we see that while all stress the role of both grace and human responsibility, some prefer to speak almost exclusively in terms of being continually conformed by God to the imago, chastising those who would stress the Christian's active role in patterning themselves after Christ. Writers such as Stuart Briscoe center their discussions upon such passages as Romans 8:29 and 2 Corinthians 3:18 and stress the idea that God desires and brings about the continual conformation of his children to the image of Christ so that the image within them may be restored. The emphasis is put upon the converted Christian being constantly shaped by the Spirit in submission to Christ. The "imitation" is not something done by the individual. Thus Briscoe writes that

the Christian is not to endeavour to emulate the glorious life of Jesus Christ, the Supreme Example, because if he does he is bound to fail ... but the man in whose soul the sin-defying properties of the Risen Christ are made real can constantly be experiencing a series of miracles whereby he is translated into a new strata of spiritual experience.[22]

This sense of being the recipient of God's conforming action should not, I think, necessarily be classified as theologically conservative. It is found in the writings of authors of radically different persuasions. In some writers, however, the concept takes a deeply conservative turn, because it is set in a cosmology of the traditional Neo-Platonic variety where the essence of perfection is to understand one's place in the chain of being and to reflect like a polished mirror the image of the image. C. S. Lewis, one of the great father figures of modern evangelical theology, spoke in rapt terms of this picture:

In the New Testament the art of life itself is an art of imitation. . . . "Originality" in the New Testament is quite plainly the prerogative of God alone; even

netus." "Epistle to Diognetus," in vol. 2 of *The Apostolic Fathers* (trans. Kirsopp Lake; LCL 25; Cambridge, MA: Harvard University Press, 1913) 10.4.

[22] Briscoe, *Fullness*, 44–45.

---

within the triune being of God it seems to be confined to the Father. The duty and happiness of every other being is placed in being derivative, in reflecting like a mirror. Nothing could be more foreign to the tone of scripture than the language of those who describe a saint as a "moral genius" or a "spiritual genius" thus insinuating that his virtue or spirituality is "creative" or "original". If I have read the New Testament aright, it leaves no room for "creativeness" even in a modified or metaphorical sense. Our whole destiny seems to lie in the opposite direction, in being as little as possible ourselves, in acquiring a fragrance that is not our own but borrowed, in becoming clean mirrors filled with the image of a face that is not ours. . . . the highest good of a creature must be creaturely—that is, derivative or reflective—good.[23]

Although few of the writers state the matter so clearly, this hierarchical view of the universe still seems to prevail at least in a sketchy form in the mainstream of Protestant Christianity despite objections that it is an unwarranted hellenistic intrusion into the Christian tradition. Where it prevails and is the context of discussion of imitation and discipleship, the element of knowing one's place is necessarily present and there tends to be a deep suspiciousness about persons who do not recognize the limits of their place in the scheme of things. The conservative tendency is compounded by the view of the depravity of the will that generally accompanies the hierarchical cosmology— leading the person to be seen not only as ontologically destined for a role in which imitation of God is the greatest achievement, but also as thrown by the effects of sin into a state where the most they can *hope* to do is imitate a clear example, and even then as needing extensive outside assistance. Augustine's theology with its bringing together of hierarchical cosmology and the idea of the vitiating effects of original sin with their resultant need for submission to the authority of Christ and of Christ's appointed teachers, has left its permanent mark on much of Protestantism. The result is a language of discipleship which expresses conformation to the image in terms of total submission and obedience to the teacher and master:

[A] disciple must submit completely to the Master's will. The Master desires to put His own truth into the mind of the disciple and His own affections into the heart of the disciple. He puts His own will before the disciple so that the disciple knows nothing, loves nothing, obeys no one other than the Lord Jesus Christ.[24]

[23] Lewis, "Christianity and Literature," in idem, *Rehabilitations and Other Essays* (London: Oxford University Press, 1939) 191.
[24] Pentecost, *Design*, 35.

The disciple's own nature and reason are not sufficient to allow correct knowledge and action. The Lord must take over. This dynamic is generally discussed by Protestant writers under the terminology of the "lordship of Christ" and discussion of discipleship in its terms tends to proceed via an incitement to check each aspect of one's life to see if Christ's lordship is visibly present in it. The language of control generally moves into the language of subject and Master and servant and Lord and this will be discussed later.

This kind of view is an anathema to many modern Christians whose theological universe is more of a horizontal democracy and who do not share the dismal view of the corrupt reason and nature that tends to go hand in hand with the hierarchical world view. Carl Jung's words capture the spirit of impatience with what is conceived to be a static notion of imitation:

> The modern man does not want to know in what way he can imitate Christ, but in what way he can live his own individual life, however meager and uninteresting it may be. It is because every form of imitation seems to him deadening and sterile that he rebels against the force of tradition that would hold him to well-trodden ways.[25]

Protestants, says Jung,

> must sooner or later face this question: Are we to understand the 'imitation of Christ' in the sense that we should copy his life and, if I may use the expression, ape his stigmata; or in the deeper sense that we are to live our own proper lives as truly as he lived his in its individual uniqueness?[26]

In response to this kind of heady blend of Pelagian faith in human possibilities and Romantic notions of the special nature of the individual and the greatness of "creativity," conservative writers like Elizabeth Elliot snap back:

> The disciple is not on his own, left to seek *self-actualization*, which is a new word for old-fashioned *selfishness*. He is not "doing his thing" to find his own life or liberty or happiness. He gives himself to a Master and in so doing leaves self behind.[27]

---

[25] Jung, "Psychotherapists or the Clergy," in Herbert Read, Michael Fordham, and Gerhard Adler, eds., *The Collected Works of C. G. Jung*, vol. 11: *Psychology and Religion: West and East* (Bollingen Series 20; 2d ed.; Princeton: Princeton University Press, 1963) 341.

[26] Ibid., 340.

[27] Elliot, *Discipline: The Glad Surrender* (Old Tappan, NJ: Revell, 1982) 25.

More liberal treatments tend to be characterized by their construal of imitation or discipleship in terms of Jesus' socially oriented teachings about the Kingdom. Generally they eschew detailed discussion of cosmology and eschatology and concentrate on Jesus' compassion toward the outcast and on his ministry of reconciliation as lived by example. Sometimes this is described in more abstract ethical terms as imitating his qualities or disposition or responding humbly and obediently to God's will as revealed in events. More generally, the writers pass over into the language of "servanthood." The idea of servanthood is one upon which I would like to focus particular attention. It is perhaps the fundamental image of the Christian life.

3

Servants of All

The language of servanthood is pervasive in Christianity and has become the subject of critical scrutiny in recent years.[1] It therefore merits particular consideration here. Discussions of discipleship and imitation inevitably pass over into discussions of servanthood because Christ acted in a way interpreted by early followers, and possibly by himself, as fulfilling the prophecies of the mysterious Suffering Servant, and because his actions and words extolled a posture of sacrificial service to others and were described with language drawn from the sphere of human service.[2] Beyond this, the concept of servanthood is informed by the additional idea that all God's creatures are rightly God's subject servants—or servants of God under Christ's lordship.[3] A further twist is added when obedient service as a corollary of one's

---

[1] Not, perhaps, just so recently. Nietzsche, e.g., wrote at length on the servile aspect of Christians. See particularly his preface to, and three essays in, Walter Kaufmann, ed., *On the Genealogy of Morals* (1967; reprinted New York: Vintage Books) 15–163.

[2] *Diakonia* is the Greek term most commonly used in the New Testament to refer to the action of serving others. On its use in the New Testament and in the early church, see Werner Foerster, "διακονία," *TDNT* 2 (1964) 87–88.

[3] The term *doulos* is generally used in the New Testament to describe the one who is a servant or slave of Christ. It is a term used with greatest frequency by Paul to speak of his enslavement or service to Christ and to Christ's community. Humans have no possibility of being absolutely free: they are *douloi* always to either righteousness or wickedness. It remains for them to choose their overlord. See Karl Rengstorf, "δοῦλος," *TDNT* 2 (1964) 261–80. For a brief discussion of the various Greek concepts underlying the English terms of servant and slave, see Klaus Hess, "Serve" and Gervais T. D. Angel, "Slave" in *The New International Dictionary of New Testament Theology*.

participation in a hierarchy of God-church-humanity is introduced; servant-hood then characterizes also one's posture in relation to earthly superiors who are seen as mediating Christ's lordship. It is important when looking at the contemporary language of servanthood to differentiate between these related, but different, concepts of service to others and servanthood—even servitude—before God. They give rise to markedly different rhetoric and have somewhat different implications.[4]

Servants of the Lord and Master and Subjects of the King

The Theological Framework

At one level, then, the language of servanthood is a development of what it means to exist as one who should render obedient service to the divine lawgiver and ruler. It is the human end, together with "subjecthood" of the metaphor of divine kingship or overlordship. Directed to Christ as King, it extends and strengthens the obedience-submission language of the master-disciple relationship and shifts the focus from learning and development to grateful pleasing and honoring of the King. Presbyterian author W. Phillip Keller elaborates:

> To have a kingdom, you must have a king, a monarch, a sovereign. By the same definition, to have a kingdom you must have those in it who are subject to the sovereign. They are those who enjoy the benefits and protection of their monarch. Their lives are enriched because they allow themselves to be governed and ruled under a benign sovereignty. The subjects subscribe to and endorse the will of their monarch by being loyal and obedient to Him. They recognize that the laws and edicts of their ruler are designed and drawn up with their own best interests in mind. They are contented citizens of a special community under the control of their own special sovereign. Gladly, cheerfully, wholeheartedly, they choose of their own free will to be governed and ruled this way. Their king's will and wishes are their cherished commands, their very code of conduct. They will willingly, gladly sacrifice their lives for king and country. . . . This is the precise picture Christ endeavored to convey to His contemporaries. Few ever caught the vision. Few see it today.[5]

[4] Likewise, it should be noted that the language of "citizenship" focuses attention on the relations of citizens to one another as much as to any overlord, while the language of "subjects of the kingdom" puts the emphasis squarely on the citizens' duty to the King.

[5] Keller, *Walking with God* (Old Tappan, NJ: Revell, 1980) 111. Keller is described on the book jacket as a noted photographer, agrologist and ecology consultant, and as "a popular lecturer and lay speaker" and "the prolific author of nineteen books."

It should be stressed that for Keller, as for most other Christian expositors, *Christ* as much as the Father is the King of the new kingdom, and their rule is also carried out by the Spirit:

> Our God has established the Kingdom of heaven—or Kingdom of God—His Kingdom. He invites us to become citizens of that community . . . to give our allegiance to Christ, the king of kings. But . . . the conditions for becoming a party of that unique and privileged community is that we shall be willing a) to be governed by God; b) to come under Christ's control; c) to be subject to the Sovereignty of His Spirit.[6]

The Father is, of course, also conceived of as King.

In contemporary American treatments, some writers display a distinct problem with the notion of kingship and find it necessary to recast the first person of the Trinity parabolically as, for example, a corporate president. Consider the way Clem Walters puts across the point the servants should always be at the ready and never mind if someone else gets picked for a job they want to do:

> Remember whom you serve. The sovereign Lord of the universe is free to use his servants as he wills. You are like a member of a corps of chauffeurs assigned to a top-level executive. . . . Each one is trained. . . . The executive walks down the line and says, "You." This chauffeur helps him into the limousine and drives off. The other nine are still standing there at attention, glad they put themselves at the employer's disposal. Nobody cries and kicks and says, "Hey, how about me? I want to drive it!" . . . For you as a Christian servant, what matters is the disposition to be of service. Whether or not your services are employed, you are cheerful and submissive.[7]

The Implications for the Christian Life

If you question why you must think of yourself as a servant of the King, two answers are typically given: (1) God created us and is our ultimate overlord and serving him is both our duty and a joyous result of our gratitude to him; (2) All humans are necessarily either enslaved to righteousness or to sin, they are necessarily servants of God or of themselves and the devil. The first

---

[6] Ibid., 111–12.

[7] Clem J. Walters, *To Serve as Jesus Served: A Guide to Servanthood* (South Bend, IN: Charismatic Renewal Services, 1983) 9–10. Walters is described on the jacket as "a leader of People of Praise, an ecumenical community based in South Bend, Indiana." He has worked in missions and is one of the leading figures in the Charismatic renewal movement. Although this fact is not made fully explicit, some of the discussion of obedience in this book appears to have as its context the obedience of new disciples to their discipleship "leaders" in the church.

answer tends to be more fully drawn out in works on stewardship. It is the second answer that seems to be developed more fully in literature focusing on servanthood. Writers like to make much of the great irony that only in servanthood to Christ is freedom possible. "Absolute freedom is absolute nonsense," writes Paul W. Powell. "It leads to complete frustration and emptiness. It is only as we attach our lives to Jesus Christ that we can ever fulfill our intended purpose."[8] You cannot avoid being subject to something or someone. There is no autonomous neutrality possible. At its most extreme, this notion of being on the side of or enslaved to God or Satan develops into the cosmologically expressed understanding of Christian life as warfare. We shall examine this later. In the interim, it should be noted that this picture of things lends itself to (or was originally the product of) a sanctioning of and fostering of the character traits or virtues of obedience, humility etc. (Authors are quick, however, to point out that this is no mere grovelling before an "oriental despot.") The obedience is both to God and to those closer at hand.

The implications for action do not, however, stop at the idea that our behavior should be in obedience to God. In conservative literature we find the hierarchical cosmology and its attendant hierarchical politics continuing to inform the broader image of servanthood to God. There is a chain of submission to be observed. God has deputies here on earth and they are to be obeyed accordingly.[9] In the sphere of lay existence, in line with the kind of household codes introduced into Ephesians and the Pastoral Epistles, children are to submit to parents and women are to submit to men as the church to Christ etc. This hierarchy of submissive servanthood is prominent in Christian life literature written by or for evangelical women. A special kind of language of powerful humility is used when talking of both "servant-leaders" in the Church and in the home. Clergy and husbands alike are to imitate Christ's special servant leadership:

> Jesus Christ, who was God in the flesh, has demonstrated with His own life that it is possible to be a servant leader. This is not a contradictory concept. It is uniquely Christian. It is possible to lead strongly and deliberately and to

---

[8] Powell, *Dynamic Discipleship* (Nashville: Broadman, 1984) 113.

[9] This is less of an emphasis in non-episcopal Protestant writings. Theoretically, in these contexts, the leader does not represent Christ in quite such an authoritarian mode. Thus, e.g., T. B. Maston writes, "The basic call of God, which is one to every child of His, is to serve or minister. ... [A]ll of us should remember that as far as our Heavenly Father is concerned, there is no 'hierarchy of calling' " (*To Walk as He Walked* [Nashville: Broadman, 1985] 97). Maston is a retired professor of Christian Ethics who taught at Southwestern Baptist Theological Seminary.

"manage well." But it is possible to do so with humility, compassion, and with a servant's heart.[10]

In the family context, the precise meaning of this is almost always drawn out with the assistance of Eph 5:22–30.[11] Writers hasten to assure the woman that her duty is submission, but in this lies her dignity and good fortune.[12] There is nothing humiliating about submitting to her husband. God intended things this way. All will be fine if the husband responsibly carries out his duty to love and look after the wife as Christ did the Church.[13] Despite the voices of such women as Patricia Gundry and the (once more overtly evangelical) Virginia Ramey Mollenkott, this remains the general line of discussion. It is found as much, if not more so, in the writings of conservative women authors. Sometimes the language of submission is relatively dilute and barely different from that of, say Stuart Briscoe, talking about his own (male) submission to Christ. An example of this would be Ruth Mead's *No One Wins Like a Loser*.[14] For the most part her book talks in highly general terms about submission to God's will and acceptance of His plans for her. However, all tied up with her discovery of this great truth is the following discovery:

> God doesn't leave us in the dark, without symbols and signs . . . He has taught me the meaning of both responsibility and "letting go" through the double symbol of the husband-wife relationship. . . .
> Christ does the work; the church receives, accepts, rejoices in that work. Christ's work is the doing, the church's work is receiving. The husband must

[10] Getz, *Serving*, 104.

[11] Especially of verses 22–25: "Wives, be subject to your husbands, as to the Lord. For the husband is the head of the wife as Christ is the head of the church, his body, and is himself its saviour. As the church is subject to Christ, so let wives be subject in everything to their husbands. Husbands, love your wives, as Christ loved the church. . . ."

[12] Mary is also evoked as an example of dutiful submission. Her significance for Protestant women of this century would appear to be limited judging by the materials on the market. For a discussion of the general issue of the role of Mary in shaping women's experience, see Elizabeth A. Johnson, "The Marian Tradition and the Reality of Women," *Horizons* 12 (1985) 116–35.

[13] Since this is the standard tack, examples could be multiplied indefinitely. See, e.g., James Montgomery Boice, "How to Be Happy as a Family," in idem, *How to Live the Christian Life* (Chicago: Moody, 1982) 65–73. Boice is described on the cover as pastor of a Presbyterian church in Philadelphia, a speaker for the radio "Bible Study Hour," and a graduate of Harvard College. The chapters of this book grew out of a series of talks that he gave on his radio show (p. 7.)

[14] Mead, *No One Wins Like a Loser* (Harrisburg, PA: Christian Publications, Inc., 1976). Mead is an American writer. Her denomination is not given. She appears to have belonged to some form of charismatic Protestant church in West Germany at the time of writing.

grow in responsibility, must demonstrate responsibility to his children; the wife symbolizes to her children the whole concept of letting go.

Love in two persons. The male love, Christ's love, that wills, plans, initiates, takes responsibility. The female love, the love of the church, that surrenders in childlike abandonment of spirit.[15]

And although she generally avoids extended reflection on the meaning of feminine submission and polemic against other views, the author cannot resist getting in a few shots at "women's libbers":

The thing that distresses me most is that a modern intelligent woman can be just as trapped, just as bound, in the absolute *littleness* of a life of demanding her supposed rights as her forbears in Victorian times before the emancipation of women was even *thought* of. . . .

Whether Merrie develops into an aggressive, unlovely, demanding, abrasive woman with her frayed-by-now list of supposed rights, or whether she develops into a truly intelligent feminine woman wanting to discover God's laws, wanting to fit in with reality rather than expecting reality to fit in with her own subjective reality, is going to make all the difference in the world as to whether Merrie finds happiness or not.[16]

The language of servanthood in this kind of writing has a tendency to pass over into the language of sexual submission of bride to groom, and we should consider this language briefly.

In the monastic traditions of East and West, and in the forms of lay spirituality influenced by these, the notion of the Church and the individual's soul as the faithful Bride of Christ has held a position of great importance. Yet despite its prominence in Protestant literature of meditation before the late nineteenth century, it does not seem to have retained its place in American or English Protestant devotional theology. As a structuring and extended image, it appears with frequency only in literature directed toward the conservative woman.

One may conjecture about the reasons for this. In works written recently by liberal and radical Christians, the avoidance of the image may be motivated by awareness of feminist critiques of the equation of Church and soul with the "feminine" or "passive" and the equation of the divine with the "masculine" bridegroom understood, patriarchally, as the active force. Yet this does not explain the fact that the image is also scant in more conservative literature. Why? Two reasons suggest themselves: one historical and the other structural.

---

[15] Ibid., 40.
[16] Ibid., 125.

Historically, one may suspect that among Protestants the image of the feminine soul surrendering to the embrace of her groom went the same way as did "feminine" portrayals of Jesus and of the ideal Christian early this century. During the early and mid nineteenth century, a clearly documented "feminization" of Christ occurs.[17] Women are taken to be paradigms of the true spiritual virtues, and these virtues are seen to be compassion of an endlessly self-giving and denying sort, and sympathy of a passive variety. This phenomenon was experienced both in England and America. Reminding women readers of his altruistic and biblically based reasons for wishing to keep them in their homes sympathetically ministering to their menfolk, Horace Bushnell writes:

> Oh! if there were nothing in this world but these workers in will and war and wrong, called men, it would be a most unblest and wretchedly dry concern. Nothing can ever lift the picture till a subject nature appears, milder, truer, and closer to the type of God's own dear submissions in the cross of his Son; allowing us to bless our sight in the beholding of so many women, by graces and benignities of self-forgetting love and sacrifice.[18]

This kind of glorification of the passive dimensions of spirituality continued to appear in the context of justifications for keeping women in their place, but it was on the way out as far as the broader conception of spirituality was concerned. Bushnell himself, outside this particular polemical context, joined Henry Ward Beecher and others in calling for a more "manly" spirituality. The 1890s saw the appearance of what has been called a "cult of virility." Theologians and pastors tumbled over themselves to demonstrate that Jesus was a man's man and religion a manly enterprise.[19] Notions of surrender in the spiritual life were only proposed in the context of the idea of gaining some kind of spiritual "power" or "victory"; the appeal was to the hard-nosed realist who saw the natural and social world in terms of struggle, testing and victory. This attitude has far from disappeared. "God don't make

[17] On this phenomenon, see Ann Douglas, *The Feminization of American Culture* (New York: Knopf, 1978).

[18] Bushnell, *Women's Suffrage; the Reform against Nature* (New York: Scribner, 1870) 99. Bushnell was a Congregationalist minister and theologian. For a similar offering from the English context, see William Landels, *Woman's Sphere and Work Considered in the Light of Scripture* (London: Nisbet, 1861). Landels was minister of Regent's Park Chapel in London.

[19] For an excellent brief overview of the phenomenon of the transition to muscular and manly Christianities, see Holifield, *History of Pastoral Care*, 159–84. On the decade of the 1890s specifically, see John Higham, "The Reorientation of American Culture in the 1890s," in idem, *Writing American History: Essays on Modern Scholarship* (Bloomington, IN: Indiana University Press, 1970) 77–100.

no wimps," declares the title of the second chapter of Stephen Brown's *No More Mr. Nice Guy.*[20] Brown enthusiastically sets about proving that Christian saints have never been "wimps," and teaching his readers that God does not wish them to be doormats.

In this kind of environment, it is not hard to see why male writers on the Christian life would fight shy of imagery which cast them as fainting brides on the arm of a bridegroom. Writers continue to speak of the Church as the Bride of Christ and themselves as part of this, but do not encourage reflection on the self as feminine spouse of Christ.[21] Contemporary Jungians intent upon recapturing the feminine dimension of their personalities have reopened this avenue of reflection on the spirit, but as yet their influence does not seem to be spreading among writers on the Christian life. The only place where one finds extensive use of the marriage imagery is in writings by or for conservative women. There the tendency is to focus on Eph 5:21–23 and to focus more generally on woman's duty to submit to her earthly spouse as the church submits to its heavenly groom. This is somewhat different from speaking of oneself or one's own soul as the Lord's bride. Parallels are however drawn: "The freedom that a wife has, living peacefully within the embrace of her husband's rule, is a type of the freedom that the committed soul has within God's embrace."[22]

The second reason that marriage imagery is not especially pervasive in contemporary literature on the Christian life may be that it is limited in its possibilities for explicating the full nature of Christian existence. It speaks of the soul or spirit's[23] relation to the divine and, in its eschatological context, of

[20] Stephen Brown, *No More Mr. Nice Guy!* (Nashville: Nelson, 1986). Brown is a Presbyterian writer.

[21] One should note, however, that contemporary Christians continue to purchase and read works from previous eras where this language is prevalent. The emphasis on the fact that it is the Church per se as bride is, in fact, truer to the New Testament message which clearly indicates, as Edward Taylor (*The Poems of Edward Taylor* [ed. Donald E. Stanford; New Haven: Yale University Press, 1960] 324) put it:

Whom Christ espousseth is his Spouse indeed.
His Spouse or bride no Single Person nay.
She is an agrigate so doth proceed
And in it sure and cant be stole away.
And if you thus be members made of mee
He'l be your Bridegroom, you his Spouse shall be.

[22] Judith M. Miles, *The Feminine Principle: A Woman's Discovery of the Key to Total Fulfillment* (Minneapolis: Bethany Fellowship, Inc., 1975) 63. Miles is described in the preface as a member of the Lutheran Church (Missouri Synod), a happily married mother of four who did doctoral studies in English (and presumably gave them up) and who describes herself as one who "has astoundingly received grace and mercy from the Lord despite her resurgent pride of intellect and hardness of heart" (p. 6).

[23] "Spirit" would appear to be used in much contemporary theology in preference to "soul."

a final reuniting with the groom at the Messianic banquet, but it has little to say about the living of the Christian life (unless one count the inculcating of obedience). Its sphere is what has traditionally been demarked as the "spiritual life." Because Christian life literature is as much, if not more, geared to the ethical, it is not surprising that the language of union does not receive great development here. To use Abraham Edel's language, in this context spousal union with Christ is a "casual" model or metaphor, rather than a heuristic or structural one. It appears on isolated occasions and is not elaborated or put to analytic use.[24]

Servants of One Another:
A Call to Action and to Suffering

A Shift in Theological Emphasis

It is important to distinguish between the kind of language of servanthood just described, and that which takes as its imitative basis Christ's compassionate servanthood to humanity, rather than his disposition of obedience to the Father. The two things are not divorced since it is in obedience to God's loving will that this compassionate ministry is exercised; nevertheless, there is a difference in the two starting points for discussion of servanthood. The following comment from Chuck Swindoll points up the difference and the connection well:

> We find it encouraging to think of ourselves as God's servants. Who would not want to be a servant of the King? But when it comes to serving other people, we begin to question the consequences. We feel noble when serving God; we feel humble when serving people. Serving God receives a favorable response; serving people, especially those who cannot repay, has no visible benefit or glory from anyone—except from God! Christ gave us the example: "The Son of Man did not come to be served, but to serve, and to give His life as a ransom for many" (Matt. 20:28). To be a servant of God we must be a servant of people.[25]

An understanding of the Christian life (and indeed all human life) as a

---

In the Pauline anthropology, there is a tripartite anthropology of spirit, soul, and body. This is rarely encountered in contemporary writers.

[24] Abraham Edel, "Metaphors, Analogies, Models, and all That, in Ethical Theory," in Sydney Morgenbesser, Patrick Suppes, and Morton White, eds., *Philosophy, Science, and Method: Essays in Honor of Ernest Nagel* (New York: St. Martin's, 1969) 366–67.

[25] Swindoll, *Improving Your Serve*, 97.

process of ministering to one another in love need not necessarily be set into the kind of hierarchical cosmology and politics that we saw in the previous section. Indeed, some authors ignore the language of God as ruler and say that in fact since Jesus is said truly to reveal God, and Jesus sees himself primarily as a servant, then God Godself is to be understood as servant, as humble etc. Insofar as God is still thought of as King, God is King of a kingdom of reversals where even kingship will not mean rule as we now understand it.[26]

These are the emphases of Christian liberation or social justice theology in its Catholic and Protestant forms. In the Protestant context, one finds the servant/kingdom theology present in most works on Christian living produced by authors of a liberal or radical persuasion. One finds them, perhaps, in their greatest clarity in the works of social justice oriented evangelicals such as Jim Wallis.[27] Servanthood is understood in terms of working as laborers in the vineyard of God's kingdom, of responding to God's gracious call to work in the spirit to help usher in the kingdom. What it means to do this is understood in the light of Jesus' teachings about the signs of the Kingdom:

> [H]is agenda for the kingdom hasn't changed since he called those first disciples. We are still called to heal the sick, proclaim the good news to the captive, and restore sight to the blind. As disciples we are all called to be involved actively and regularly in making a difference for the kingdom in our own society—right now.[28]

And it is understood also in the light of Jesus' own mode of life as a servant.

The concern with social action is also beginning to show itself again in somewhat more conservative Protestant writings on the Christian life. On retiring from his post as Professor of Ethics at Southwestern Baptist Theological Seminary, T. B. Maston set about introducing the notion of the Christian life as servanthood to a conservative audience. His 1985 work *To Walk as*

---

[26] See, e.g., Donald B. Kraybill, *The Upside-Down Kingdom* (Scottdale, PA: Herald, 1978).

[27] See, e.g., Wallis, *Agenda for Biblical People* (New York: Harper & Row, 1978). Wallis is, however, also drawn to the language of pilgrimage and sojourn—perhaps not surprisingly given his connection with the Washington based Sojourners Community. The epilogue of this book, "Sojourners in the Land," brings together servanthood and sojourn, concluding: "The servant community is the gathered style of biblical people. It is the style of those who live as sojourners in the land, and it is the way that God has so mightily used a faithful people in history and will use them again in our own day" (p. 139).

[28] Tom Sine, *Taking Discipleship Seriously: A Radical Biblical Approach* (Valley Forge, PA: Judson, 1985) 23. Sine teaches at Seattle Pacific University and Fuller Theological Seminary and works with Evangelicals for Social Action.

He Walked is a particularly good example of the kind of text which gives the reader a simplified "life of Jesus," a grounding in all the doctrines the author feels are central, and a single image framework—servanthood—with which to draw all together. Maston, like Sine, is particularly concerned to make the reader understand that social justice and evangelism are not irrevocably opposed concerns. Jesus commanded them both, and in fact one's servant life is a key form of witness to the truth of his message:

> Many fail to give proper attention to the life that Jesus lived while He walked among people. This area, as is true of many aspects of the Christian life, should be both/and rather than either/or: Christ was both human and divine. He was and is deeply concerned about our salvation, but He was and is deeply concerned about the kinds of lives we live. Will you not agree that those of us who are conservative in our theology should give more attention to the kind of life He lived and the kind of life He wants us to live for Him? . . .
>
> What we believe [theologically] . . . is tremendously important. I will seek to emphasize in this book that equally important is the kind of lives we live, including the spirit we manifest toward those with whom we may disagree theologically. After all, the lives we live are more convincing to the rank and file of people . . . than our position on any theological matter.[29]

It bears emphasizing that servanthood in the kingdom remains a primary category for evangelical Protestants as well as for their Catholic counterparts involved in liberation theology. They have more in common with each other than they do with those in their own traditions who espouse spiritualized notions of the Kingdom or who do not believe that the Kingdom will be ushered in until after the Second Coming. The precise use one makes of a symbol such as the Kingdom, or a self-understanding such as oneself as servant, will be shaped by its place in the general configuration of one's beliefs. It is not a symbol whose consequences are self-explanatory.

Implications for the Christian Life

The emphasis on servanthood of the kind displayed by Jesus necessarily brings with it the ideas of self-denial and suffering. Suffering is generally seen as incidental to the work, not as an end in itself (except insofar as God sends it to test and improve the person). There is no implication that God is an intentionally harsh taskmaster. The idea of self-denial provokes more disagreement in interpretation. What does it mean to "deny yourself"? Primarily, in the context of discussing servanthood, the authors construe it to mean the putting aside of all interests that run contrary to those of the Lord.

---

[29] Maston, *To Walk*, 10.

This, of course, can mean any number of different things according to circumstance. When are our interests selfish and when not? How can we be sure? Who establishes the guidelines? It has been pointed out in numerous works that religion works to keep people in their place insofar as it offers them a postponed reward for obedience sometime in the next life, and insofar as it fosters an attitude of self-sacrifice which benefits certain sectors of society (e.g., the government, white slave owners, males). This kind of observation is behind the writings of James H. Cone when he writes of the dangers of the logic of self-sacrifice when it comes to the oppressed:

> Jesus' exhortations "turn the other cheek" and "go the second mile" are no evidence that black people should let white people beat the hell out of them. We cannot use Jesus' behavior in the first century as a literal guide for our actions in the twentieth century.[30]

Similar concerns motivate such remarks as those of Valerie Saiving to the effect that the ideal of self-denial can be dangerous for women since it was and is a response to the particular forms of sinfulness more common to the male, namely those of pride, and that it does not assist women whose forms of sinfulness "are better suggested by such items as triviality, distractibility, and diffuseness; lack of an organizing center or focus; dependence on others for one's own self-definition . . . in short, underdevelopment or negation of the self."[31] There is, of course, an assumption at work here that self-development is a good thing. This is precisely what would have been denied during the greater part of Christian history. The courageous self-sacrificing woman is, for example, the perfect paradigm of Christian behavior for Horace Bushnell: "Her type of life is more like that of Christ than any man's can be."[32] And Paul Tillich asserted with some vigor that

> Self-sacrifice is not a character of male as male or female as female, but it is, in the very act of self-sacrifice, the negation of the one or the other in exclusion. Self-sacrifice breaks the contrast of the sexes, and this is symbolically manifest in the picture of the suffering Christ, in which Christians of both sexes have participated with equal psychological and spiritual intensity.[33]

[30] Cone, *A Black Theology of Liberation* (Philadelphia: Lippincott, 1970) 68.

[31] Saiving, "The Human Situation: A Feminine View," in Carol P. Christ and Judith Plaskow, eds., *Womanspirit Rising: A Feminist Reader in Religion* (San Francisco: Harper & Row, 1979) 37.

[32] Bushnell, *Women's Suffrage*, 80.

[33] Tillich, *Systematic Theology*, vol. 3: *Life and the Spirit: History and the Kingdom of God* (1963; reprinted Phoenix Books, 1976) 294.

The difficult problem is how to construe servanthood in such a way that it does not lead to an unhealthy disregard for one's own person, but—on the other hand—is not reinterpreted so broadly that it turns into self-serving. It may be true that a healthy "self-love" must be the basis of any healthy serving of others—you cannot love another truly if you have no love for yourself. But this line of reasoning can easily lead down the path of extensive self-culture and self-nurture and away from the path of suffering servanthood trodden by Christ. The writer must needs steer a passage between the Scylla of narcissism and the Charybdis of unhealthy disregard of self. When one encounters such statements as that of Stanley C. Baldwin to the effect that "if we define love as caring, and if caring about our own character development is our duty, then 'self-love' is a Christian virtue,"[34] one feels the danger of narcissism is imminent.[35]

Some Problems and Possibilities of Servanthood

The idea of serving others is at the heart of Jesus' message. To dilute the idea of service beyond a certain point is to depart from meaningful participation in the tradition. Given this fact, a particular dilemma presents itself: namely, how to understand the idea of servanthood in such a way that it cannot lead to the oppression of particular groups of people. This involves careful reflection on the point at which a person has actually attained the kind of selfhood that can freely choose to make sacrifices. It raises particularly interesting issues for the parent and the educator. Should you raise a child up to be unselfish from the earliest time, or should you inculcate a degree of selfishness as a necessary element in the development in the sense of self—which is then to be consciously deconstructed?

The idea of human service to God is likely to be viewed positively by most if what is being stressed is obedience to laws which benefit all. God's dominion is rarely seen as problematic so long as it is understood to be equitable. Indeed, God's servants may invoke their service to a higher Lord to overthrow earthly oppressors, just as much as kings may, rely upon divine sanction of their own positions to perpetuate their subjects' earthly servitude. Historically, the concept of a hierarchical serving of the divine by the human appears to have been accompanied by parallel arguments for serving of the

[34] Baldwin, *How to Build Your Christian Character* (Wheaton, IL: Victor Books, 1982) 113. Baldwin is the author of numerous "how-to" works.

[35] On the ambiguous status of the concept of "self-love" in Christian thought, see Gene Outka, "Agape and Self-love," in idem, *Agape: An Ethical Analysis* (New Haven: Yale University Press, 1972) 55–74.

male human by the female. One might say that there was no internal logical reason why this need be so. One could just as well follow the logic of appeal to a horizontal egalitarianism under a relativizing divinity; however, caution needs to be exercised here.

Perhaps the most troubling dimension, for many today, of the notion of being servants of a divine master is the radical gap between God and human that characterizes the relationship. This is built into the way that the greater part of the tradition has understood the language of servant and Master, subject and King. "In essence," says Don Cupitt,

> the more seriously the imagery of lordship and servanthood be taken the more it diminishes the believer's moral stature. If the believer, in his enthusiasm, declares that of himself he is depraved, that he cannot tell right from wrong, that he can do no good thing, that God must enlighten his conscience, fortify his will, direct his path, inspire and assist all his acts—then such language, the more literally it be taken, the more it offends against our post-Kantian sense of ourselves as responsible moral agents.[36]

No easy resolution is possible. One cannot have the comfort of the traditional language of submission and guidance, while espousing a rugged self-sufficiency in daily life. Indeed, says, Cupitt, it is dangerous to cling to the old imagery of vassal and lord as if it were the best available because that "suggests that religious people regard the social order which that imagery reflects as the best form of society, because it was the form of society which best imaged the nature of God."[37] "What the believer wants to express," he continues, is

> his sense of the all-encompassing total adequacy and beauty of God, and the over-riding character of God's claims, promises and consolations. He wants to convey a sense of fullness and completeness, experienced in an ecstasy that frees him from himself. It was, formerly, right to express this by saying that he found himself in the service of the greatest and most munificent of lords. But that is not the right way to express it today.[38]

[36] Cupitt, Crisis of Moral Authority (Philadelphia: Westminster, 1972) 119.
[37] Ibid., 120.
[38] Ibid.

4

Stewards of God,
Stewards of Life

The Rediscovery of a Self-Image

The last two decades have witnessed the strong resurgence of "stewardship" as a metaphor for the Christian life, and it provides us with a most interesting example of the rediscovery and revivification of a theme. Despite its solid biblical origins it appears to have exerted little appeal on the imagination of Christian writers until about two hundred years ago. The basic premise of human trusteeship of the world and accountability to God found its way into the mainstream of European thought, but few treatises were written specifically on Christian life as stewardship. God's own *oikonomia* or providential ordering of the cosmos and of the salvation of his creatures was a common theme in patristic literature, but the idea of each Christian as a trustee of the Lord's creation and of their own life was not developed in the language of stewardship.[1] Stewardship as a metaphor for the responsible Christian life experienced its first real rise to prominence in early nineteenth century America, apparently as the result of two developments in American Protestantism. One of these developments was the increasing desire to fund mission activity at home and abroad. This connection is highlighted by George E. Salstrand:

---

[1] On the theme in patristic literature, see G. L. Prestige, *God in Patristic Thought* (1936; reprinted London: S.P.C.K., 1952) 57–67; 98–102.

The missionary enterprise challenged Christian leaders with the realization of the great need, financial and spiritual. The effect was a re-examination of the scriptures with the intention of seeing what was taught regarding the relation of man to his money. The result was Stewardship, the American contribution to theological thinking.[2]

Salstrand stresses the Americanness of the discovery of the importance of stewardship, and indeed it was only in America that the metaphor came to have such importance during this period, even though the overseas missionary impetus was also strong in other Protestant countries.[3] Why was the image of the "steward" so much more compelling to Americans than to others?

The reason seems to lie in the second development which was more clearly restricted to North America: the necessity for many American churches of gaining congregational funding where little or no support from state or denomination was forthcoming. It has been argued that only in such a context could it have become necessary for the churches to court the individual believer and to appeal to images which would foster sound financial management and a sense of obligation to return some of one's possessions to God via a worthy (and needy) channel, the church.[4]

The idea of thinking of life in terms of stewardship very much caught the imagination of American Protestants, and what became known as the "stewardship movement" gathered momentum during the late nineteenth and early twentieth centuries. One suspects that this popularity may have had something to do with the fact that the stewardship literature had a tendency to focus on the idea of increasing one's "talents," and effectively constituted a ringing endorsement of the entrepreneurial desires of the day. The main emphasis of the literature was, however, on stewardship as grateful financial response to God's gifts. Despite more rounded and socially responsible developments of it by writers such as Ralph S. Cushman,[5] the concept of stewardship became increasingly tied to the tithing movement and to fundraising schemes. By the mid twentieth century, any broader possibilities or deeper implications that it might have had looked as though they were going to fall by the wayside.

Yet there were a small number of writers during the mid 1950s who devoted considerable energy to reestablishing these broader possibilities. They refused to surrender the symbol to the fundraisers since they were

[2] Salstrand, *The Story of Stewardship in the United States* (Grand Rapids, MI: Baker Book House, 1956) 25.

[3] Hall (*Steward*, 2) points out that it had little or no usage in the European tradition.

[4] Ibid., 39–40

[5] Cushman, *The Message of Stewardship* (Cincinnati: Abingdon, 1922).

convinced that it somehow captured the heart of Christian existence. The Mennonite author Milo Kauffman, and the Lutheran T. A. Kantonen proved the most influential of these writers.[6] Kantonen enthusiastically described stewardship as the "vita nova," the believer's whole life as a response to the revelation of divine truth.[7] Despite the energetic espousal of the metaphor of stewardship by these authors, it only inspired a handful of extended theological expositions over the next fifteen years.[8] However, it was beginning to attract attention, and now a new generation of writers, notably Douglas Hall, has reiterated its importance for Christians today.

Hall describes the symbol of the steward as "the gospel *in nuce.*"[9] In a similar vein, Wallace E. Fisher asserts that "The church's effective witness during the remainder of this volcanic century will depend substantially on its rediscovering and shaping its life to the *biblical* concept of stewardship."[10] At one level, the image of the steward has continued to be used for fundraising purposes. However, by comparison with much of the nineteenth century and early twentieth century stewardship literature there is much less of a tendency to equate "steward" with "tither" or "successful capitalist," and most of the writers protest such reductionistic equations vigorously. What we see is a concerted attempt to liberate the symbol from the constrictive environment that its partial development in the context of biblical passages concerning the tithe originally produced. Mc Kay writes that the Christian steward "must see his life and his stewardship against the pattern given in that Life poured out on Calvary's lone summit. And when he does, he will not regard the statistics of budgetary increase as a proper equivalent of 'sacrificial' giving."[11] Even writers of denominational literature which is geared explicitly toward fundraising appear to feel obliged to include at least a cautionary introductory chapter explaining the merits of understanding all

[6] Kauffman has written a number of works on stewardship. His first extended treatment was *The Challenge of Christian Stewardship* (Scottdale, PA: Herald, 1955). His most recent is *Stewards of God* (Scottdale, PA: Herald, 1975).

[7] Kantonen, *A Theology for Christian Stewardship* (Philadelphia: Muhlenberg, 1956) 22.

[8] Two extended treatments appear during this period: Arthur Mc Kay, *Servants and Stewards: The Teaching and Practice of Stewardship* (Philadelphia: Geneva, 1963); and Helge Brattgard, *God's Stewards: A Theological Study of the Principles and Practices of Stewardship* (trans. Gene J. Lund; Minneapolis: Augsburg, 1963) appeared in translation.

[9] Hall, *Steward*, 28. This conviction has led Hall to write in quick succession three books on the topic of stewardship. His most recent is *Imaging God: Dominion as Stewardship* (Grand Rapids, MI: Eerdmans, 1986 [with the Friendship Press, for the Commission on Stewardship of the National Council of the Churches of Christ in the U.S.A.]).

[10] Fisher, *A New Climate for Stewardship* (Nashville: Abingdon, 1976) 13. Fisher is an American Lutheran pastor from Lancaster, Pennsylvania.

[11] Mc Kay, *Servants and Stewards*, 18.

of life as stewardship before they launch into the business of how to raise dollars.[12] This new awareness about the dangers of reductionistic equation of stewardship with wise financial management and faithful tithing seems to be linked to a gradual realization on the part of North American Protestant churches that, during the first flush of enthusiasm for tithing and financial stewardship, there had been an unfortunate and unbiblical tendency toward seeing all Christian life in constricted, money-centered terms and toward a new kind of insidious legalism that conflicted with the gospel of liberty. As one might expect, Lutheran theologians such as Kantonen were among the first to pick up on this error.[13] A contemporary Lutheran, Waldo J. Werning, makes the point most forcefully. He warns clergy against invoking the symbol of the steward in the context of demanding obligatory tithing, and says that it is vital to remember that stewardship is not a new law, but part of the Christian's sanctified life lived in response to God.[14] Clergy should instead be fostering an ethical consciousness which will lead to true stewardship.[15]

Although some writers continue to talk of stewardship as a mode of life that will bring definite rewards in the form of God blessing those who tithe and in the form of one's fostering of one's talents paying off, the majority of writers feel uncomfortable with this notion. It is another interpretation from which they feel they must free the idea of stewardship before it can be truly helpful. Kauffman does uphold the idea that the faithful steward will be rewarded by God, saying, "Stewardship is a law of first magnitude in the economy of God, a primary principle in God's universe which if observed will bring great blessing and harmony."[16] Others, however, are troubled by this kind of assertion, and point out that such an attitude can easily lead one into a works righteousness frame of mind[17] or to a very transactional notion of religion with a kind of cosmic banker deity who repays good management with material blessings.[18]

[12] As is the case, e.g., in Lee E. Davis and Ernest D. Standerfer, *Christian Stewardship in Action* (Nashville: Convention, 1983). At the time of writing, they both worked for the Southern Baptist Stewardship Commission.

[13] Kantonen, *Theology for Christian Stewardship*, 23.

[14] Werning, *Christian Stewards: Confronted and Committed* (Saint Louis: Concordia, 1982) 3. Werning is a Lutheran minister who has spent most of his career working on fundraising and stewardship projects. At the time of writing he was Director of Development at Concordia Theological Seminary in Fort Wayne, Indiana. According to the book jacket, he has the distinction of being described by Robert Schuler as "perhaps the foremost authority on church funding."

[15] Ibid., 5.

[16] Kauffman, *Stewards of God*, 19.

[17] Brattgard, *God's Stewards*, 162.

[18] They are, however, then stuck with the problem of what to do about the scriptural passages that do seem to promise reward. Lutheran author Carl W. Berner Sr. (*The Power of Pure Stewardship* [Saint Louis: Concordia, 1970] 81) neatly encapsulates the dilemma posed by

Such critiques of certain types of use of the "steward" image show an awareness on the part of the authors of the inappropriateness of using it in ways that are out of keeping with the broader message of the gospel (as they understand it). However, the critiques do not merely reflect unease with poor theology, they also reflect a desire to rescue what is perceived as an image with great potential vitality from the truncated treatments that it has been receiving. From the mid fifties on, and especially after 1970, we find an increasing number of works which take up the issue of its other possibilities. Two groupings stand out. One—by far the smaller—consists of material that picks up on the Pauline idea of the duty to be stewards of God's mysteries and focuses on this as a mandate for evangelism. This directly mission-oriented literature focuses on passages such as 1 Cor 4:1–2 and 9:17 which allude to a responsibility for Christians to be stewards of the mysteries of God. It discusses the responsibility of churches and individual Christians to guard the gospel message and to carry it to the world, increasing its treasure like the trustworthy steward of the parable. In such interpretations, stewardship becomes equated primarily with mission or witness. It may even become subsumed by the metaphor of life as "witness." An extreme example of this is Virginia Ely's 1962 work *Stewardship, Witnessing to Christ* which is entirely given over to the idea of bringing people to Christ through the witness of one's words and deeds.[19]

The other grouping consists of material that discusses stewardship as a way of conceiving of *all* of one's duties and opportunities as a Christian. It stresses the importance of both stewardship of the gospel (variously understood) and stewardship of all the resources of human life in the service of the God behind this gospel. Indeed, one is seen as leading naturally to the other. Many of the texts make a strong call for commitment to ecological issues and social justice work in the name of responsible stewardship.[20]

It is to this second group of texts with the broader focus that the main body of this chapter will be devoted. It will look first at the understanding of the nature and relationship of God, creation and humanity that is found in the typical theological explanation of the meaning of Christian life as stewardship. It will then examine two different directions in which the writers develop the image of the Christian steward in the context of the discussion of living the Christian life. Particular attention will be paid to the issue of how

---

conflicting scriptural messages on the point: "We do not become good stewards or practice good stewardship because we have our eyes on rewards. Rewards are not the motive, but they certainly will be the result of stewardship faithfulness. God has made this unmistakably clear."

[19] Ely, *Stewardship: Witnessing for Christ* (Westwood, NJ: Revell, 1962).

[20] The term "stewardship" has, of course, also become common in literature on the environment and global resources which has no overtly Christian or Jewish context.

far specific ethical directives or principles may be said to arise clearly from
the metaphor. The chapter will conclude with a discussion of the possible
strengths and weaknesses of the metaphor in particular contexts and with a
special study of the way in which women may profit from its development
along one particular line of exegesis, and be endangered by another.

The Theology of Stewardship

As we saw earlier, large claims are made for the special ability of the metaphor of stewardship to illuminate the true meaning of the Christian life.
These claims rest on a belief that it encapsulates in microcosm the message
of the gospel and the essential truths about how human beings should live in
relation to God and to each other. The basic exegesis underlying these
claims varies little and runs as follows:[21]

The Hebrew Scriptures give us a clear picture of God as the Creator and
Sustainer of all, to whom all the universe belongs. All that He creates is
good. In the Book of Genesis we are shown how Adam and Eve were
created by Him and given the task of "dressing and keeping" the garden
(Gen.1:15). They were also given "dominion" over the earth (Gen. 1:28);
their task was therefore one in which they had some definite degree of power
and autonomy. They were to help God and to carry out his purposes. However, they were not the owners of the garden. They were expected to treat it
properly; they could not do whatever they wished. The forbidden apple was
a symbolic reminder of God's ownership and overall power.[22] They were
trustees or stewards; managers of the property of another who were expected
to carry out his purposes to the best of their ability. Unfortunately, they
betrayed their trust. They behaved in a way that was out of keeping with
God's law and purposes. Depending on how literally you take the story of
Adam and Eve, you may say that all the ills in the world are to be traced back
to this initial sin of bad stewardship, or you may construe the incident as a
mythic paradigm of failed stewardship and its consequences. Either way, it
was necessary for God to bring about the reconciliation to Himself of creation through the work of his Son. Christians understand that God is the
Owner of all that exists twice over: once by virtue of creation, and once by
virtue of redemption.

Christians also understand that they have been given a fresh chance to live
as responsible stewards—carrying out God's purposes in the world. They

[21] See, e.g., Kauffman, *Stewards of God*, 44–57.

[22] This interpretation does seem to overlook the whole significance of the apple as the locus of
knowledge of good and evil. The exegesis is perhaps most strained at this point.

have a double responsibility: to act as stewards of the gospel message itself, and to live lives which are models of careful stewardship of all personal resources and resources of the material world. As Adam and Eve were stewards of the old creation, so Christians are now stewards of the new creation. They are unusual stewards, in that they are also "sons" and "daughters" of God who shall "inherit the earth." This gives them a special interest in their work. They are partners with God in helping Him carry out his purposes. They may perhaps even be described as "co-creators."[23] Non-Christians are also stewards of creation but they may be unconscious of this, and even at best they do not have such a deep knowledge of God's purposes as do Christians, and therefore may not exercise their stewardship so effectively. Specifically Christian stewardship is felt to spring from grateful response to Christ's saving work, and a desire to carry out God's purposes in the light of what Christ has revealed about them. At this point the exegesis usually tries to paint a picture of Christ himself as the exemplary Steward. As Turner Clinard puts it:

> Jesus is the ground and motive of Christian stewardship, and he is even its model and pattern. For before we hear him call us into that relationship, we see him in his own stewardship role toward the Father. Jesus was a true steward: careful to reveal the truth that was his; careful to save and keep all those who have been committed to him. . . . He was a steward, being always "about his Father's business."[24]

Beyond this point the exegesis diverges since there are as many different interpretations of the precise nature of Jesus' stewardship and of the missionary and ethical import of the New Testament passages relating to stewardship as there are interpreters. To the issue of these divergences we shall turn later, but at this point, it is helpful to look at the general contours of what the authors envisage as a life lived as a steward.

---

[23] Ronald D. Petry, *Partners in Creation: Stewardship for Pastor and People* (Elgin, IL: Brethren, 1980) 22. In 1980 Petry was pastor of the Church of the Brethren, Sebring, Florida. He is described on the book jacket as having served for ten years as a member of a denominational stewardship staff, during which time he also chaired the Commission on Stewardship of the National Council of Churches.

[24] Clinard, *Responding to God: The Life of Stewardship* (Philadelphia: Westminster, 1980) 28–29. Clinard is described as a former pastor and chaplain, now Professor of English at Emory and Henry College in Virginia.

Living the Life of Stewardship

There is an almost complete consensus that the key virtues, or perhaps dispositions, of the life of stewardship are faithfulness and responsibility. Gratitude to God and a sense of accountability and desire to return or share what one has been given are its wellsprings. Judging by the greater part of writings on the subject, the idea of life as stewardship has tended to be developed in two related but rather different ways. Many of the books are written by authors who are beguiled by the notion of tidy organizing of each compartment of life; their books are "how-to" manuals for persons who would exercise their trust of each minute area of their lives. Other books are informed more extensively by a powerful sense of God's desire for humanity to participate in the process of bringing about harmony within creation. Here the small details of life may not be so painstakingly spelled out. The emphasis is more on the cosmogonic basis of stewardship and on the ecological and social-justice implications of it; in contrast to most treatments of stewardship prior to 1960, these works represent a "radicalization" of the image and its implications.

Stewardship of Life's Every Dimension

One of the reasons that the symbol seems to appeal to the tidy minded is that it brings with it the conviction that every created thing has a *purpose*. Everything has to be looked after or used in an appropriate way. Using things the right way will lead to an improvement in one's own life and in the environment and community around one. Denominational resource books and Christian self-help manuals abound in tidy-minded catchphrases such as stewardship of "time, talent and treasure." The muddly entirety of life is neatly packaged into areas to be dealt with and utilized to the greater glory of God.[25] At a more rigorous and challenging level, authors of popular stewardship theologies, such as John McMullen, provide their readers with a theologically based life blueprint of this variety.[26] McMullen takes as his basic definition of stewardship the statement adopted by the United Stewardship Council in 1945:

> Christian stewardship is the practice of systematic and proportionate giving of time, abilities, and material possessions, based on the conviction that these are

[25] See, e.g., Bill Bright, *A Handbook for Christian Maturity: A Compilation of Ten Basic Steps Toward Christian Maturity* (San Bernardino, CA: Here's Life Publishers, 1982) 273–306.

[26] McMullen, *Stewardship Unlimited* (Richmond, VA: John Knox, 1961).

a trust from God to be used in his service for the benefit of all mankind in grateful acknowledgement of Christ's redeeming love.[27]

After exploring the biblical bases of this definition, he proceeds to explore its application in various aspects of life. He discusses the making and use of money, the development of one's talents and skills, and the importance of finding the right job and of cultivating skills that are both helpful and enjoyable. Next he goes on to discuss the vital importance of cultivating the mind as one of the most valuable resources given to us. The home provides still another arena for stewardship: husbands and wives have a responsibility for managing their various resources—including the blessings of sex. McMullen goes so far as to advocate planned parenthood as good stewardship.[28] He concludes by discussing the steward's responsibilities in the political and ecological spheres.

Milo Kauffman's influential works (*The Challenge of Christian Stewardship* and *Stewards of God*) provide similar blends of carefully thought-out theology and practical advice for the would-be organized reader. He explains to his reader that stewards are those who are managing God's world to help accomplish His purposes: "We are stewards of the manifold grace of God. As stewards our primary concern is to help restore people to the image of God, to promote God's community of love and righteousness."[29] Then he breaks the steward's concerns down into three specific tasks: (1) to make disciples of all the nations; (2) to help bring the Saints to spiritual maturity; (3) to minister to the downtrodden and to share resources with the world. He discusses in detail the implications of each.[30]

Kauffman is particularly interesting because early on, back in the mid fifties, he was already focusing on the ability of the image of the steward to speak to the importance of participating in the struggle for justice in the world. His work bridges the two types of readership described earlier. His first book is impeccably tidy-minded in its discussion of the properly Christian way to deal with each area of one's personal life. Indeed, Kauffman seems to get a little too carried away with the personal piety and personality development dimension of stewardship, saying, "The outstanding purpose of stewardship of possessions is the development of Christian character and Christian personality."[31] But then he moves tidy-mindedly into areas requiring considerable risk and courage, bridging the two genres of stewardship

[27] Ibid., 6.
[28] Ibid., 60–61.
[29] Kauffman, *Stewards of God*, 13.
[30] Ibid.
[31] Kauffman, *Challenge of Christian Stewardship*, 32.

literature described above. Proper stewardship requires insisting upon ecologically responsible farming and treatment of the environment.[32] Proper stewardship does not allow working in munitions plants. Proper stewardship
particularly excludes making atomic bombs. It even precludes helping
manufacture liquor. "Earning money in working against the purposes and
interests of God is not Christian stewardship."[33] In the more recent *Stewards
of God*, the same balance of personal development and social justice is found
but with even greater emphasis on the latter and with more warnings that the
modern world does not permit of absolute tidy mindedness. He has moved
firmly into the category of stewardship writers who have radicalized the
metaphor of stewardship in a way that reflects their interest in issues of social
justice and whose writings appeal to people with similar concerns.

"Radicalization" of the Image

This radicalization of the image of the steward is to be found in many writings of the seventies and eighties, particularly in those dealing with ecological issues. It may be helpful to set the texts we are examining in a broader
context. During the last two decades many North Americans and Europeans
have become increasingly aware of the effects of their lifestyle on the world
around them. They have also become more aware of the inequities of wealth
and resources. People have asked how the ecological crises can have come
about. Are they in some way linked to our religious world views? Some
scholars, such as Lewis W. Moncrief and Alan S. Miller, have argued that
there is no direct correlation.[34] Eastern scientists such as Yi Fu Tuan have
pointed out that ecological atrocities have been perpetrated by persons with
supposedly much more benign attitudes toward nature.[35] Nevertheless, many
have voiced suspicion that Judaism and Christianity are in some way to
blame for many of our Western excesses, and there has been long and
animated discussion among ecologists and scholars in the humanities about
whether the Judaeo-Christian tradition (or the Hellenistic Christian tradition)
is to blame for Western people's cavalier or destructive attitudes to the
natural world.[36] Some feel that the presence in Genesis of the commands to

[32] Ibid., 56.

[33] Ibid., 47.

[34] Moncrief, "The Cultural Basis for our Environmental Crisis," in David and Eileen Spring,
eds., *Ecology and Religion in History* (New York: Harper & Row, 1974) 76–90; Miller, *A
Planet to Choose: Value Studies in Political Ecology* (New York: Pilgrim, 1978) 71–79.

[35] Yi-Fu Tuan, "Discrepancies between Environmental Attitude and Behaviour: Examples
from Europe and China," in Spring, *Ecology and Religion*, 91–113.

[36] See, e.g., Lynn White, Jr., "The Historical Roots of Our Ecologic Crisis," *Science* 155
(1967); reprinted in Spring, *Religion and Ecology*, 15–31.

subdue, or have dominion over, the earth and to populate it make the whole tradition dubious from the moment go.[37] Others choose to interpret "dominion" in the light of the accompanying command to dress and keep the garden and view it as benevolent management that is being urged upon Adam and Eve and all humanity. Those who take this last point of view remain comfortable with the metaphor of stewardship and feel that there is nothing intrinsically wrong with its presupposition of human superiority to nature, providing humans do not construe this to mean that nature exists merely for their own interests. They feel that the idea of accountability will be sufficient to provide safe parameters for the exercise of dominion. The metaphor of stewardship is, therefore, one which they enthusiastically endorse.[38] Even though he does not believe it will happen, John Black says:

> One way in which a sense of responsibility for the use of the earth could be inculcated would be a widespread acceptance of the Christian doctrine of stewardship, a belief that we are accountable at the end of the day for the manner in which we have used the resources entrusted to us. There can be no doubt that a return to this view, if it were universally accepted, could develop the sense of sacrifice and restraint which is at present lacking.[39]

The metaphor has also been taken up by those who have chosen to cut it out from its traditional religious roots, instead of accountability to God making accountability to future generations or to the earth itself the watchword. An abundance of works discussing the moral claims of unborn generations and our responsibilities to them have appeared in recent years.[40] Likewise, a new area of ethics is developing which is trying to find grounds for speaking of duties and responsibilities to non-human creation. Judging by the frequency with which the term occurs in such contexts, stewardship appears to have

[37] See, e.g., Elizabeth Dodson Gray, *Green Paradise Lost* (Wellesley, MA: Roundtable, 1981) 3–8.

[38] See, e.g., Roger L. Shinn, "Eco-Justice Themes in Christian Ethics since the 1960s," in Dieter T. Hessel, ed., *For Creation's Sake: Preaching, Ecology, and Justice*, (Philadelphia: Geneva, 1985) 96–114. "After hearing all the tirades that have been uttered against that doctrine for its destructive consequences," says Shinn, "I want to say a good word for it. Christian faith affirms a human dominion—a reverent, creaturely dominion, not a renunciation of dominion. To appreciate dominion is to accept freedom, foresight, and power—and to exercise them responsibly" (p. 113). Shinn is Reinhold Niebuhr Professor of Social Ethics at the Union Theological Seminary.

[39] Black, *The Dominion of Man: The Search for Ecological Responsibility* (Edinburgh: Edinburgh University Press, 1970) 120. At the time of writing, Black was Professor of Natural Resources at Edinburgh University.

[40] See, e.g., R. I. Sikora and Brian Barry, eds., *Obligations to Future Generations* (Philadelphia: Temple University Press, 1978).

proven more exciting to ecologically minded humanists than to Christians during the seventies. However, some Christians who had written the concept off as moribund, or at very least uninteresting, were now prompted by circumstances to give it new thought. Hall speaks of how he came to recognize the potential of the image almost by chance after being asked to speak at a stewardship conference and doing some research on its history. He says:

> [W]e Christians have been carrying about with us a highly provocative and even revolutionary symbol—whose power we have unfortunately muffled in ecclesiastical wrappings. While the churches trudge along with this ancient metaphor, rather embarrassed by its association with money and properties, the contemporary world of environmentalists and peace marchers and others has been discovering its radical potential. It seemed to me that it's time had come, that we might redeem it for Christian use too![41]

He went on to devote several years work to expounding the metaphor's importance for contemporary life. He develops its ecological implications and, like Kauffman, he takes up its social justice implications. However, the tidy-mindedness framework is gone.

For Hall, the keynote of stewardship is the conservation of life itself, and the total commitment to stewarding the world's resources in such a way as to meet this goal in the fullest sense. He stresses that the image of the steward has clear potential for raising commitment to establishing economic and social equity. For one thing, with its assertion of God as the only true Owner, it presents a critique of the whole idea of private ownership and of any supposed accompanying right to use things selfishly for our own purposes. We must use our resources according to God's will, and that means to help other people. And we must throw our energies fully into this. Stewardship, says Hall, is "a plan of action, a style of confrontation, a resistance and a protest that is at the same time the presentation of a radical alternative."[42] The same idea is taken up by the Southern Baptist writer Richard B. Cunningham:

> The Christian steward works with all people for human rights, justice, equality, peace, equitable distribution of the world's resources, and the care of the good earth. As a steward in the world, the Christian labors with God to bend the secular historical process toward the horizons of the coming kingdom of God.[43]

---

[41] Hall, *Steward*, iii.

[42] Douglas John Hall, *The Stewardship of Life in the Kingdom of Death* (New York: Friendship Press for the Commission on Stewardship of the National Council of the Churches of Christ in the U.S.A., 1985) iv.

[43] Cunningham, *Creative Stewardship* (Nashville: Abingdon, 1979) 27.

This thoroughgoing emphasis on equitable distribution of resources and on working for a new social order is a relatively new feature in stewardship literature. Although early twentieth century leaders such as Ralph Cushman had a strong social-gospel orientation, they did not critique the overall structures of capitalism. As Cushman's son Robert put it: "[T]he Stewardship Movement did not so much challenge the economic structures of capitalism as place individual capitalists under the judgement of their own Christian profession."[44] Again, "The movement more or less accepted the prevailing individualistic conception of salvation and Christian vocation that had emerged out of 150 years of American evangelical experience. It undertook to make it socially responsible and morally significant."[45]

Writers such as Cunningham and Hall take the metaphor's logic a stage further and see its condemnation of autonomous private ownership as implying an ethical responsibility to participate in the radical restructuring of society. For them, the issue is not mercy or charity, nor philanthropy. It is global justice.[46] There is a world of difference as Joseph Fletcher points out in his essay "Wealth and Taxation":

> The sub-Christian twist comes when we begin to think of our giving and sharing as *our* mercy to the less fortunate, instead of seeing that it is a stewardly handling of God's wealth to fulfill God's purposes. We are not our own stewards, being generous to our neighbours out of our greater wisdom and wealth; we are God's stewards, acting for God in the distribution of *his* wealth to his family on earth.[47]

The question of to what ultimate end people are exercising their stewardship is answered variously. As noted above, Cunningham speaks of helping "bend the secular process toward the horizons of the coming kingdom of God."[48] On a similar note, Hall speaks of stewards of the king, helping to

---

[44] Robert E. Cushman, "Twentieth Century Development in Stewardship," in Edwin A. Briggs, ed., *Theological Perspectives of Stewardship* (Evanston, IL: The General Board of the Laity, the United Methodist Church, 1969) 108. Cushman is a Methodist writer who was Dean of the Duke Divinity School. His essay provides a most interesting discussion of the links between the Social Gospel movement and the Stewardship Movement in early twentieth-century Protestant America.

[45] Ibid., 109

[46] See also Ronald J. Sider, "A Biblical Perspective on Stewardship," in Mary Evelyn Jegen and Bruno Manno, eds., *The Earth is the Lord's: Essays on Stewardship* (New York: Paulist, 1978) 1–21; and William J. Byron, *Toward Stewardship: An Interim Ethic of Poverty, Power and Pollution* (New York: Paulist, 1975).

[47] Fletcher, "Wealth and Taxation: the Ethics of Stewardship," in T. K. Thompson, ed., *Stewardship in Contemporary Theology* (New York: Association, 1960) 214.

[48] See n. 45 above.

bring about the kingdom.[49] By contrast, those writing out of traditions which do not think of humans as effective participants in the process of bringing about or building the kingdom naturally have a different view. In his book *Man's Responsibility for Nature*, John Passmore blasts this kind of attitude as representing a new Pelagianism.[50] And, as Jeremy Rifkin and Ted Howard point out in *The Emerging Order*, the general position of evangelical theologians is that human beings can never restore the world back to its pre-fall state; indeed, they see the natural order as moving irrevocably toward a state of chaos. Stewardship in this context takes a less positive cast; it is a desperate rearguard action. As Rifkin and Howard put it:

> The choice, put rather simply, is whether the individual will align himself with the forces responsible for speeding up the entropy process, or the forces attempting to preserve God's creation.[51]

It may be that God will intervene and reverse the process of entropy and usher in the kingdom, but this will not be due to human efforts. So, instead, stewardship has more the character of *witness* to the coming of the kingdom: "Serving witness means respecting and protecting God's created order to the fullest, even while knowing that all of one's efforts are ultimately insufficient to the task."[52] This is very much the approach taken by Arthur Mc Kay and Francis Schaeffer, who emphasize the importance of stewardship as grateful and grace-empowered response to God, and offer no promises about its effects on the world.[53] Clearly understandings of the motive and end of life lived under the guiding metaphor of stewardship differ, although the disposition encouraged may be the same, and some of the practical implications for living may be similar.

An Example of the Limits of Ethical Extrapolation from an Image

Ecological ethicists and theologians alike have commented on the common ground that the metaphor affords in its idea of responsible trusteeship. Hall

---

[49] Douglas John Hall, "Mission as a Function of Stewardship," in W. Donald Goodger, ed., *Spotlighting Stewardship* (Ontario: The United Church of Canada, 1981) 44.

[50] Passmore, *Man's Responsibility for Nature: Ecological Problems and Western Traditions* (London: Duckworth, 1974) 20.

[51] Rifkin, with Howard, *The Emerging Order: God in the Age of Scarcity* (1979; reprinted New York: Ballantine Books, 1983) 234.

[52] Ibid.

[53] Mc Kay, *Servants and Stewards*, 62–63; Schaeffer, *Pollution and the Death of Man: The Christian View of Ecology* (1970; reprinted Wheaton, IL: Tyndale House, 1981) 92.

discusses this ecumenical potential at some length.[54] Stripped of its evangelistic dimension, the metaphor can function to help bring Christians together with others who share their concern for justice and for harmony with the natural world. However, one might question just how far this consensus based on shared use of metaphor will go. Let us consider some of the difficulties that may dog attempts to move toward agreement.[55]

The problem is that it is one thing to talk about stewardship, but quite another to discuss its specific implications.[56] Even within Christianity, there is likely to be disagreement. Most Catholic theologians would be unlikely to see eye to eye with McMullen over his statement that birth control represents good stewardship. Just as problematic are decisions about what constitutes good stewardship in the areas of scientific experiment. Is genetic engineering, for example, good stewardship? How is one to know what constitutes use of nature in accordance with God's will? Can one even be sure what is "natural" in a given situation? The concept of stewardship is tied inextricably to prevailing understandings of the nature of Nature. As understandings of the latter diverge, so one may expect consensus on the implications of stewardship qua ecological/ethical principle to fragment.

Another related set of divisive problems is likely to accompany any discussion of what constitutes good global stewardship. Many ecologically motivated users of the stewardship metaphor manifest a certain ambivalence about the relative rights of individual human beings vis-à-vis the rest of the natural order. The ecological outlook reflects a holistic metaphysics which sees the value of all things as conditioned by their place in the total network of creation. The overall objective is sustaining the balance of harmony within the chain of being. For those Christians, humanists and others who value human life above other forms of life, problems arise when the stewardship of the whole biosphere which is being advocated by ecologists conflicts with the needs of individual human beings. What do you do when crop land is desperately needed but rain forest will have to be destroyed to create it? To give a specific example that has been in the news recently, the Indian government's Save the Tiger program has run into difficulty. When Indira Gandhi originally set it up, it commanded great public support. Certain "core" forest areas were made reservations where no one was allowed to enter or to graze cattle. Around these core areas, buffer zones were

[54] Hall, "Mission as a Function," 18–44.

[55] As mentioned in the Introduction, I will follow some of the problems through into forms of literature other than those which provide the main basis for this study. I do this to make it clear that the shortcomings discussed are not simply the result of the confines of the genre.

[56] The same point could, of course, have been illustrated in relation to the idea of servanthood, and will be made in relation to the idea of warfare against the world's evils.

established where young male tigers could roam during the years that the older males kept them away from the core area, and where local people could also graze their cattle. The programme was extremely successful. The number of tigers doubled. But in recent years tiger attacks on humans have increased, and drought and growing population numbers have led the local people to invade the core areas desperately seeking enough grazing ground. Many of the reserves have been destroyed overnight. Apparently, stewardship of part of India's natural heritage is causing its people additional poverty and hardship. The decisions to be made are difficult.

Persons who take their stewardship obligations to include protection of animals and plant life have been working on the development of extended ethics which accord "rights" to animals (and even plant life) by analogy with human rights and provide grounds for giving them priority in certain situations. Their arguments have a high degree of cogency. But, as Thomas Derr argues in his book *Ecology and Human Need*, the Judaeo-Christian tradition does appear to assert that human life is always more important than any other form of life, this principle must govern our actions even if it redounds unfavourably to a non-human life. He argues that ecological strategies must be based on a sense of stewardship that works ultimately for the good of human beings. Given what we know of the interconnectedness of humans with the rest of the natural world, this will involve the ecologically sound goals of stabilizing and preserving the natural order. But this will be primarily for the sake of human beings now and to come.[57] It is most improbable that Derr and an animal rights activist would see eye to eye over the implications of stewardship in every situation.

Derr also speaks to the issue of the problematic aspects of the metaphor of stewardship as transformed into an ultra conservative principle for guiding scientific experiment and technology. He notes the rise of a new form of nature romanicism which glorifies nature in its raw state and understands stewardship to involve preserving it in that glorious rawness. He comments that

> an uncritical reverence for unaltered nature would oblige acceptance of disease and passive acquiescence in the face of other natural disasters such as floods, earthquakes, and forest fires. It requires a very selected sensitivity to build ethics solely on nature's workings.[58]

And he later underlines the point:

> Knowledge of the facts about the natural world does not bestow meaning on the process, nor dictate ethical priorities and proprieties. Meaning and meaningful,

[57] Derr, *Ecology and Human Need* (Philadelphia: Westminster, 1975) 83–86.
[58] Ibid., 59.

responsible choice, i.e., ethics, belongs to another order entirely, to a vision of the *place* of this scientific data in the history and purpose of the whole, a vision of the destiny of the cosmos and of man within it.[59]

Stewardship, he believes, does not simply involve letting nature take its course. What is, is not necessarily what ought to be. As in the realm of human relations, intervention is part of stewardship. He feels that the early Hebrews were recognizing this need for intervention when they accepted that in some real sense nature does require to be "subdued." However, Derr does not answer the question posed earlier: At what point does intervention in nature cease to be good stewardship? Is genetic engineering "natural"? Is it good stewardship or mismanagement of nature?

It would appear then, that agreement on the importance of stewardship will not necessarily bring agreement on practical issues in its wake. The inclusiveness of the metaphor can be overstressed. It is not the perfect locus for agreement beween persons of different faiths or denominations. It would seem truer to say that it simply provides some promising common ground from which productive discussion may begin.

Let us turn now from these larger ethical issues to look in more general terms at the adequacy or otherwise of the metaphor for use as the primary guiding metaphor for an individual's life. We have seen that it has indeed caught the imagination of many, but is it an exhaustive or fully sufficient interpreter of experience? Also, what might be the practical implications of visualizing oneself primarily as a steward? Are there some for whom stewardship may prove a dangerous image?

Some Problems and Possibilities

The Scope of the Metaphor

One criticism that has been made of stewardship theology is that it overstates the extent of the metaphor's scope. James Mark makes the observation that it is misleading to try to make stewardship the only metaphor or image necessary to convey the fullness of a Christian life. He points out that many writers, such as Kantonen, have a tendency to conflate stewardship with vocation, overlooking the fact that vocation may actually be a stage or factor which precedes the exercise of stewardship and actually determines the shape it takes. He even suggests that vocation is a better overall category for understanding the Christian life, since it points to the idea of what a person *is*,

[59] Ibid., 72.

rather than what they *have* (be it personal possessions or qualities).[60]

Other writers have suggested that the image of stewardship is not exhaustive enough in other respects and needs to be supplemented with some further image to make it more effective as an interpreter and shaper of the Christian life. Perhaps the most convincing partner image is that of the "pilgrim." S. Paul Schilling says that the stewardship metaphor is always in danger of becoming too static when people think of it as being a kind of "householder" for God. He says:

> The house which he [the steward] administers for his Lord is not a luxurious suburban estate, but a trailer, a mobile home which supplies his minimum needs yet allows maximum freedom for movement. Christians are pilgrims on the way to a kingdom that cannot be shaken. Therefore they are called to worship and serve the living God who brings the kingdom, and to use all his gifts here and now in active love toward their fellow wayfarers.[61]

This changes the complexion of the metaphor to a noticeable degree.

General Drawbacks and Advantages

It is interesting to consider the practical implications of adopting the metaphor of stewardship as the framework for one's life. What might be the dangers and the advantages? One of the dangers, as implied by Schilling, is a certain staticness, even smugness. Most stewardship writers compartmentalize life to the nth degree in order to render it amenable to a tidy programme of stewardship. If a person faithfully followed one of their blueprints, he or she might easily develop a false sense of security, of being in control of every necessary aspect of life.

Another problem with the idea of stewardship is that, as discussed above, its actual content will depend upon a Christian's understanding of the Bible as a whole and what it says about Christ and about God's purposes. If one grasps onto the concept without having thought through the theology that is to inform it, the result is likely to be somewhat trivial—a mechanical following of time and management plans. Even for those who have thought their theology through, certain problems may remain. At the level of ethical decision making, the implications of stewardship are not always clear.

However, the metaphor has many practical advantages. It presupposes the basic goodness of creation and fosters an attitude of care and responsibility

[60] Mark, *The Question of Christian Stewardship* (London: SCM, 1964) 87–88. Mark is an English Anglican writer.

[61] Schilling, "A Theological Interpretation," in Briggs, *Theological Perspectives*, 17. Schilling was Professor of Systematic Theology at the Boston University School of Theology.

toward it. Even though the precise implications may not always be clear, the underlying attitude seems sound. The idea of stewardship can also serve as an antidote to apathy. Built into it is the idea that what one does has a real and tangible effect on one's life and on the world around one. And the positive side of very programmatic stewardship thinking is that it can counteract the despair at the world's muddliness that often stymies people's impulse to act responsibly in the world. If life is broken down into clearly delimited areas and one's responsibilities in each are spelt out clearly, the task becomes somewhat easier.

The stewardship literature also fosters the idea of the importance of self-development and of helping others develop. Depending on one's understanding of the nature of God and God's purposes it could help one grow in justice and compassion. The strongest feature of the metaphor is perhaps its radical critique of the idea of possession. As a child of God, one may inherit the earth. But as a steward one realizes that in this life nothing belongs to one in a private sense. As Hall says, "The whole doctrinal area of redemption is embraced in the metaphor of stewardship. For redemption in a real sense has to do with our being liberated from the need to possess."[62]

An Image with a Limited Constituency?

I have talked in rather general terms of the pros and cons of stewardship as one's primary framework for understanding the Christian life. But before continuing on to examine another image, we need to ask a further question of this one. Is the idea of stewardship likely to appeal to everyone, or are there groups of people to whom it might appear inappropriate, unhelpful, or even dangerous?

A question mark perhaps hangs over its usefulness where disempowered groups are concerned. Most stewardship discussions speak to the dilemmas of first-world people with enough possessions or resources to find the concept of stewardship meaningful. Does the symbol have much meaning beyond this sphere? Eugene F. Roop remarks:

> We have appealed to these [biblical] texts when the question involved the way in which people in positions of power are to deal with the issue of injustice and oppression. Seldom have we asked what stewardship means to the oppressed, to the people who have little power to manage their own affairs.[63]

[62] Hall, "Mission as a Function," 40.

[63] Roop, "Stewardship and Persons in Transition," in Nordan C. Murphy, ed., *Teaching and Preaching Stewardship: An Anthology* (New York: National Commission on Stewardship of the National Council of the Churches of Christ in the U.S.A., 1985) 67. At the time of writing, Roop was Professor of Biblical Studies at Bethany Theological Seminary in Oak Brook, Illinois.

Unfortunately his essay gives little answer. One is left with the suspicion that although stewardship may be possible where only miniscule resources are available, the metaphor may not be so compelling. And the accompanying idea of sacrificial giving may be quite inappropriate—fostering acquiescence to poverty or powerlessness rather than inspiring opposition to their causes.

One of the most important questions from my own point of view is how the image of stewardship may be appropriated by women, if at all. Certain aspects of its traditional development should make one cautious about embracing it too swiftly. For women the validity of the idea of stewardship may well be compromised by its hierarchical presuppositions. As the earlier overview of standard "stewardship exegeses" made clear, it has traditionally entailed the idea of responsible service to a masculine "Lord" or "Master" God. As William J. Keech put it:

> The Christian idea of stewardship is based primarily on belief in a sovereign God who created and directs the universe he made to his own self-appointed ends. . . . Man can achieve his real manhood and stature only as he becomes an honest, responsible, and faithful manager of God's things for God's end under the lordship of Jesus Christ.[64]

Now, on the one hand, the concepts of divine lordship and ownership relativize all our selfish claims of autonomy, power, and possession. They are limiting, or humbling, concepts with possible salutary effects. On the other hand, as we saw in the discussion of servanthood, where one has a concept of the relationship of God and humanity as essentially hierarchical, whether Lord and Servant or Owner/Master and steward, there is always a danger of this serving as a model and legitimizer for human relationships of a domination-submission pattern. In particular, we are used to seeing the following parallel: woman is to man as man is to God; if the male is God's servant or steward, so is woman man's servant or steward. This danger for women is compounded by the fact that in the literature on Christian life as stewardship a definite God-human-nature hierarchy is usually assumed. If one construes stewardship in terms of a command to have "dominion" over nature, this may well entail males having dominion over females insofar as the latter have tended, in the Christian tradition, to be subsumed under the realm of "nature" rather than that of "spirit."[65] A particularly egregious

---

[64] Keech, *The Life I Owe: Christian Stewardship as a Way of Life* (Valley Forge, PA: Judson, 1963) 16.

[65] For a discussion of the issue of parallelism between human/nature and male/female ordering see, e.g., Sherry B. Ortner, "Is Female to Male as Nature is to Culture?," in Michelle Zimbalist Rosaldo and Louise Lamphere, eds., *Woman, Culture, and Society* (Stanford: Stanford University Press, 1974).

example of this crossover thinking in a stewardship context may be found in Francis Schaeffer's *Pollution and the Death of Man*. He tells the reader that Christians are called upon to exercise dominion properly—unlike fallen "man." Explaining what this means, he says that the parallel to "man's" dominion over nature is "man's" dominion over his wife (which is loving but firm, etc., etc., etc.). He then goes on to say that just as we Christians must refuse men the right to ravish our wives, so we must refuse men the right to ravish our land.[66] The English term "steward" seems to have unavoidable patriarchal connotations, evoking the picture of a male retainer or administrator. As we shall see, some of the women writers of the fifties and sixties called themselves "stewardesses." This does not seem to have had any negative connotations for them, but today it is strongly colored by its most common use, and tends to conjure up pictures of smiling aircraft attendants in uniform. In a patriarchally shaped culture, the idea of a manager with some autonomy and authority tends to dissipate the moment the feminine suffix is added. The individual writer will need to decide whether she wishes to adopt and attempt to revalidate the feminine form or whether she would rather seek a (slightly) less masculine synonym such as "custodian," "caretaker" or perhaps "guardian."

Another dangerous aspect of the theme, as traditionally presented, is that it emphasizes "sacrificial giving" of money and energies as a response to God's generous giving. As feminist writers from Valerie Saiving onward have emphasized, many women are rather *too* susceptible to giving of a self-denying variety; commands to put the interests of others ahead of oneself and to give all that one can may play into the dynamic of keeping women at the service of others.[67]

Despite these problems, the idea of stewardship has a strong theological appeal to some feminist writers because of the seriousness with which it takes the idea of care for the earth. There is an attempt to retain the strengths of the theme and to avoid its dangers. In the hands of, for example, Letty Russell, *koinonia* is the concept that comes to the forefront in discussion of stewardship; the aspects of dominion and subservient servanthood are downplayed.[68] Similarly, Dorothee Soelle and Shirley A. Cloyes redefine the concept to remove the unwanted aspects of otherness and mastery:

[66] Schaeffer, *Pollution*, 72; 84. The pagination refers to the 1981 reprint of this work. It is not described as a new edition, but its pagination appears to differ from the 1970 printing. The page references for the older printing are 52–53, and 60.

[67] Saiving, "Human Situation," 37–41.

[68] Russell, "Partnership in Stewardship: Creation and Redemption" in Murphy, *Teaching and Preaching*, 2–8. Russell is Professor of Liberation Theology at Yale Divinity School.

The earth does not belong to us. It is not something that we are allowed to plunder and exhaust at will. On the contrary, it is the human being who belongs to the earth, and to belong means to live in mutual dependence . . . We must affirm our dependency between humanity and the earth, for we are the stewards of the earth.[69]

Although spirit/matter, human/nature, and male/female dualisms are embedded in many traditional interpretations, nevertheless the idea of life as stewardship of creation (human and non-human) seems close to feminist concerns insofar as it focuses strongly on the "now," on the way to live in the midst of God's good creation. It is rooted in a positive evaluation of the material world. Insofar as women find the nurturing, as opposed to questing, images more congenial one would expect them to be more drawn to the stewardship imagery. However, a strong caveat should be entered at this point. There is a risk of stereotyping here. There is no reason why questing should remain the province of the male and nurturing that of the female. This point will be investigated further in the chapter on pilgrimage.

A Case Study in the Hidden Potential of an Idea

During the nineteen fifties there seems to have been a sudden growth in books on life as stewardship written by Protestant women. There is no doubt that stewardship as a theme appealed to many traditional women of the era partly because of its potential for a theological sanctioning of roles of nurturing and caring. The theme had great power to illuminate the tasks of the wife and mother, and to show their importance in the divine scheme of things. In 1956, Lutheran writer Eleanor Bockelman published a book called *The Stewardess*. I want to quote at some length from it so that its flavor is not lost. She wrote the book, she says, because the multiple demands on her time and energy prompted her to reflect on how to respond to these so as to live her life in the best way.[70] The usual theological themes are present, but Brockelman addresses herself to the immediate sphere of her life and to the problems in hand:

We call it stewardship—this matter of scheduling time and energies to get the most accomplished. The Germans have a word for it. . . . They say— *Haushalter*. With a little prompting I learned this means "householder," and with a little imagination I interpreted it to mean housekeeper or homemaker.

[69] Soelle with Cloyes, *To Work and To Love: A Theology of Creation* (Philadelphia: Fortress, 1984) 33–34. Soelle is a German theologian of Lutheran background who now teaches at Union Theological Seminary. Cloyes works for Orbis Books.

[70] Bockelman, *The Stewardess* (Columbus, OH: Wartburg, 1956) 1.

For us stewardship is as simple as that—homemaking—homemaking for myself and for my family and all that it entails for friends and neighbours . . . and all of this for God. Stewardship means that I am a stewardess. . . .

Time that is spent in sewing a dolly's nightie could be just as good a stewardship of time as that used in church projects or service. Stewardship involves the time we use for cooking and canning and sewing and wiping noses just as much as the time we devote to calling on prospective church members or attending circle meetings.[71]

Here we see a woman redefining stewardship to assert the importance of her contribution over and against "official" church stewardship.[72] In the book every aspect of domestic life is considered as it relates to stewardship. Marriage and the raising of children as works of stewardship are given much attention by women authors of the fifties and sixties.[73] Of children, Helen Kingsbury Wallace writes:

Every child born into a family widens the scope of its stewardship. The personality of each child is different and requires individual guidance. . . . There are few phases of stewardship more important than that of bringing up a child.[74]

A whole essay in the Mennonite collection *A Farthing in Her Hand* is devoted to the stewardship of the children that God "entrusts to us for a time."[75] This particular collection of essays provides a good example of the way in which an attempt is made to give meaning to all aspects of women's

[71] Ibid., 5; 7.

[72] The context for this theological polemic may well be the extended debate among Protestant women of the period about how much and in what ways they should participate in churchwork and, more particularly, in fundraising. These kinds of issues are discussed more fully in such popular works as Carolyn P. Blackwood, *How to Be an Effective Churchwoman* (Philadelphia: Westminster, 1955). See esp. chaps. 12 and 13 on the "trusteeship" of women and their ways of raising money.

[73] For a development of the theme of marriage as stewardship of each other's talents see Florence M. Sly, *Your Family and Christian Stewardship* (Saint Louis: Bethany, 1958).

[74] Kingsbury Wallace, *Stewardship for Today's Woman* (Westwood, NJ: Revell, 1960) 43–45. According to the Foreword, this book was written at the request of the National Council of American Baptist Women. It was Wallace's third on the topic of stewardship. Her earlier works were *Stewardship in the Life of Women* (New York: Revell, 1928), and, with Robert Donald Williamson, *Stewardship in the Life of Youth* (New York: Revell, 1926).

[75] Phyllis Martens, "Stewardship of Children," in Helen Alderfer, ed., *A Farthing in Her Hand: Stewardship for Women* (Scottdale, PA: Herald, 1964) 40. Martens spent her childhood in India, went to school in Kansas, taught English at Pacific College in Fresno, married a Mennonite pastor, and at the time of writing was raising three small children and considering the issue of personality development in the Christian context (p. 58).

lives through the theme of stewardship. Alta Mae Erb tackles the stewardship of possessions. She writes:

> The Christianizing of her possessions is a great task that confronts the Christian
> woman in this twentieth century.
>   Scan any current periodical with many advertisments. The great majority of
> ads are planned to catch the eyes and hearts of women. This assumes that the
> woman is the prime influence in securing the family's possessions.[76]

Out of their love and sense of responsibility to their families, women try to
create the perfect home. Unfortunately, advertisers play on this and try to
foist endless items onto them. Erb remarks that women run a great danger of
being "mastered by things"; it is important for them to keep in mind the true
status of possessions and to remember that they are partners with God in running their home:

> God owns all that is found in the house. The housekeeper is the manager for
> God. We do not call the house furnishings secular and the housekeeping
> sacred. All things when used for God have a spiritual significance and are
> sacred. The woman's motive in keeping the house clean, in selecting furnish-
> ings, in buying food at the mart, in deciding on the line between necessity and
> luxury, is very important. . . . Her many possessions are held as a trust from
> God, as a loan to her. Her housekeeping is a practical expression of her experi-
> ence with God.[77]

In the same collection of essays, however, there are articles that suggest
that a woman's stewardship may take her out of this sphere of the home.
Eleanor Beachy, writing about the stewardship of one's energies, remarks
that "God has given women brains and talent. With the new freedom of
choice women are more responsible for the development and use of these
assets than ever before."[78] An apparently conservative symbol starts to show
glimmerings of radical potential. We see this also in the other works mentioned above. Helen Kingsbury Wallace devotes a chapter to the "Career
Woman" in which she earnestly, if rather nervously, suggests ways for business "girls" and women to exercise stewardship in their work sphere.
Again, it is worth quoting at some length to capture the spirit of her writing:

---

[76] Erb, "Stewardship of Possessions," in Alderfer, *Farthing*, 61. Erb, says the editor, "has
served the church she loves as minister's wife, church school teacher, writer and speaker." She
taught at Hesston College and Goshen College and, at the time of writing, worked for the Mennonite Publishing House in Scottdale, Pennsylvania.

[77] Ibid., 65.

[78] Beachy, "Stewardship of Energy" in Alderfer, *Farthing*, 188.

The business woman's job is a most important part of her stewardship. . . . One's job, if it is ideal, is creative. . . . The really smart girl will look for a job that suits her taste, her personality, through which she can best express herself and make a significant contribution. She feels that it is not enough just to earn her living. As a part of her stewardship she puts forth every effort to find a rewarding job, and, having found it, she stays in it in spite of attractive offers of higher salaries. If she finds herself miserable in a job, she seeks to get a new one as soon as possible. . . .

An element in a satisfactory job is its challenge to develop one's potentialities, to rise to one's capabilities. . . . The professional woman may try to excel in her profession and to be alert to all the fresh developments in her field. She may be flexible and mobile, rather than static, in her work. The concept of stewardship is broader than a woman's responsibility to be what she is and use what she has: it also includes becoming what she is capable of becoming and developing all her possessions. Growth, expansion, investment, all are inherent in Christian stewardship.[79]

These kinds of writings represent a type of embryonic vocational theology which suggests that women should consider, as men have always been permitted to, in which directions their God-given talents should take them. The writings also provide a window onto early discussions about the relative demands of career and family. As one might perhaps expect, given the period, most of the writers are disinclined to see the "home" and "career" areas of stewardship as fully compatible. Beachy remarks trenchantly that she is convinced that a married mother with small children cannot give to her profession what a man or unmarried woman can give.[80] The issues of how best to use one's energies and which talents to develop at which time are present in the writings of most of the women authors whose works I have examined. These issues of what good stewardship means are still very much with us. The drawback of the concept of stewardship is similar to that of most theologies of work or vocation: specific guidance for decisions is lacking. This is, of course, one instance of the wider group of theological/ethical difficulties discussed earlier that arise from the openendedness of such a concept as stewardship.

This example of women's writing has been discussed at some length because it is a fine illustration of the way that themes such as stewardship

[79] Kingsbury Wallace, *Stewardship*, 22–23.

[80] Beachy, "Stewardship of Energy," 193. Beachy grew up in Menagha, Minnesota. She received a B.A. in English from Goshen College and edited the magazine *Agape* while working for the Mennonite Board of Missions and Charities. She married a school teacher, and at the time of writing appears to have been engaged in raising a young son and doing voluntary work (p. 199).

often take on a life somewhat independent of their "deep" theologies; selectively used in manuals on the religious life they become organizers of experience, marshallers of possibilities. Authors stress some aspects of a theme more than others in the context of responding to particular concerns and needs of the readers. The parable of the talents may, for example, be lifted out of the more fully developed theological context and used as the basis for meditation on personal growth. Conversely, care for the earth may be stressed, while self-development is disregarded. One of the effects of this pragmatic pastoral use of symbol is that certain themes or symbols which one might see as "bad" in their anchoredness in patriarchal notions of deity can, in the short term when selectively developed, provide great impetus for individual women in the direction of growth and power. The question is whether one can use the concepts safely in the religious life without changing their dubious underpinnings; whether the longterm dangers of the fundamental theology may outweigh the immediate gains from the pragmatic use of selected dimensions of the theme.

Allowing for this usefulness in a restricted context, I would argue that it is dangerous to use the idea of stewardship in this decontextualized way; the woman who would speak of her life as stewardship would be wise to follow the lead of Soelle and other feminist theologians such as Rosemary Ruether in reinterpreting its cosmological underpinnings before proceeding further.

Stewardship, then, has proven to be a model of great complexity. Having come to the fore in the last century, it has been appropriated by persons of very different theological outlooks and developed in diverse ways. Another area of metaphor which has received much less attention is that of Christian life as organic development toward fruition. Here the Christian, not the world around him or her, is the garden to be kept and dressed. To this image we now turn.

5

Shoots of the True Vine
and Seed Beds of the Spirit

Stewardship with its picture of God as overlord of the good creation and humans as God's stewards is, as we have seen, a model rooted in a developed cosmology and with the potential for an extended theological outworking. More restricted and restrictive is the related symbolism of spiritual horticulture where God is the pruner of the vine, or Gardener of the garden of the Christian soul. Despite the growing interest in ecology and horticulture mentioned in the last chapter, this language of spiritual horticulture does not seem to be experiencing a noticeable revival. It is interesting to look at the reasons why, and to consider whether one would wish to foster its wider usage or think of one's own relationship to God in its terms.

The Language of Vine and Garden
in Christian Reflection

The Bible is replete with parallels between organic and spiritual growth. The fields are white and ready for the harvest. The grain of wheat must first die before it grows. The Word is like seed scattered upon the ground. Even salvation history has its organic analogy, the Gentiles being like a graft into the olive tree of Israel.[1] As Christians are all part of the Body of Christ, so they

---

[1] John 4:35; 1 Cor 15:36–7; Mark 4:14–20; Rom 11:13–24.

are all shoots of the True Vine. "I am the True Vine," says John's Christ,

> and my Father is the vinedresser. Every branch of mine that bears no fruit, he
> takes away, and every branch that does bear fruit he prunes, that it may bear
> more fruit. You are already made clean by the word which I have spoken to
> you. Abide in me, and I in you. As the branch cannot bear fruit by itself,
> unless it abides in the vine, neither can you, unless you abide in me. I am the
> vine, you are the branches. He who abides in me, and I in him, he it is that
> bears much fruit, for apart from me you can do nothing. If a man does not abide
> in me, he is cast forth as a branch and withers; and the branches are gathered,
> thrown into the fire and burned. If you abide in me, and my words abide in
> you, ask whatever you will, and it shall be done for you. By this my Father is
> glorified, that you bear much fruit, and so prove to be my disciples. As the
> Father has loved me, so I have loved you; abide in my love. (John 15:1–9)

Through union with God, Christians draw their strength. And their hearts
should be to God like the garden of the lover of the Song of Solomon, who
cries:

> Awake, O north wind,
>   and come, O south wind!
> Blow upon my garden,
>   let its fragrance be wafted abroad.
> Let my beloved come to his garden,
>   and eat its choicest fruits. (Song of Solomon 4:16)

The tradition of speaking of the religious life in terms of horticulture has
continued down the centuries. Hermas, for example, picks up on the note of
judgment sounded in Jesus' words about the true vine. In Hermas's vision,
the Shepherd shows him "many trees, some budding and some withered,"
and says to him:

> These trees . . . which are budding are the righteous, who are destined to live in
> the world to come; for the world to come is summer for the righteous, but
> winter for the sinners. When therefore the mercy of the Lord shall shine, then
> the servants of God shall be made plain and all men shall be made apparent.
> For, just as in the summer the fruit of each individual tree is made plain, and
> they are recognized for what they are, so also the fruit of righteousness will be
> plain, and they will all be known, by blossoming in that world. But the heathen
> and the sinners—the withered trees which you saw—will be found to be such,
> dried and fruitless in that world, and they shall be burnt up like wood and shall
> be made manifest. . . . Be therefore fruitful, that your fruit may be known in
> that summer.[2]

---

[2] *Herm. Sim.* 4. Hermas's use of plant and tree imagery is quite remarkable. His eighth par-

The Puritan poet Edward Taylor, by contrast, meditates upon Christ as the tree of life and upon the meaning of this union. The following poem provides a particularly good example of how the language of organic union spills easily over into that of familial union; a family tree in actuality:

> My shattred Phancy stole away from mee,
>   (Wits run a Wooling over Edens Parke)
> And in Gods Garden saw a golden Tree,
>   Whose Heart was All Divine, and gold its barke.
>   Whose glorious limbs and fruitfull branches strong
>   With Saints, and Angells bright are richly hung.
>
> Thou! thou! my Deare-Deare Lord, art this rich Tree
>   The Tree of Life Within God's Paradise.
> I am a withered Twig, dri'de fit to bee
>   A Chat Cast in thy fire, Writh off by Vice.
> Yet if thye Milke white-Gracious Hand will take mee
> And grafft mee in this golden stock, thou'lt make mee.
>
> I being grafft in thee there up do stand
>   In us Relations all that mutuall are.
> I am thy Patient, Pupill, Servant, and
>   Thy Sister, Mother, Doove, Spouse, Son, and Heire.
>   Thou art my Priest, Physician, Prophet, King,
>   Lord, Brother, Bridegroom, Father, Ev'ry thing.
>
> I being grafft in thee am graffted here
>   Into thy Family, and kindred Claim
> To all in Heaven, God, Saints, and Angells there.
>   I thy Relations my Relations name.
>   Thy Father's mine, thy God my God, and I
>   With Saints, and Angells draw Affinity
>
> But Lord, as burnish't Sun Beams forth out fly
>   Let Angell-Shine forth in my Life out flame,
> That I may grace thy gracefull Family
>   And not to thy Relations be a Shame
> Make mee thy Grafft, be thou my Golden Stock.
>   Thy Glory, then I'le make my fruits and Crop.[3]

---

able is an extraordinary allegory in which an angel with a great pruning hook cuts branches from a "great willow, covering plains and mountains" and gives twigs to all those called by the Lord. Depending on their lives, their twigs and they themselves fare differently (*Herm. Sim.* 8). Hermas lived in Rome and his text dates from ca. 120 CE.

[3] Taylor, *Poems*, 47–48.

Taylor's poetry also offers us an example of another aspect of traditional reflection on the horticultural dimensions of spiritual development, namely that of Christ as gardener of our souls:

> My Gracious Lord, I would thee glory doe:
> But finde my Garden over grown with weeds;
> My soile is sandy; brambles o're it grow;
> My stock is stunted; branch no good Fruits breeds.
> My Garden weed: Fatten my Soile, and prune
> My Stocke, and make it with thy glory bloome.[4]

The late seventeenth century was a time when horticultural metaphor or trope was particularly popular. John Flavel's *Husbandry Spiritualized* and Cotton Mather's imitative tribute *Agricola, or the Religious Husbandman* set a fashion for extracting moral messages and spiritual parallels from every minute aspect of the agricultural process.[5] Jonathan Edwards avoided the excesses of the vogue and reflected at length in a more traditional mode on spiritual ingrafting. His treatment is interesting because he speaks both of the grafting of the natural or bad branch of the believer into the good stock of Christ, and then by contrast of the ingrafting of the life-giving twig of Christ into the wild or barren tree of the believer:

> Grace in the soul is the infant Christ there, a tender twig ingrafted from a heavenly stock in the soul by which it bears all its fruit. The nature is sanctified, the sap sweetened, and the tree made fruitfull.[6]

These writings develop horticultural images in quite overt and technical ways. Often, however, the idea of spiritual "fruit" functions in devotional literature as a "dead metaphor," one which is used by the writer without any thought to the material genesis of the term. Paul himself when writing of the "fruit" of the Spirit may have used it this way. As Herbert M. Gale observes,

> Numerous words may suggest pictures of certain phenomena or life situations, but when they become widely used in a figurative sense their appearance need not necessarily indicate that the writer was consciously intending to present pictures *as pictures* to the mind of the reader. Thus, when Paul uses the verb "to bear fruit," he may simply be employing a term that had become a familiar

---

[4] Ibid., 87.

[5] For a discussion of this, see Perry Miller's Introduction to Jonathan Edwards, *Images or Shadows of Divine Things* (New Haven: Yale University Press, 1948) 12–17.

[6] Edwards, *Images*, 114–15. The type is developed at some length.

substitute for "to produce results." In some cases, the actual picture of an agricultural phenomenon need not be involved at all; in other cases the picture might have been intended to have relevance.[7]

Undeveloped usages aside, one can see from this cluster of historical examples that the organic imagery of the vine and other related images of horticultural nurture were felt to offer many possibilities for theological reflection. The imagery is not usually used in such a sustained way in popular theological texts today. "Spiritual Fruit" are frequently discussed in the quasi-literal way referred to immediately above without any sense of the horticultural overtones of the term.[8] In only a few texts that I have seen does the author keep the context alive and use the imagery in a sustained way to discuss the various dimensions of the Christian life. A number of possible reasons may exist for this.

One problem may be that it is hard for the majority of modern North Americans and British people to think of God as, say, Vineyard owner or Dresser of the Vine, except insofar as they have been educated since childhood to do so. They are also likely to have little or no sense of the finer points of the horticultural and agricultural imagery, and are therefore likely to miss the point of detailed exegeses, or to fail to be very interested even when they do follow them.[9] This, of course, is not a new problem. Augustine cautioned the readers of his *De Doctrina Christiana*: "An ignorance of things makes figurative expressions obscure when we are ignorant of the natures of animals, or stones, or plants, or things which are often used in the Scriptures for the purpose of creating similitudes,"[10] giving as one example of the problem:

[T]here are many who because of an ignorance of hyssop—being unaware of its power either to purify the lungs or, as it is said, to penetrate its roots to the rocks in spite of the fact that it is a small and humble plant—are not at all able to understand why it is said, "Thou shalt sprinkle me with hyssop, and I shall be cleansed."[11]

For centuries, it has been a stock in trade of pastors to tackle zealously the

[7] Gale, *The Use of Analogy in the Letters of Paul* (Philadelphia: Westminster, 1964) 19.

[8] See, e.g., Getz, *Serving*, 49–50.

[9] One would imagine that the imagery would be drawn upon with greater enthusiasm in agricultural areas. Its basic lineaments would have a more visceral appeal to those from whose livelihood it was drawn.

[10] Augustine, *On Christian Doctrine* (trans. D. W. Robertson; Indianapolis: Bobbs-Merrill, 1958) 50.

[11] Ibid., 51.

explanation of these figures. Luckily for them, some Christians seem to manifest a great love for the *oddness* of biblical pictures and to evince a particular fondness for the more complex details of imagery drawn from a world that they have never known.

Two examples of modern writers who do take the time to explain and develop the horticultural imagery are John H. Timmerman and W. Phillip Keller. Just as Mather and friends came (with some effort) to see every aspect of husbandry replete with spiritual significance, so Timmerman and Keller. In the case of both men, their personal experience of working the land appears to have fed their love of horticultural imagery. Timmerman is a Vietnam veteran now teaching English at Calvin College who at some point became an avid gardener and thus found the imagery coming alive for him. Here, for example, is his discovery of the significance of *weeds*:

> When I first started gardening, I did it with a deliberation that both amused and astounded my wife and friends. As early as November I amassed seed catalogs. . . . By February, I had my orders placed, sometimes to a half-dozen different companies whose seeds for one particular vegetable or herb I thought superior. During winter months I made plans on sheets of paper for the garden layout—trellised vegetables here, marigolds spaced there to keep out certain bugs, and so forth, even down to a fence of old tin cans tied together to frighten off the rabbits and woodchucks that I would spot on the hillside as they greedily eyed the patch. Almost before the snow melted I was turning compost into the soil. The one thing I couldn't plan for was the weeds. They always came up, more regular than rain. Once I was out of town for a few days and returned to find my wife weeding in the garden. A sudden July rain had brought out the quackgrass with a vengeance. If it wasn't rooted up right away, the weeds would surely damage the crop that summer. My wife knew this. Like the poor farmer, I was out of town. . . .
>
> She gave me a good lesson . . . the matter of pruning and weeding is *urgent*. Left alone, those weeds will choke the crop.
>
> When we take inventory of our spiritual garden, it is good to bear two principles in mind. First, pruning and weeding are urgent tasks. they can't be delayed, however precious the junk in our lives seems to us. Second, they must be done thoroughly.[12]

Keller's early years were spent in Kenya, watching his father create crop land from rocky ridge ground. His book *A Gardener Looks at the Fruits of the Spirit* begins with chapters explaining the meaning of the parable of the seed that falls on the pathway, the rocky ground, and the thorny ground, and he draws upon his memories of Africa to explain these.[13] In the chapter on

---

[12] Timmerman, *The Way of Christian Living* (Grand Rapids, MI: Eerdmans, 1987) 18–19.

[13] Keller, *A Gardener Looks at the Fruits of the Spirit* (Waco, TX: Word Books, 1979).

the rocky ground of the unbelieving heart he writes:

> The second type of rocky ground is what we generally call stony soil. This is
> land littered with loose stones and boulders varying in size from that large eggs
> to random rocks weighing hundreds of pounds. Frequently this is very fertile
> soil which requires enormous labor and expense to clear for proper cultivation.
> My boyhood home in the heart of Africa was located on such land. My
> father had acquired 110 acres of desolate land on a high ridge. With tremen-
> dous toil, using teams of oxen, he literally tore thousands of stones from the
> ground. . . . And where the stones had lain there were planted thousands of
> trees of all sorts—fruit trees, coffee trees, ornamental trees, and firewood trees.
> . . . It was, in fact, a down-to-earth demonstration of the prophecy foretold by
> Ezekiel. It was a garden of Eden flourishing where before there had been noth-
> ing but stones, scrub thorn, and the cry of the jackals in the wilderness.
> In the Christian experience there are likewise wilderness areas. There are
> areas of stony soil, ground in which the good seed of God's Word has been
> dropped. It germinates, flourishes briefly, comes up against rocks of resistance,
> then withers away to nothing. . . .
> By His Gracious Spirit, God wants to clear the stony, stubborn soil of our
> souls. He wants to plant the trees of his own righteousness in every spot from
> which a stone of disobedience has been dug . . . to cultivate a gorgeous garden
> where before there were only barren boulders of bald resistance to His Word.[14]

Keller also draws upon his training in agricultural research, land management, and ecological studies to give more detailed analogies between the
state of the soul and the state of various types of soil.[15]

Fundamental Theological Limitations of the Images of Vine and Garden

One of the reasons that Vine language is not used extensively in theological
treatises on the Christian life may be that the writers see it as more overtly
metaphorical than, say, the language of servanthood. There seems to be no
assumption that we are in any real sense "shoots of a vine" or that Christ
really *is* a vine in the same way as he is Lord or even Captain of the church
militant.[16] No cosmology underlies the image, and it is difficult to develop a

---

[14] Ibid., 39–41.

[15] See, e.g., his discussion of shallow soil on basement rock (ibid., 33–34).

[16] The writers would appear to take the same view as Stephen Brown (*Image and Truth*, 154)
who said that "when Christ said 'I am the vine, you the branches,' He expressed the truth that
there exist between Him and every Christian relations as intimate and necessary as those that link
the branches to the vine, relations so intimate and necessary that Christians derive from Christ
the supernatural life of their souls in as real a sense as the branches derive their life from the

doctrine of God or of God's action with its aid. It appears to be a very partial image—one designed to highlight certain dimensions of the Christian's existence. Timmerman, for example, makes it clear that in his mind he is dealing with an analogy, albeit one understood as a "divine principle *rooted* in physical reality."[17] What this appears to mean for him, is that nature offers true and edifying parallels for the discussion of the Christian life but cannot be said to provide a locus for the most accurate picturing of God. Horticultural images are simply apposite subsidiary modes for expressing the more fundamental idea of God's loving action.

Even where Father, Son, and Spirit are pictured as gardeners, as in the case of Keller, the theme receives little development. The idea of the divine as gardener is less overtly metaphorical than that of Christ as Vine in that agency and personhood are present in the image of the garden. Nevertheless, Keller does not feel the need to provide a theologically complete matrix for his discussion of God's dealings with the soul.

Understanding the Christian Life in Horticultural Terms: Similar Imagery—Different Conclusions

Both Timmerman and Keller draw upon horticultural imagery primarily to address dimensions of Christian existence (rather than to convey information about the divine nature or the world at large). The first half of Timmerman's book is a reflection on the passage about the True Vine.

> This is the great blessing and the terrible reality of Christian living. It is a threefold process of fruit bearing. Grafted into Jesus as the True Vine, the Christian is expected to bear fruit. The life of the Christian needs pruning to bear abundant fruit. If the Christian doesn't bear fruit, his branch withers and is doomed.[18]

Having said this, Timmerman then branches out into more general horticultural discussion to make his point:

> Pruning is the hard, merciless thing to do. One always hopes for transformation, is reluctant to hack out the blighted or constricting branch. Any farmer, any backyard gardener, knows this feeling.
> That branch of the rose with the mottled leaves—maybe if I let it go it will

---

parent stem. The scope or point of the metaphor is the entire dependence of the Soul on Christ. With that point the resemblance between Christ and a vine begins and ends."

[17] Timmerman, *Way*, 8.

[18] Ibid., 10.

improve. But letting the blight of black-leaf have its own way impoverishes
not just the one rose but all the others in the garden. . . .

And then too that tomato plant—every branch seems to promise fat red
fruit. How can one snip off those tiny sprouts. . . .[19]

The lesson drawn from this is that Christian lives need pruning both to
remove sin and to produce greater moral fruit. These are urgent tasks that
cannot be put off. Timmerman also uses the traditional image of weeding
one's spiritual garden of sins, likening the desires of the flesh to dandelions
whose giant taproots cut a foot into the ground to leach out every drop of
nutrient and water, and which if only partially removed seem to come back
stronger than ever.[20] He provides the reader with a traditional list of
"weeds" and "fruit" of the spiritual life to aid them in their business of
extracting the former.[21]

Within the confines of the imagery, a number of theological issues are
explored by Timmerman, notably the relative roles of divine and human
action in the process of sanctification. In a wilful piece of mis-exegesis, Timmerman says: "The analogy Jesus draws in John 15 is clear—the Christian
must prune his life of the things that will destroy or diminish the fruits of the
spirit," and goes on to speak of the Christian's responsibility to prune and
weed.[22] In fact, in the passage of John referred to, despite the context of
injunction to love each other and bear fruit, the pruner is most specifically the
Father, not the Christian. The emphasis is on the goodness that flows from
abiding in Christ. We are at the heart here of the problem of grace and
human effort as it is construed within the limits of the image. Perhaps even
without noticing, Timmerman has shifted the onus to the Christian's
willpower. Even though he speaks consistently throughout his book of the
way that God prunes us with sufferings, he also speaks as if it were the
reader's responsibility and ability to get about his or her own self-
improvement, to cooperate with God in the cultivation of his or her own
character. The assistant gardener appears to have taken over from the head
gardener. Perhaps horticultural and agricultural imagery has an almost
irresistible pull in this direction. The farmer knows that it is only with human
cooperation that the land brings forth its crops, and the one who has observed
this is inclined to think that surely the same must hold good of the spiritual
life. James Gustafson remarks in a footnote that his Father was wont to tell a
particular joke in Swedish to the effect that the pastor says to Farmer

[19] Ibid., 15–16.
[20] Ibid., 16–19.
[21] Ibid., 18.
[22] Ibid.

Lindstrom: "That surely is a beautiful cornfield the Lord has given you, Lindstrom," and Lindstrom replies, "Ya, Pastor, but you should have seen it when the Lord had it alone."[23] Timmerman puts it thus:

> We nurture and consciously develop the fruits of the spirit and yet we also recognize that they are blessings upon our Christian life. We might say that though we nurture the fruit on our human spiritual ground, God rewards our attempts by sending the rich rain of his Spirit to make the fruit flourish.[24]

Not only does observation of actual agriculture or horticulture prompt one to try and inject agency into its spiritual metaphorical counterpart, so also does experience of oneself as an *agent*. Thinking of oneself as a vine shoot or as a garden tended by the Divine Gardener leaves very little room for the dimension of one's own will and agency as experienced in everyday life. As we see, Timmerman has come up against this problem and has resolved it by departing from his biblical sources.

Keller differs markedly from Timmerman, both in his choice of specific horticultural image and in his understanding of the relative roles of divine and human. He focuses on biblical passages relating to transformation of barren ground; what interests him is the image of the Christian, or the Christian's soul, as a garden tended, by the "Great Good Gardener." The first half of his book describes the states of the soul that prevent the seeds of the Spirit being planted and taking root, and the ways that the soul can be properly prepared so that they will take root. The second half describes the "fruits" of the Spirit in terms of the characteristics of God which will take root and produce a harvest in the Christian who lets them be planted.

The emphasis in Keller's book is squarely on divine action. The Gardener and not the garden is the focus:

> Christ comes to us in compassion to implant the seed of His own special Word. He endeavors to cultivate the soil of our lives by the inner working of His own gentle Spirit.[25]

It is the divine gardener and not the human gardener that takes care of the garden, unlike in Timmerman's book:

---

[23] Gustafson, *Ethics from a Theocentric Perspective*, vol. 1: *Theology and Ethics* (Chicago: University of Chicago Press, 1981) 106. Similar jokes turn up in many of the books that I have looked at, and I remember hearing an English version of this joke in a sermon a number of years ago.

[24] Timmerman, *Way*, 59.

[25] Keller, *Gardener*, 19.

The weeds of self-assertion, self-aggrandizement, self-serving, self-importance, self-assurance must go. All the old worldly concepts of personal grandeur and greatness which so readily invade our thinking will have to be plowed under by the deep in-working of the Good Gardener.[26]

Such fruits as are produced, are the work of God or God's Spirit:

> Such fruit can and does come only from above. It is not something which we can counterfeit. The very life of God, epitomized in the love of God, originates only and always with Him.
>
> Like good seed introduced into good garden soil, it must come from a source outside the garden. It does not, nor can it ever spring from the soil of our own souls and spirits spontaneously.
>
> There may be theologians, scholars, and teachers who would try to tell us that there is inherent good in man which if properly tended and cultivated can be gradually improved so that it ultimately becomes divine. This . . . is not the teaching of God's Word. . . .
>
> The picture presented to us in unmistakable language is that there must be the divine life of the living God implanted in our spirits. The very seed of the life of Christ sown in us by the Spirit of God can germinate in the ground of our being to mature into magnificent fruitage if we permit it to happen.[27]

The Christian's responsibility is simply to present the soil or ground of the soul for the Divine Gardener to act upon. What does this involve? "There are three simple steps that can be taken to break up our unbelief under the dynamic impulse of God's Spirit," writes Keller:

> 1) Ask God in sincerity to show you Himself. Ask Him to let you see what He is really like. When you discover that he is the Good Gardener who loves you immensely and longs to make your life productive it will pulverize your proud stony heart.
>
> 2) Ask Christ by His Spirit to show you yourself and the hard condition of your own inner will. When it dawns upon your dull soul how defiant and difficult you can be, it will break your heart and prepare it for His deep work.
>
> 3) Ask God by His Spirit to impart to you great faith—the faith to trust him implicitly. . . .[28]

We are responsible for that to which we expose our mind, emotion, will, and spirit,[29] but beyond that we can claim no responsibility for anything good that

---

[26] Ibid., 114–15.
[27] Ibid., 82–83.
[28] Ibid., 39.
[29] Ibid., 21.

comes about since it is not our independent action that has brought it about. In fact a patient and productive submissiveness is the hallmark of the good person, "the one great, essential ingredient for good soil to be productive under God's good hand is obedience or responsiveness."[30]

The Disposition Fostered by Horticultural Metaphor

Timmerman and Keller clearly have different ideas about the degree to which human agency is exercised in the process of growth in the Spirit, and this shows itself up to a point in their resultant slightly different understandings of the disposition that should mark the Christian's conduct. Timmerman's picture of the Christian as gardener allows for a certain zealous self-judgment—an attacking of the weeds of one's life and an acting fostering of good around one. Keller also emphasizes the importance of active virtue, but his conception of the self as friable soil awaiting the seeding of the Spirit is one which leads to a concentration of focus on humble acceptance and patience as the proper Christian disposition. He is keen to emphasize that this is not just a cowed or spineless acquiesence. Nor is it "a grudging, shriveled sort of sour stoicism," but rather

> a cheerful delight in the divine work of the Master Gardener in my life. The deep spading and the heavy plowing of God's Spirit in my soul are what eventually will produce the rich fruit of His own patience in my character. It can come no other way.
>
> In all of this as I continually remind myself that He, God very God, is dealing with me in patience and perseverance, I will lift up my heart and spirit to rejoice. I will rest in the sure confidence and quiet knowledge that He does all things well, both for my sake and His own.[31]

Not surprisingly, Keller's high estimation of patient acceptance of God's providential treatment of all persons, leads him to draw also upon other images which highlight this disposition. "[W]e face whatever arrangements God our Father makes for us as His proper and appropriate provision for us," he writes, and

> we accept these as the great good mills of God that will grind us into fine flour to feed His hungry people. We recognize our trials as the winepress of God's own creation in which our lives can be so compressed that there will flow from us refreshment for the weary, thirsty world around us.[32]

---

[30] Ibid., 76.
[31] Ibid., 124.
[32] Ibid., 123.

His theology of submission to God's will and opening to God's being also leads him to bring in the language of divine lordship and control at frequent intervals.[33] Timmerman does not emphasize submission to the same degree. He does, however, share Keller's appreciation of the virtue of patience. He deems impatience one of the worst of the weeds of the spirit, and presents patience as one of the key lessons to be learnt from the example of the farmer tending the land.[34]

One of the interesting aspects of the metaphor of the self as garden, is that its development is usually accompanied by a kind of "catalogue" of weeds and fruits. This convention allows the writer to highlight pretty much any virtues and vices she or he pleases. The same basic metaphor can provide the context for quite different presentations of the ideal Christian character. The weeds and flowers are like the "talents" in the stewardship model and the pieces of the Christian's "armour" in the context of soldiery: they provide room for variables within the model.

Some Conclusions

The writings of Timmerman and Keller have illustrated a number of important points: how particular images come alive in the hands of those for whom the metaphorical domain is familiar at first hand; how similar images can be developed in different directions by persons with differing notions of the nature of God's action; and how the internal structure of particular metaphors can constrain the discourse that they shape. Yet again, we have seen also how specific moral guidelines are tacked on, rather than arise organically out of, the images.

The language of the vine is really not susceptible of evaluation in the same way that, for example, that of stewardship may be. It is clearly a limited and more overtly figurative image which serves to highlight the importance of abiding in Christ. The metaphors of garden and gardener merit closer attention. The image of the garden slowly coming to fruition offers, in some ways, a good analogy for the way that human lives develop slowly and in response to a nurture which does, indeed, have much in common with the feeding and pruning of plants. One needs to use the language of "pruning" with some caution, though. It can be too easy to construe instances of

---

[33] For example, "God's Gracious Spirit is given only to those who obey (Acts 5:32). He will not enter nor reside where there is rebellion or resentment against His Royal Presence. He who is sovereign seeks for, expects, and counts on our complete cooperation and compliance with His commands in all areas of our lives" (ibid., 76).

[34] Timmerman, *Way*, 90.

adversity as God's intended pruning, when in fact they may be troubles for which humans alone are responsible and which humans should correct. The language of pruning can also be dangerous in contexts where its user thinks of himself or herself as responsible for someone else's growth. Used in the context of Christian parenting it offers unpleasant possibilities for the sanctioning of punishments intended to lead to the child's ultimate better growth.

Other possible problems with the image of self or personality as garden, lie in the way that the gardener is envisaged. Keller's kind of picture of the Christian as friable soil is only appropriate if one espouses the kind of notion of human depravity which necessitates having the seeds of goodness planted from outside and all horticultural attention directed from above.[35] For most contemporary Americans and English, the kind of joint gardening venture envisaged by Timmerman is likely to have greater appeal because it appears to make more room for human agency.

In some respects, however, the language of the garden is very attractive. It assumes a kind of fundamental continuity between the human personality and the rest of creation: all living things seeking to come to their fruition under God's hand. Despite the unpleasant elements of pruning, blights etc., it has the added attraction of being a relatively *irenic* mode of discourse. In sharp contrast stands the language of Christian warfare, to which we now turn.

[35] Keller's kind of emphasis on the seeds coming from without also plays into the traditional tendency within Christianity to envisage the Christian as the passive recipient of seed from outside, like the woman who receives the male seed. It may, therefore, reinforce a patriarchal conception of the divine as the male who kindly fertilizes his creation (viewed as female).

6

Fighting the Good Fight

The image of the Christian as a faithful soldier, fighting with principalities and powers which assault the soul and, more mundanely, with the obstacles presented to faith by the world of daily life, has been a persistant and popular one throughout the centuries. It was much favoured by certain New Testament writers. Perhaps the best known passage is that of the Epistle to the Ephesians:

> Put on the whole armor of God, that you may be able to stand against the wiles of the devil. For we are not contending against flesh and blood, but against the principalities, against the powers, against the world rulers of this present darkness, against the spiritual hosts of wickedness in the heavenly places. Therefore take the whole armor of God, that you may be able to withstand in the evil day, and having done all, to stand. Stand, therefore, having girded your loins with truth, and having put on the breast plate of righteousness, and having shod your feet with the equipment of the gospel of peace; besides all these taking the shield of faith, with which you can quench all the flaming darts of the evil one. And take the helmet of salvation and the sword of the Spirit, which is the word of God. (Eph 6:11 – 17)[1]

[1] See also Rom 13:12 – 14; 2 Cor 6:7; and 1 Thess 5:8. Other examples in the New Testament include: 2 Tim 2:3 – 4; 1 John 5:4; Heb 4:12. The social and historical context of the use of military imagery by Paul and the Pauline writers is explored by numerous authors. See, e.g., Brown, *Image and Truth*, 102 – 4; and Markus Barth, *Ephesians: Translation and Commentary on Chapters 4 – 6* (Garden City, NY: Doubleday, 1974). The cosmological context of the principalities and powers, and the idea of Christians wrapping themselves in the armor which was traditionally that of the divine warrior (not of his faithful) is addressed in the recent dissertation by Thomas R. Yoder Neufeld, ''God and Saints at War: The Transformation and Democratization of

In later centuries, the image proved dear to such diverse writers as Prudentius, Lorenzo Scupoli, William Gurnall, Horace Bushnell, and Hannah Whi-
tall Smith.[2] In many periods, of course, the image became a reality, not just
in the religious life of the Christian, but on the battlefields of Christendom.
The phenomenon of actual holy warfare is only a step away from the self-
conception of oneself as a member of God's church militant or holy empire.[3]

The Chequered Fortunes
of Warfare as a Guiding Image

A Fall from Grace in Some Quarters

The fortunes of the metaphor of warfare in the modern postwar period have
been chequered. In an article written in 1973, Nancy M. Tischler speaks
regretfully of the reverse it has suffered:

> One hymn you don't hear much in church these days is that old favourite
> "Onward, Christian Soldiers." The tune is certainly not one that offends the

---

the Divine Warrior in Isaiah 59, Wisdom of Solomon 5, 1 Thessalonians 5, and Ephesians 6"
(Th.D. diss., Harvard University, 1989). Also, see Walter Wink, *Naming the Powers: The
Language of Power in the New Testament* (Philadelphia: Fortress, 1984); and Clinton E. Arnold,
Ephesians: Power and Magic (SNTSMS 63; New York: Cambridge University Press, 1989).

    [2] See, e.g., Prudentius "Hamartigenia" and "Psychomachia" in *The Poems of Prudentius*,
vol. 2 (trans. Sister M. Clement Eagan; Washington, DC: Catholic University of America Press,
1965); Erasmus, *Enchiridion Milites Christiani* (ed. Anne M. O'Donnell; Early English Text
Society; Oxford: Oxford University Press, 1981); Lawrence [Lorenzo] Scupoli, *The Spiritual
Combat, and a Treatise on Peace of the Soul* (trans. rev. William Lester and Robert Mohan; New
York: Paulist, 1978) first published in 1589; William Gurnall, *The Christian in Complete
Armour*, vol. 1 (rev. ed.; 1864; reprinted Edinburgh: Banner of Truth Trust, 1964) first published
1665; Horace Bushnell, "The Military Discipline," in idem, *Sermons on Living Subjects* (New
York: Scribner's Sons, 1876); Hannah Whittal Smith, *The Christian Secret of a Happy Life*
(1870; reprinted Old Tappan, NJ: Revell, n.d.) 15–16. The metaphor operates in a number of
different ways in these and other works. An introductory overview would prove, I think,
unwieldy. Instead I draw upon historical examples during the course of discussion of present
works to illustrate continuities and departures. For those interested in the general use of the
language of warfare in particular periods of history, the following may be of interest: Adolf Har-
nack, *Militia Christi: The Christian Religion and the Military in the First Three Centuries* (ed.
McInnes; Philadelphia: Fortress, 1981), McInnes also surveys more recent works in his Introduction (ibid., 9–22); Thomas M. Greene, "Renaissance Warfare: A Metaphor in Conflict," in Thomas Patrick Murphy, ed., *The Holy War* (Columbus, OH: The Ohio State University Press,
1976). Useful footnotes and bibliography are also to be found in Barth, *Ephesians*, 759–829.

    [3] On the concept of the church as the army of Christ, see Hans-Ruedi Weber, *The Militant
Ministry: People and Pastors in the Early Church and Today* (Philadelphia: Fortress, 1963).

sensitive Christian ear; rather it is the notion that a Christian can be a soldier even metaphorically.[4]

We are presented with a classic example of how the changing nature of the realm of experience from which a symbol is drawn may render it unfit, in the eyes of many, to be applied to the realm of the religious life. Carnage of war, the unquestioning obedience and supremacist thinking that led to the holocaust, shocking photographic images of the human consequences of the armed conflicts of our century, the constant threat of nuclear annihilation— all these have contributed to a deep-seated distrust on the part of many of all thought systems and allied symbolisms with a remotely military cast. Believing firmly that symbol systems do shape behavior, many have rejected the concept of warfare as a metaphor for the Christian endeavour because of a conviction that it fosters violent attitudes and triumphalism in those for whom it becomes compelling.

We are also presented with an example of the rejection of a cluster of symbols because of a conviction that they legitimize or glorify the wrong dimensions of the mundane realm from which they are drawn: many Christians see the military metaphor as indissociable from an undesirable idealization of the warrior and they emphasize the potentially lethal consequences of continuing to idealize the soldier in an age where the actuality of war can be so terrible. Quaker author William Myers writes: "[T]he mere existence of nuclear weapons means that the warrior ideal can no longer be part of the way nations define their relations with one another."[5] In an excellent article on the problems of using battle imagery in hymns, Brian Wren looks at early Christian usage of battle symbolism and then at modern usage of it and the new twist that has been given to it by modern warfare. His observations bear quoting at length:

> The early church used such language [imagery of war], to suggest how God would protect the faithful witness ("the whole armour of God"), and to indicate the "weapons" available to a Christian. The idea of being a soldier for Christ may also have suggested the strong fellowship of people committed to a common cause. . . .
>
> Our first century Christian ancestors were unlikely to be fooled into taking

[4] Tischler, "Onward Christian Soldiers?," *Christianity Today* 17 (February 1973) 15. The interesting issue of the decline-of-battle symbolism in twentieth-century hymns is taken up by Methodist laywoman Anastasia Van Burkalow, "In Defense of Battle Symbolism in Hymns," *The Hymn* 17 (April 1966) 37–41; and idem, "A Call for Battle Symbolism in Hymns," *The Hymn* 38 (1987) 14–17.

[5] William A. Myers, *Replacing the Warrior: Cultural Ideals and Militarism* (Pendle Hill Pamphlet no. 263; Wallingford, PA: Pendle Hill, 1985) 25–26.

such language literally, since they were a persecuted minority. They were also, for several centuries, *pacifists*, who did not bear arms. *The context of language-use changes language meanings.* It is one thing for people who didn't carry weapons, and who were renowned for loving each other, to speak metaphorically in terms of "spiritual battles". It is quite another for us to use such language, since we live in a militarized culture, most of us are not pacifists, and we all too easily turn "spiritual" battles into material ones. If we use battle imagery, the experience we have to draw on is not that of Paul, or a first century slave in the arena, but our own. . . .

Modern war is *total war*. It involves whole populations and ravages the good earth God gives us. If we use battle imagery in worship today, the experience we are being asked to draw on, or will inevitably call to mind, is not the experience of earlier times, but our own. Can we draw on the experience of World War Two, Korea, Vietnam, Iran's human waves, or the IRA's suburban slayings, to describe the Christian life? . . .

Pacifist or patriot, we know—or ought to know—that war is hell. How can hell serve as a metaphor for the work of God?[6]

Another reason for the metaphor's decline in popularity in some circles may be that its appropriateness as a mode of describing the Christian life is closely bound up with a strong awareness of hostile sinful forces within and without one that are to be fought. Many liberals do not have a pronounced sense of sin as an enemy within that calls for combat; under the influence of modern psychological findings, it has come to be more common to construe sin as the unfortunate product of alienated conciousness and/or accumulated bad habit and to see it as needing behavioural therapy rather than arduous battle.[7]

As for the enemy without, evil and oppression have become so incredibly complex in their manifestations that it is unclear how they are to be attacked. It is difficult to have a sense of purposeful engagement in the *militia Christi* when there appears to be no universally recognized diagnosis of the enemy or plan of campaign, and when you feel (as do many Christians) that some of the worst enemies are in your own camp. Internecine strife scarcely has the appeal of a crusade against the infidel or against the forces of evil.

A further factor connected with the metaphor's decline in liberal Christian intellectual circles may be the rise of an awareness of the relativity of one's own religious beliefs. The metaphor of warfare tends to presuppose and

---

[6] Wren, "Onward Christian Rambos? The Case Against Battle Symbolism in Hymns," *The Hymn* 38 (July 1987) 13–15. Wren is a minister of the United Reform Church in England and Wales, and himself a hymn writer. He is described as "actively involved in movements for justice and peace" (p. 13).

[7] See, e.g., the discussions of this phenomenon in: Shirley Sugerman, *Sin and Madness: Studies in Narcissism* (Philadelphia: Westminster, 1976); and Karl Menninger, *Whatever Became of Sin?* (New York: Hawthorne Books, 1973).

foster a more absolutist understanding of truth. When the writer of Ephesians speaks of girding up one's loins with truth, he clearly envisages no dispute about what that truth is. Even though a case can be made for there being New Testament bases for universalist soteriology and even for sympathy for people of other religions, the witness of the texts overall suggests a belief that Christians alone possess the final revelation and that they can expect to have to struggle to make their truth prevail in a hostile world. There is a sense of urgency of mission, of the need to fight to free other souls from Satan's grasp. In modern writings the warfare metaphor is often accompanied by a similar note of spiritual belligerence. For example, in his 1964 Morgan memorial lecture David Martyn Lloyd-Jones lambasts liberals, accommodators, and others who no longer see faith as a fighting matter.[8] The world of mutual learning and respect for the other's tradition advocated by such historians of religion as Wilfred Cantwell Smith or Diana Eck is a far cry from such views. Spiritual belligerence is an attitude consciously rejected by many engaged in the process of trying to understand the faith of others. The metaphor of pilgrimage, which can be used to present a more open-ended understanding of truth as a destination still to be reached, appears more appropriate in this context.

These, then, may be some of the factors that have led to disenchantment with the imagery of war among certain sectors of the Christian population: fear of the practical consequences of adopting militaristic modes of thought; lessened awareness of sin as a force needing to be fought; bafflement and paralysis in the face of the complex forms of evil and oppression in the modern world; heightened awareness of the value that lies in other faiths, and desire to learn from rather than combat these.

It should also be said, that even among circles where the metaphor has continued to be used, it has not always retained its vigor. The language has survived, but it fails to move or persuade. Back in 1960, British author T. Austin-Sparks noticed that even his acquaintances who used the language of warfare to describe the Christian life seemed curiously unconvinced by it:

> I wonder whether we have made enough of this matter of our being, as the Lord's people, really on a *war footing*. Has it really come home to us that we,

---

[8] Lloyd-Jones, *The Weapons of Our Warfare* (Glasgow: Pickering and Inglis, 1964) 9. Lloyd-Jones (d. 1981) was one of the foremost figures in British evangelicalism. He spent his youth doing missionary work among miners and dock workers in South Wales. He later became minister of the Westminster Chapel in London, and his sermons are considered by British and American evangelicals to be some of the best preached this century. His devotional writings and biblical commentaries remain best sellers in conservative quarters. Many of these works deal with the issue of spiritual warfare.

the people of God, are supposed to be in the field under war conditions? Is there the mentality and consciousness in every section and in every individual that we are in a great campaign; that there is no let up in this matter, and that we are in it up to the hilt? There may be, and indeed often is, a real gap between our teaching, instruction, information, on the subject of Christian soldiering, and the assured conviction of being actually in a war—on active service. So many of the Lord's people listen to the teaching, and are interested in it, but they are not really in the fight, not really counting in the battle.[9]

The Continuing Power of the Image in Other Quarters

Having said all this, it is nevertheless obvious from a survey of popular theological literature of the last thirty years that not all North American or British Christians share these reservations about the idea of Christian soldiery.[10] Some are not even aware of the kind of objections discussed above. Others, such as Arthur Wallis, are aware of them but consciously choose to go on using military metaphor with a few caveats: "In using the military analogy throughout this book I am not expressing sympathy with the brutality of human warfare. I am simply taking my cue from the Bible."[11]

What are the factors that contribute to the continued popularity of this image in some quarters? I think one would have to point to the influence of Scripture, the liturgy, and devotional literature, also to social factors, to the life experience of the Christian, and to the structural richness of the image itself.

The influence of scripture plays an important part in the continuing popularity. The image of the soldier remains compelling to numerous Christians who have grown up with frequent sermons on such passages as the description of the armour of faith in Ephesians 6, and with the tales of the warrior heroes of the Hebrew Scriptures. Popular writers on the Christian life, such as Theodore H. Epp, move comfortably between the tangible earthly trials of the Hebrew warriors and the ethereal New Testament battles against principalities and powers, finding types of the latter in the former and using both to explicate the everyday battles of the Christian. Epp wrote an entire book on Joshua, *Joshua: Victorious by Faith*, because, as he puts it, "Joshua, in an outstanding way, exhibits many of the things that will help us in our own

---

[9] Austin-Sparks, *Our Warfare* (London: Witness and Testimony, 1960) 43–44.

[10] "Soldiery" can be used to connote either a body of soldiers or "military skill, soldiership." It is used here in its latter sense. I use the term because devotional and popular theological literature on the Christian soldier generally claims to be teaching the Christian the spiritual equivalent to military skill; it is in effect, "soldiery" of the spiritual realm.

[11] Wallis, *Into Battle: A Manual of the Christian Life* (Eastbourne, E. Sussex: Kingsway Publications, 1973) 7–8. Wallis is a British writer.

spiritual lives. We often consider the matter of the victorious Christian life and wonder how we can attain it. Joshua's life furnishes us with many fine illustrations of how this can be done.''[12] He rejects the more common interpretation of Canaan as a type of heaven and presents it as a type of the Christian struggle:

> Rather it is a type of the Christian's battle against sin and his victory over it as he seeks to live for the Lord. Canaan was a scene of conflict, not of complete peace and rest as heaven will be. The nations in Canaan become types of the principalities and powers we read about in Ephesians 6:12.[13]

Here we have a clear example of a person whose sense of the Christian life as combat has been shaped and informed by the Scriptures and, in particular, by typological interpretation of them.[14]

The resonances of the liturgy are also evident in some of the treatises on Christian soldiery. J. R. Richards, a bishop of the Church in Wales reminds his readers of the baptismal vow "manfully to fight under his [Christ's] banner, against sin, the world, and the devil,'' and says:

> When at our Confirmation we reaffirmed the promises made on our behalf at baptism, we of our own volition opened our hearts afresh to receive from God the gift of his Holy Spirit, to abide in us and to be our strength and stay. Signed with the sign of the Cross at our baptism, we were enrolled under Christ's banner as his soldiers, as members of the Church militant, to be sent forth, equipped with the armour of God, to wage war against sin, the world and the devil.[15]

In Britain, the continued practice of hymn singing in mandatory religious assemblies in many schools probably contributes to the continued power of the language of soldiery. Despite the new and more irenic hymn books created for use over the last twenty years, it would seem that many schools continue to use old stalwarts containing such perennial favorites as Onward Christian Soldiers. In parts of America where religious programming on the

---

[12] Epp, *Joshua*, 9. At the time of writing, Epp was director of the Back to the Bible Broadcast. The book grew out of radio bible "messages" (p. 6).

[13] Ibid., 15.

[14] This typological trend is much more pronounced in American literature where we find a continued presence of the Puritan love of typological exegeses which make the figures and events of the Old Testament both adumbrations of Christ's work and of the occurrences of the individual Christian's spiritual life.

[15] Richards, *Under His Banner* (Penarth: Church in Wales Publications, 1973) 44.

radio is prevalent and popular, the theme of Christian soldiery may be heard on the airwaves repeatedly.[16]

There is no doubt that in their choice of theological directions Christians are affected by the general social forces of their day, just as much as they influence the latter. Brooks Holifield's book, mentioned earlier, provides an illuminating discussion of the rise of the language of power, control, and muscularity in Christian writings from the late nineteenth century. He observes the shift in the writings of such theologians as Gladden and Bushnell to speaking of the natural world in terms of struggle, force, and survival of the fittest, and he comments upon the way the language of technology of the day is employed in devotional rhetoric, infusing "pious discourse with a recurring tone of power and energy." In America, these tendencies were compounded by the cult of virility that arose after the civil war with its calling forth of a new heroic and stoical ideal of manly virtue. This tendency was further reinforced by the rise of "muscular Christianity" with its emphasis on the strenuous life and mood. "From every side," says Holifield,

> from science, technology, the war, the economy, and popular culture—the message was the same: Power and vitality stood at the center of things. The imagery of power was by no means alien to the Christian tradition. The Old Testament exalted feats of physical strength; Jesus promised that his followers would receive "power;" Paul compared Christians to athletes running in a race. But antebellum Protestants had not made much of those themes. Only in the postwar cultural atmosphere did the churches recover (and distort and exaggerate) them. The result was a new setting for Protestant pastoral care.
>
> Throughout the religious spectrum, ministers announced that Christianity was a source of power.[17]

In such a context, the language of battle and victory easily becomes normative. In England, similar forces were at work, with the Empire perhaps providing the fillip to the language of manliness that the civil war provided in America.[18]

---

[16] I base this observation on listening to gospel stations while in North Carolina and Georgia. The one station available in the Boston area tends to focus on preaching and exhortation and to skimp on rousing hymns.

[17] Holifield, *History of Pastoral Care*, 169.

[18] The First World War was to lead to a general disillusionment with war as a heroic activity. The accounts of the sheer hell of the filthy trenches, the chaos of the war and its dubious reasons for even being conducted, led a strong strain of pacifism in British society and a resistance to the glorification of war. The Second World War, despite its horrors, was felt to be a more "just" war; its soldiers were fighting for a clearer purpose and more self-evidently with right on their side. One would expect this to have contributed to a condoning or reenergizing of military metaphor in Christian circles.

Other forms of influence aside, though, it would be unusual to find a person drawing upon biblical and liturgical analogies that did not resonate to some considerable degree with her or his own life experiences. With the military analogy in particular, it is very clear that many of the writers find it a strongly convincing way to describe the Christian life. This is especially true of those such as Arthur Wallis who have been involved in actual warfare, and can draw parallels between this and the Christian life from personal experience of both,[19] but such writers as Ray C. Stedman feel that even for those who have never served in an army, the nature of life as a battle should be self-evident. Speaking of Eph 6:10 – 13 he says:

> It is very clear in this passage that Paul's view of the basic characteristic of life can be put in one word: *struggle*. Life, he says, is a conflict, a combat, a continual wrestling. This is, of course, confirmed constantly by our experience.[20]

Some writers go even further and insist that it is inappropriate to speak of warfare merely in terms of metaphor, symbol or analogy. For them, Christian life *is* warfare. Wallis says:

> [T]he call of Christ is a call to arms. The Christian life means warfare. This is not to use a metaphor or a figure of speech but to state a literal fact. It is simply that the sphere, the weapons, and the foe, are all spiritual rather than material.[21]

John White takes the matter a stage further yet:

> War is not something that illustrates aspects of Christian living. Christian living *is* war. Indeed I would go further. Earthly warfare is not the real warfare. It is but a faint, ugly reflection of the real thing.[22]

[19] C. Day-Lewis (*The Poetic Image* [1947; reprinted Los Angeles: Tarcher, 1984] 110) wrote of the poet of the war era: "The idea of war had been colouring his poetry and shaping his images before 1939, of course: but now war was a subject which spoke to him with all the authority of common suffering, all the buoyancy of man's resistance and resilience." The number of English writers and readers who saw combat duty or who witnessed and participated in the smaller acts of heroism amid the air raids at home during the Second World War may also account for the greater popularity of the metaphor in postwar English writings and for the greater realism of the imagery used. At very least it created a greater toleration for the language of warfare. To reject it forcibly would have been to manifest a disrespect for those who had died for the country's sake.

[20] Stedman, *Spiritual Warfare* (Waco, TX: Word Books, 1975) 15. Stedman was trained at Dallas Theological Seminary and was, in 1975, pastor or the Peninsula Bible Church in Palo Alto, California.

[21] Wallis, *Into Battle*, 7.

[22] White, *The Fight* (Downers Grove, IL: InterVarsity, 1976) 216.

For such writers, the presence of the satanic, the evil and the sin in oneself has a sense of real enemy presence as real as any soldier feels on the battle field. Likewise, the struggle or combat has a very real quality.[23]

There may also be structural reasons for the continuing appeal of the metaphor of warfare. Few other images carry with them so *many* possible parallels, and several of the books by English authors betray a positive glee on the part of the authors over the serendipity of the multiple points of correspondence. Austin-Sparks takes his chapter titles wholesale from Field Marshall Slim's volume *Defeat into Victory*: "Supreme Command," "The Twofold Objective," "Morale," "Discipline," "Provisioning and Flexibility." He says that he has had to concentrate on only a few of Slim's headings, although he would have liked to have treated all of them:

> The discerning will recognize that these ten points could provide scope for valuable consideration for a long time. If all that were translated and interpreted into spiritual terms, and the Lord's people were in possession of such strategy spiritually, what a tremendously efficient people they would be![24]

Peter Gammons uses similar types of title: "The Divine Transfer" (moving from Satan's control into the army of Christ); "Victory!," "Dynamite" (empowerment by the Holy Spirit), "Signing Up," "Reveille" etc.[25] Arthur Wallis aims at even greater precision: "The Rescue Operation" (the atoning work of Christ), "Time to Enlist" (conversion), "Put on the Uniform" (baptism), "Equipped" (baptism in the Holy Spirit), "Lines of Communication" (prayer), "Posted to a Unit" (joining a local church) and so on.

Let us now turn and look more specifically at the ways in which the metaphor of warfare and soldiery operates. What does it really mean to speak of the Christian life as warfare? Does there appear to be a common theology behind the majority of works which speak of it as such? If so, how is God understood? Who or what is the enemy? What is the nature of the struggle? What are the exact parallels with physical warfare? What attitudes and qualities are being evoked and lauded when the Christian is exorted to be a faithful soldier?

---

[23] This pronounced sense of demonic onslaught is, of course, not merely a modern phenomenon. See, e.g., the account of Abba Macarius's brush with the demons of Terenuthis, "The Sayings of the Desert Fathers," in Owen Chadwick, trans. ed., *Western Asceticism* (LCC; Philadelphia: Westminster, 1958) 84.

[24] Austin-Sparks, *Our Warfare*, 11.

[25] Gammons, *Battle Stations* (Eastbourne: Kingsway Publications, 1984). Gammons is a British writer. He is described on the book jacket as an international evangelist and conference speaker and a member of the Good News Crusade team.

The Theology of the Image of Warfare

The General Outlines of the Theology

There does indeed appear to be a relatively consistent theology behind the majority of treatments of the theme. It is a theology where the cosmic battle of good and evil has prominence and where the work of Christ as atoner and victor over the forces of evil is of paramount importance. God created a good world, Satan engineered its downfall (with the complicity of humans), humans became sinful and liable to an unpayable penalty. God sent his Son to redeem humanity and to defeat the forces of evil; to offer to humans the possibility of an imputed righteousness and the possibility of personal victory over sin through appropriation of his victory.[26] It is asserted that the cosmic war between Satan and God continues, but that Satan has in reality been defeated by Christ and that anyone who puts their faith in Christ may appropriate his victory and may stand firm against the assaults of the principalities and powers and their worldling tools and be enabled to hold the sinful desires of the flesh at bay. The key scriptural text for belief in this promise is Rom 8:37: "In all these things we shall be more than conquerors through him who loved us."[27] Another important text is that of 1 John 5:4–5: "For whatever is born of God overcomes the world; and this is the victory that overcomes the world, our faith. Who is it that overcomes the world but he who believes that Jesus is the Son of God?" Passages from Revelation provide a mandate for battle; the fight is offensive not merely defensive.[28] The important thing always to remember is that Satan has been defeated; he is just a terrifying paper tiger. As Epp puts it:

> It needs to be repeated again and again that in our spiritual warfare as believers we fight against a defeated foe. This does not mean there will not be a battle, but it does mean we do not need to be worried about the outcome. Satan is not afraid of us but he is afraid of Christ, and as long as we walk with Christ, victory is assured. As we press forward in aggressive warfare on the spiritual battlefield, we will find as did the two spies in Jericho that terror has already

---

[26] Many examples could be given of this theological exposition. A good one is to be found in Roger Price, *Victory in Jesus* (Basingstoke, Hants.: Marshall Morgan & Scott, 1982) 15–89.

[27] This was a favorite text of John Wesley and, through his influence, its theme came to have a central place in Methodism and later in the Holiness movement. Holifield (*History of Pastoral Care*) appears to overlook this earlier infusion of spiritual victory language into the tradition.

[28] See Rev 2:7, 17, 26 and 3:5, 12, 21. For an example of exegesis of these passages, see Corrie Ten Boom, *Marching Orders for the End Battle* (Fort Washington, PA: Christian Literature Crusade, 1969) 21–24.

laid hold of the enemy; and they anticipate nothing but defeat. The powers of darkness tremble when we come in the strength of the Lord.[29]

Ultimate victory for the forces of good awaits the second coming of Christ, but victory at the personal level is possible now.

In the context of this theology, God the Father is seen as king or ruler at war, as the "Commander." The imagery owes much to the picture of the masculine warrior God found in some of the Hebrew Scriptures.[30] Austin-Sparks, for example, speaks of the Father in terms of a warlord king whose supreme objective is "the Throne"—the rights, claims and influence of the heavenly throne, and the well-being of the people over whom it is set.[31] In a similar vein, the late David Watson, an Anglican evangelical, speaks of the Lord of hosts who has designed suitable equipment for the struggle and devised the strategy for the defeat of Satan's forces.[32] This is not to say that the writers try to obscure the divine characteristics of love or mercy; rather, they are dealing with the aspect of God which leads him to act as a "man of war," namely, his wrath against sin. However, the literature as a whole is noticeably lacking in any hope of the possibility that God's love or mercy might extend to those who remain wilfully without the Christian fold.

Jesus is first and foremost the Commander or Captain. Epp writes:

> As our spiritual Captain he leads us in spiritual warfare, giving us the power to pull down strongholds and cast down imaginations and every high thing that exalts itself against the knowledge of God.[33]

He is also the supreme example of good soldiery, "our perfect example of how to conduct spiritual warfare."[34] In this context, the earthly figure of Christ is evoked, complete with the public humiliations that were part of his martyrdom. His obedient furtherance of the Father's cause and suppression of his own will are presented as the paradigmatic actions of the soldier who has been trained to lay down his life. Paul E. Billheimer stresses the importance of this, reminding his readers of the words of Marshall Foch: "Battles

[29] Epp, *Joshua*, 95.

[30] See, e.g., Exodus 15:3. On the origins of the warrior dimension of the divine, see Frank Moore Cross, "The Divine Warrior," in idem, *Canaanite Myth and Hebrew Epic: Essays in the History of Israel* (Cambridge, MA: Harvard University Press, 1973); and Patrick D. Miller, Jr., *The Divine Warrior in Early Israel* (HSM 5; Cambridge: Harvard University Press, 1973).

[31] Austin-Sparks, *Our Warfare*, 25–27.

[32] Watson, *Hidden Warfare* (rev. ed.; 1979; reprinted Eastbourne, E. Sussex: STL and Kingsway Publications, 1983) 102.

[33] Epp, *Joshua*, 172.

[34] Michael Harper, *Spiritual Warfare* (rev. ed.; Ann Arbor, MI: Servant Books, 1984) 21.

are won by teaching soldiers how to die, not how to avoid dying,'' and calling on them to imitate Christ's example.[35] He laments what he sees as the present day loss of willingness to sacrifice one's wishes and even one's own life, saying:

> [W]e have surrendered the central principle of Christianity to patriots. That is why nations deify their war heroes, because men instinctively recognize the divine quality of self-sacrifice.[36]

Despite these examples of reference to the trials of Christ, it should be said that the Christ evoked in the literature tends to be mainly the risen and triumphant Christ. This is to be expected in a theology where the major emphasis is on his victory over the forces of evil and on the possibility of the Christian's appropriation of this victory. In her short work *The Spiritual Warfare*, Jessie Penn-Lewis says emphatically:

> Your reliance should never be *upon a Christ within*, but upon a Christ on the Throne in heaven, who by His Spirit will energize you for all He wants you to do. Your faith is to rest upon the glorified Man in heaven, and as you look to Him there, His Spirit is poured into your spirit, making him a reality to you.[37]

And she continues:

> It is very important that you do not rely upon an inward subjective experience, *but upon God and Christ* in the glory. *The reliance upon an inward experience opens the door to Satan's counterfeits.* The faith of the Church is to be centred upon Christ on the Throne, even as He is set forth in the Word. The apostles preached a glorified Christ in heaven.[38]

It is the Holy Spirit who is the presence which continually abides with the Christian. He is the one who empowers Christians in such a way that they are able to fight the good fight and to appropriate Christ's victory.[39] He is the ''armorer'' of the faithful. His gifts or charismata are construed as weapons or equipment necessary for the fight. In this regard, some of the authors insist upon the importance of ''spirit baptism'' as a necessary stage following

---

[35] Billheimer, *Overcomers Through the Cross* (Eastbourne, E. Sussex: Kingsway Publications, 1982) 43. Billheimer is an elderly American writer who has written prolifically on all dimensions of Christian soldiery. His best-known book is *Destined for the Throne* (Minneapolis, Bethany House, 1975), a particular favorite of Billy Graham (*Overcomers*, 13).

[36] Ibid., 42.

[37] Penn-Lewis, *The Spiritual Warfare* (Poole, Dorset: Overcomer Publications, n.d.) 37.

[38] Ibid., 36–37.

[39] Without exception, the writers use the masculine pronoun to describe the Spirit.

upon water baptism. Michael Harper writes: "To lead a person to Christ and not to show him how he can be filled with the Holy Spirit is like recruiting him for the army and not providing him with adequate weapons."[40] Such, then, are the divine leaders in the cosmic struggle against evil. Let us turn now to consider the enemy forces.

Traditionally the enemies are listed as threefold: the devil, flesh or sin, and the world. Ranged against the divine Trinity and its cause are the external enemies: Satan and the principalities and powers. Ranged against the Christian and fallen humanity in general are the internal human enemies: the prompting of sin or desires of the flesh; the "old man." At loose in the world are the legions of Satan, and the effects of human sinfulness which together produce "the world" as a negative entity faced by the Christian.

The context for speaking of the Church as the *militia Christi* is the cosmic battle, raging also on earth, against the forces of evil:

> For the spiritual conflict with Satan, God too recruits and trains his own fighting forces: Christians make up the army of the Lord on earth. In the heavenly realms, he deploys legions of angels and archangels, of cherubim and seraphim. In this world, he primarily uses men and women specially picked and prepared. They are people who have been reborn spiritually, made partakers of divine life, and endowed by the Holy Spirit with particular individual abilities to serve Christ's cause.[41]

By contrast, the struggle against internal sin forms the backdrop for discussion of interior warfare in the spiritual life. As we shall see later, different writers focus on different battle fronts; the literature of soldiery ranges from an apocalyptic realism dealing with battling principalities and powers to a gentle exegesis of the metaphor in terms of assisting the Christian in conquering personal sins and worldly opposition.

The Nature of the Struggle Engaged in by the Christian

Fighting the Principalities and Powers

Let us turn now to look in greater detail at the nature of the warfare, beginning with the genre of literature which deals primarily with the battle against the principalities and powers. Its subject matter often goes under the heading of "spiritual warfare." Sometimes the term achieves a broader significance, but traditionally it has usually been attached mainly to these more specialized

---

40 Harper, *Spiritual Warfare*, 57.
41 Watson, *Hidden Warfare*, 45.

works which continue the exposition of the theme of *psychomachia*, first presented in the works of Prudentius.[42] In our century, such works have tended to be produced only by very conservative authors with what might be described as "charismatic" leanings. That is not to say that others have not taken seriously the principalities and powers. Most systematic theologians at some point take up this subject.[43] However, few have written books specifically on the topic.

"Spiritual warfare" literature focuses most strongly on the business of fighting principalities and powers; on recognizing their presence and their attacks and repelling them. The writers emphasize the reality and power of the enemies:

[42] It is rare, however, for modern authors to take up the allegorical dimension of the treatments of *psychomachia* pioneered by Prudentius and found in such works as Gregory's *Morals on the Book of Job* A Library of Fathers (Oxford: John Henry Parker, 1844), and John Bunyan, *The Holy War* (London: The Religious Tract Society, n.d.; reprinted Grand Rapids, MI: Baker Book House, 1986). Of the *topos* of *psychomachia*, Martin Irving writes: "There are actually two closely related motifs...The first is the representation of diabolical agression against the soul in metaphors of battle, hunting, or robbery (flaming arrows, spears, snares, and so on), and the second is the expansion of this metaphor into a full-scale allegory with the personalized virtues and vices as individualized representations of the primary spiritual struggle. The main elements of the *topos* in either form usually include: the machinations of the devil and his agents against the soul, the weapons of the diabolical forces, the wounds of sin inflicted by the enemy, God's ability to defend the faithful, the fortress of the soul, the use of heroic conventions and the diction of epic poetry" ("Cynewulf's Use of Psychomachia Allegory: The Latin Sources of Some 'Interpolated' Passages," in Morton W. Bloomfield, ed., *Allegory, Myth and Symbol* (Harvard English Studies 9; Cambridge: Harvard University Press, 1981) 53. The patristic and pagan origins and developments of the idea of psychomachia in the Christian latin context are explored by Macklin Smith in his fascinating book *Prudentius' Psychomachia: A Reexamination* (Princeton: Princeton University Press, 1976). One of his key points is that although such writers as Tertullian and Cyprian picked up and developed Paul's language of spiritual warfare, Prudentius was the first to provide a detailed and extended psychological presentation of this, and he did it by means of employing epic allegorical narrative (pp. 130–31). The theme of the psychomachia has retained a place of great importance in both Catholic and Protestant writings over the centuries. Bunyan's treatment is perhaps the best known and widely used Protestant example. In the Catholic tradition, Scupoli's *Spiritual Combat* holds a place of honor. Francis de Sales held it to be as great a classic as the *Imitation of Christ*. This same work was taken up, put together with another of Scupoli's works *Path to Paradise*, and translated with the latter as *Unseen Warfare* and edited by Nicodemus of Athos in the eighteenth century, and again reedited by the Russian Bishop, Theophan the Recluse, in the nineteenth century. In these forms it has become a text of major importance in the Orthodox Church. Nicodemus of the Holy Mountain and Theophan the Recluse, *Unseen Warfare* (trans. E. Kadloubovsky and G. E. H. Palmer; Crestwood, NY: St.Vladimir's Seminary Press, 1987).

[43] See, e.g., Karl Barth, *Church Dogmatics*, vol. 3.3: *The Doctrine of Creation* (Edinburgh: T. & T. Clark, 1961) esp. 289–531.

Humanity is beset by a host of self-conscious evil spirit personalities called demons who are responsible for much, if not most, of the personality difficulties, complexities, spiritual pressures, strains and the aggravated forms of evil that characterize our modern social order.

The fallen condition of mankind, the sin of the human heart alone, does not explain the abnormal psychoses and the universal snarling and fouling of human relations. This constant and fiendish disruption of the human social order is explained only by the mass activity behind the scenes of a vast, well-organized host of wicked spirits under the control of their master prince. Any spiritual method or technique which ignores the presence and activity of these occult forces cannot possibly offer an adequate solution for the problems plaguing mankind.[44]

Great attention is paid to using the authority Jesus gave to all his disciples to trample such evil beings under foot, to expel or bind them in his name and to counteract their doings with concerted prayer. Prayer is perhaps the key weapon. Says Penn-Lewis:

Briefly, prayer warfare simply means holding unceasingly the power of the "finished work of Christ" over the hosts of evil, in their attack upon some place or person, until the victory is won. Just as Moses lifted his hands stedfastly until the victory was won, so the prayer warrior holds up stedfastly the victory of the Cross—the finished victory of Christ over Satan—until the forces of evil retreat and are vanquished.[45]

She tries to convey something of the intensity of the engagement:

In union with the enthroned Lord, the believer in due time finds the conflict of Ephesians 6 open to him, and discovers that there is a prayer-warfare where he needs, not only Christ as his life within, but "the whole armour of God", or Christ as his covering, without. Where he will meet in direct combat, without the intervention of "flesh and blood", the satanic principalities and powers, and learn, by standing on the firm foundation of the Gospel (e.g. *Christ crucified*) to overthrow the foe, and then with "unwearied persistence" to hold the victory for himself and others.[46]

Penn-Lewis believes that such terrible conflicts come only to the more advanced believer.[47] God would not permit a new Christian to be tested so, or

[44] Paul Billheimer, *Destined to Overcome: The Technique of Spiritual Warfare* (Minneapolis: Bethany House, 1982) 21–22.
[45] Penn-Lewis, *Spiritual Warfare*, 6.
[46] Ibid.
[47] Ibid., 19.

thrown into the front line of the cosmic battle. Hal Lindsey is inclined to agree: "Not many believers are called upon to endure direct Satanic attack in the way that Job was. Only those who are specially prepared and called are thrust into that conflict. But rest assured that these battle-tested warriors will be given special eternal rewards."[48] However, he does warn the reader that it looks suspiciously as if we are living in the beginning of the end times and that if this be the case, we can expect renewed and unusually deadly onslaughts from Satan's cohorts.[49] Michael Harper concurs in this assessment: "We are living at a time of expanding supernaturalism, good and bad. On the one hand, there is the charismatic revival . . . on the other hand, there is the resurgence of the power of evil supernaturalism on a truly daunting scale."[50]

Writers on spiritual warfare differ in their understanding of the precise workings of the powers and in the extent to which they feel that it is important to detail these for the reader. Penn-Lewis (*Spiritual Warfare*) restricts herself to discussion of battle being waged in an entirely spiritual realm, whereas writers such as David Watson (*Hidden Warfare*) deal with specific onslaughts in the physical realm. This latter approach involves the broadening of scope to discuss "the world"; the second enemy or battlefront and to more tangible discussions of disciplining the flesh.

The World

The concept of "the world" as enemy is susceptible of very different treatments. For those with a strong belief in the operation of principalities and powers, "world" is synonymous with the arena of their power and lingering authority. The Christian soldier is exorted to discern and deal with the many ways that Satan is trying to thwart God's plans for him or her. For example, in *The Battle for Your Faith*, William M. Aldrich discusses in detail how Satan operates. He says Satan disseminates lies so as to undercut Christian faith and prevent successful mission. He also is perverting the educational and political systems:

> Loyalty to the nation is being discouraged and loyalty to world government fostered. And in the meantime the alien enemy who is succeeding in destroying

---

[48] Lindsey, *Combat Faith* (New York: Bantam Books, 1986) 164. Lindsey is a converted seaman who became a self-taught expert on Bible prophecy. He is a premillenialist who might perhaps be described as a freelance prophet of Armageddon.

[49] Ibid., 19.

[50] Harper, *Spiritual Warfare*, 5.

morals and loyalties in our midst is vigorously indoctrinating his own youth in the principles of communistic world revolution.

The enemy of our souls leaves no stone unturned in his master strategy of destroying faith in God, country and decency. And one of his devices is to destroy the images of national heroes of virtue and courage and to replace them with figures of men and women of moral abandon, daring violence and rebellion.[51]

He goes on to discuss Satanic use of the media, politics and all other spheres of public life. Another area of Satan's activity is the focus of David Watson's scrutiny: cults, occultism and church schisms. He calls these "three of his most effective weapons," and says that schism is the worst of the lot:

If Satan were forced to choose one weapon only out of his total arsenal, it would probably be schisms. Consider this: nothing convinces the unredeemed world more effectively that they should reject Jesus Christ as Saviour and Lord than the sight of squabbling Christians.[52]

In similar fashion we find Ray Stedman speaking of Satan orchestrating liberal attacks on the inerrancy of the Bible,[53] and Hal Lindsey describing New Age religion in terms of the one-world religion that, according to his interpretation of Revelation, Satan will set up to be led by the Antichrist during the seven year tribulation after the Christ has gone.[54]

It is noticeable how these constructions of "the world" reflect very conservative political and moral outlooks just as much as they reflect literalist interpretation of the Bible. Not surprisingly, many people of other political leanings are very wary of talk of satanic activity. History has witnessed much fanaticism and bloodshed in the name of rooting out of satanic activity—most of it directed against women and ethnic and religious minorities such as blacks and Jews.

The equation between belief in the activities of principalities and powers and extreme conservatism across the board does not always hold fully— particularly with English writers. For example, Clive Calver and Derek Copley in their book *The Fight of Your Life* affirm that the Christian life is indeed a prolonged spiritual warfare, but say:

What is needed is a new generation of Christians. Men and women utterly devoted to Jesus Christ, committed to a vision of the King and his kingdom,

---

51 Aldrich, *The Battle for Your Faith* (Portland, OR: Multnomah, 1975) 93.

52 Watson, *Hidden Warfare*, 99–100.

53 Stedman, *Spiritual Warfare*, 109–110.

54 Lindsey, *Combat Faith*, 8–9.

recognizing that spiritual warfare is not, in the main, a matter of occult activity. Men and women committed to a day by day overcoming of personal temptation to live the life of Jesus in victory through the power of his Holy Spirit.[55]

And they continue:

> Spiritual militancy might well seem to be considerably "over the top" in the pale light of much of the Christian activity in the western world. But to the early church, or to our brothers today in much of the so-called "third world," it is normal. God has always wanted an army which would stand for righteousness and justice, but whose weapons would be godly lives, compassion and the word of God.[56]

They go on to speak of warfare in terms of providing an "adequate response to the pain and depravity of a hungry hurting world," and of the great importance of avoiding cosy triumphalism.[57] Peter Gammons agrees with these emphases. Although his whole book is replete with the most militant language, he nevertheless stresses the importance of working for such goals as racial harmony.[58]

However, it has to be said that the overall flavor of the literature which takes principalities and powers seriously and speaks of combatting "the world" is definitely conservative. On the whole, liberals and radicals who have a pronounced sense of the structural evils of society and can theorize with some sophistication about how they work and are perpetuated are less inclined to see principalities and powers at work.[59] They may see, as did Walter Rauschenbusch, the tendency of society to give rise to certain forms of sinfulness and to permit and even encourage their perpetuation.[60] Or they may choose to focus on the collective manifestations of sin in particular situations or instances and to dismiss as pointless and even dangerous

---

[55] Calver and Copley, *The Fight of Your Life* (Eastbourne, E. Sussex: Kingsway Publications, 1986) 25. Calver is General Secretary of the Evangelical Alliance, and Copley the Principal of Moorlands Bible College.

[56] Ibid., 26.

[57] Ibid., 66. Racism, AIDS, and unemployment are among the social evils that they call upon the Christian to tackle.

[58] Gammons, *Battle Stations*, 132–33.

[59] They are likely to follow Bultmann in describing all talk of principalities and powers as mythological projection or metaphorical expression of the real fact that "the evil for which every man is responsible individually has nevertheless become a power which mysteriously enslaves every member of the human race" (Bultmann, *Jesus Christ and Mythology* [New York: Scribner's Sons, 1958] 21).

[60] Rauschenbush, *A Theology for the Social Gospel* (1917; reprinted Nashville: Abingdon, 1978) 69–94.

attempts to find any transcendental or universal basis for these. The latter view is discussed in a recent work by Sharon Welch. Speaking of liberation theologians, especially James Cone and Mary Daly, she says:

> These analyses of sin and redemption are historical and political, not ontological. Rather than examine the structure of the human will and its potential for sin or describe the sociality of human existence and the possibility for social deformation of individual lives (thus delineating the ontological roots of complicity in institutional evil), liberation theologians analyze particular forms of oppression. They do not address oppression as such, but challenge specific structures of oppression.[61]

In such situations, the appropriate response is to subvert the processes that keep these collective forms of sin masked, hidden and therefore powerful. Liberation theologians like Daly, Cone, and Gutierrez do not try to discover and describe universal conditions for the possibility of sin; they try to unmask the myriad manifestations of particular forms of sin, particular forms of domination. They contend that this unmasking is necessary given the collective nature of sin. Our participation in structures of oppression is largely unconscious. Our complicity is unwitting and naive. The task of liberation theology is to break the facade of innocence and expose the impact of our social system.[62]

The language of unmasking and revealing has much in common with the language used by such writers as Aldrich (*Battle for Your Faith*) who would have their reader understand how they have been duped into particular behaviours by the forces of evil. However, in the context of liberation theology as described by Welch, there is merely the mechanism of complicity awaiting revelation; no demonic puppeteers hover behind the shadow screen. Knowledge, not combat is what is emphasized; although to the extent that knowledge is power, it could be viewed as a weapon if the term were not so inappropriate in that context.

Sin and the Flesh: Interior Warfare

Although the writers tackle the issues of assaults on the soul and of evil at large in the world, it is perhaps the military disciplining of "the flesh" or the unregenerate dimensions of the self that concerns them most. Traditionally there has always been the greatest call for works which purport to help the individual Christian in his or her own battle against selfish desires; to achieve

---

[61] Welch, *Communities of Resistance and Solidarity: A Feminist Theology of Liberation* (Maryknoll, NY: Orbis Books, 1985) 48.
[62] Ibid., 49.

the "victorious" or "triumphant" life or become "overcomers" in this context of day-to-day development in holiness. The theological anthropology is Pauline: a war between the regenerate and unregenerate dimensions of the person. The basic idea is, once again, the appropriation and enforcement of the victory won by Christ. Billheimer puts it this way:

> When we consecrate ourselves wholly to be sanctified, cleansed from the carnal mind and filled with the Spirit, we agree that our "old man", who has been judicially crucified with Christ, shall be actually and practically nailed to the cross. When God sees that we mean business, that our consent is really genuine, he accepts the sacrifice.
>
> And then the battle begins. What we have done theoretically has to be practically wrought out in all the endless varieties of daily life, Christian experience and conduct.[63]

Again, the delicate tension is between a victory already gained, and yet still to be enforced. Readers are continually reminded that they are "more than conquerors in Christ," and are simultaneously urged to make the conquest real.

A distinct tension between willpower and grace and between the idea of being saved by one's own works and by God's grace is always lurking. In the interests of motivating people, some authors seem to link successful battles with personal effort and to link building up battle ability with progress in sanctification. At very least, they seem to suggest that the believer's own will and action have a very large part in determining the outcome of conflicts. William Deal, for example, writes: "Back of every really victorious Christian life are these three secrets: prevailing prayer, personal knowledge of God's Word, and perseverance in the Christian way."[64] Or we find JoAnne Sekowsky writing:

> It is not easy to accept the fact that the enemy is of our own "household," in this case our own flesh. This week, call your "enemy" to task. Determine ways you may have been cooperating with Satan and his schemes. Then take authority over the areas where you should have (self-control) and ask Jesus to strengthen you in your resolve.[65]

[63] Billheimer, *Overcomers*, 12–13.

[64] Ibid., 66. Racism, AIDS, and unemployment are among the social evils that they call upon the Christian to tackle.

[65] Sekowsky, *Spiritual Warfare: Strategy for Winning* (Women's Aglow Fellowship Workbook Series; Lynwood, WA: Aglow Publications, 1983) 65. Sekowsky is an editor and writer for the Aglow Fellowship, an evangelical women's organization with a large publications operation.

And Calver and Copley tell the reader, "Consistency in victory and strength to win the bigger and more prolonged battles can only come through steady effort."[66]

This is very much the same psychology of little-by-little, step-by-step character building that was so evident in much of the stewardship literature. We are close here to the "how-to" manuals of the secular sphere, and to the not-necessarily-religious idea of the moral life as a war.[67] Seeing this problem on the horizon, one particular group of writers under consideration made it a key part of their agenda to insist that "victory" in the battles of life can come only through total surrender and allowing Christ to work through one. These are the writers of the "Victorious Life" movement.[68] Their main spokesman, Charles G. Trumbull, spells the matter out very clearly:

> Jesus, you know, makes two offers to everyone. He offers to set us free from the *penalty* of our sin. And he offers to set us free from the *power* of our sin. Both these offers are made on exactly the same terms: we can accept them only by letting Him do it all.
>
> Every Christian has accepted the first offer. Many Christians have not accepted the second offer. They mistakenly think, as I did, that they must have some part in overcoming the power of their sin; that their efforts, their will, their determination, strengthened and helped by the power of Christ, is the way to victory.[69]

We are, he says, to use our wills to accept victory, not to make an effort to win it.[70]

This tension between submission and personal effort, worked out in the

[66] Calver and Copley, *Fight of Your Life*, 129.

[67] On this point, see e.g., William James, *The Varieties of Religious Experience* (New York: Collier Books, 1961) 53: "For morality life is a war."

[68] A fascinating account of the rise of this movement is to be found in Douglas Frank, *Less than Conquerors: How Evangelicals Entered the Twentieth Century* (Grand Rapids, MI: Eerdmans, 1986) 103–66. Frank locates the rise of the movement in a late nineteenth-century obsession with avoiding defeats in life (of both sin and circumstance). The leaders of the movement promised followers that if they totally gave up their own will and allowed Christ to act through them, they would be guaranteed victory in all areas of their lives. Frank details the miseries that ensued as the followers gradually came to realize that defeats were sometimes inevitable.

[69] Trumbull, *Victory in Christ: Messages on the Victorious Life* (Fort Washington, PA: Christian Literature Crusade, 1959) 9.

[70] Ibid., 49. In this move, they perfectly exemplify James's characterization of those who have discovered the shortcomings of robust moral athleticism and discovered with relief the state of mind "in which the will to assert ourselves and hold our own has been displaced by a willingness to close our mouths and be as nothing in the floods and waterspouts of God," (James, *Varieties*, 54). Nevertheless, they continue to talk in the language of soldiering on.

language of soldierly obedience is reminiscent of the language of the servant who does the bidding of the master and of the disciple whose development hinges on submitting to the word and will of the teacher. The same dynamic is at work in each.

A Life Lived in the Light of the Image

A Disposition Toward Disciplined Obedience

In the discussion of what constitutes the enemy to be countered in the "world" we saw again the way that specific directives for ethical dilemmas cannot be drawn automatically from an image. It is all very well to speak of battling against evil in oneself and in the world around one, but first one has to make decisions about what exactly *is* evil. Even the conservative is obliged to enter into assessments for which the Bible does not offer fixed guidelines. It is only to agreement on the general contours of faith and morality that the shared texts and tradition lead.

We see particular dispositions and virtues being encouraged in the literature. When one looks at the qualities being evoked by use of the image of the soldier, one finds that the key words are faith, obedience, and discipline. Faith and obedience are integrally linked; for one who cannot as yet see clearly, obedience to the person who can see is vital. Sekowsky likens the Christian soldier to one who does not fully understand the intricacies of the battle but does her part by obeying seemingly "foolish" commands.[71] Gammons says straightforwardly that Jesus wants obedience: "Jesus is looking for an army willing to obey and submit to his will; soldiers who will unashamedly make a stand for him, twenty-four hours a day, seven days a week!"[72] Soldiers will need to exercise some discernment, but lone rangers are not welcome; obedience and esprit de corp are the *sine* qua non of the authentic Christian life:

> Every Christian belongs somewhere! No one is called to be a Kamikaze pilot. Independent soldiers, going their own way and doing their own thing, are of no real value to God's army. Commitment to a local corp is vital![73]

The same point is made more lyrically by Corrie Ten Boom:

> When there is no unity in an army, one cannot expect victory. We need the fellowship of the saints. The fruit of the Spirit of Gal. 5:22 makes the fellowship

[71] Sekowsky, *Spiritual Warfare*, 45.
[72] Gammons, *Battle Stations*, 62.
[73] Ibid., 138.

of the children of God a joyful possibility. In this battle it is very essential that we are one in spirit with the other soldiers in the army of Jesus Christ.[74]

Discipline complements obedience. It is the necessity or quality perhaps most dwelt upon by the writers. "Unless," says Paul E. Adolph, "there is willingness to obey Christ as our Lord and accept his disciplines, the triumphant living discussed in the pages which follow cannot be ours."[75] Discipline trains one to cope with all events and builds an orderly character.[76]

Some of the writers approve of soldierly discipline for another reason. They use the metaphor of army training to provide a kind of micro-theodicy. If one sees the world as a kind of bootcamp and God or the Holy Spirit as the ultimate sargeant, all unpleasantnesses can be interpreted as intentionally imposed parts of the training. Say Calver and Copley:

> Some Christians do manage to develop spiritually in the absence of testing— but most of us don't. It's just the same in the military life. Most soldiers have to learn how to survive under rough, tough conditions. Sometimes they face harsh and cruel treatment. Yet few methods have proved to be equally effective in producing tough, obedient, self-disciplined men and women.[77]

The point is made even more categorically by John White:

> He [God] trains, disciplines, shapes you as a runner in the race of faith, as a fighter in the warfare of faith. The training involves correction and pain. Your faith will increase or decrease according to how you respond to his intervention.[78]

---

[74] Ten Boom, *Marching Orders for the End Battle* (Fort Washington, PA: Christian Literature Crusade, 1969) 50.

[75] Adolph, *Triumphant Living* (Chicago: Moody, 1959) 16.

[76] With regard to the issue of the Christian "transformation" of perennial ethical models, it is interesting to compare Christian use of warfare metaphor with that of a non-Christian writer, Paul's contemporary Seneca. Like Paul, Seneca used military metaphor very widely to convey his understanding of the proper ethical/religious stance. Gerard B. Lavery writes, "The metaphor of philosophical adherent as soldier undoubtedly appealed to the Stoicized mind of Seneca because of its emphasis on discipline, obedience, resignation, and acceptance. The paradox of the soldier is central to this appeal. The soldier is a figure both of power and powerlessness. On the one hand, the soldier, symbolizing the might and *machismo* of the *imperium Romanum*, presents an image of strength. On the other hand, the individual soldier has power only as part of a larger organization. He cannot make decisions about tactics or strategy. He can only carry out orders and indeed his chief value lies in his readiness to obey" ("Metaphors of War and Travel in Seneca's Prose Works," *Greece and Rome* 27 (1980) 147–48. In Seneca's case *fortuna* was the enemy, and *natura* the post to be held (p. 149).

[77] Calver and Copley, *Fight of Your Life*, 163.

[78] White, *Fight*, 112.

This is a picture of the divine that might not necessarily appeal to all Christians since it conceives of God as inflicting suffering rather than permitting it. It also presumes rather a high degree of passivity on the part of the Christian. It is interesting to note, however, that in the hands of Penn-Lewis, this notion of passive acceptance of suffering as part of one's "training" is balanced by the argument that the suffering may *not* be part of the training, but in fact may be part of real onslaughts from the devil:

> The true way of victory does not *always* lie in receiving power to 'bear' the imposition of others. Very often there is need of insight into the *cause* at the back of it, and prayer to God to deal with the cause. "You must *bear* this, it is your cross!" How the deceiver can get behind the very truth of God and use it to crush you! It may not be God who puts that "cross" upon you, but the enemy, and you must not passively endure suffering which comes from the devil.[79]

Beyond the basic qualities and virtues of faith, obedience and discipline, the metaphor is used in a more narrow way to serve as the focus of a stylized meditation on the major Christian virtues. The context is a formalized discussion of the "weapons of faith" which derives from extended exegesis of the passage about the armor of God found in Ephesians 6.[80] This passage is an exegete's delight, going as it does, piece by piece through the armor and the virtue or action each represents. One by one the writers run through them: the girding of the loins with truth, the breastplate of righteousness, the sandals of peace, the shield of faith, the helmet of salvation and the sword of the spirit. Roger Price even provides little pictures of the equipment,[81] and his cover sports a brightly coloured picture of a merry Roman legionary off to the wars.

The explicitness of the text about the virtues or qualities described ensures a certain constancy of interpretation. It is interesting to speculate how a different set of armor might have formed a different piety: the breastplate of social justice, the sword of compassion for example. As the matter stands, the warrior virtues relate primarily to evangelizing and remaining steadfast in one's beliefs. The full spectrum of virtues necessary to the religious life is not covered.

Before turning to look at the limits of consensus, I want to examine briefly

[79] Penn-Lewis, *Spiritual Warfare*, 34.

[80] See, e.g., David Martyn Lloyd-Jones, *Christian Warfare: An Exposition of Ephesians 6:10–13* (1976; reprinted Grand Rapids, MI: Baker Book House, 1977); and idem, *The Christian Soldier: An Exposition of Ephesians 6:10–20* (1977; reprinted Grand Rapids, MI: Baker Book House, 1977).

[81] Price, *Victory*, 129.

whether the life of warfare is presented the same way by the women authors. The number of recent female writers on the topic seems small: Corrie Ten Boom, JoAnne Sekowsky, Jessie Penn-Lewis, Nancy Tischler, and Anastasia Van Burkalow are the only ones whom I have encountered in my research.[82] Yet the image does seem to appeal to them and to many of their female readers. Van Burkalow is militantly pro militancy. "Do not be afraid to write and speak about Satan and sin and to use militaristic symbolism to describe the personal and social warfare we must wage against them," she says,

> Challenge us anew to carry on that spiritual warfare of ideas, for only when we have won the victory in this endeavour can we expect to put an end to the threat of physical warfare and achieve the peace we so much desire. Let us not forget that in pursuit of that end we as Christians are called to be the *church militant*. We must be spiritual warmongers.[83]

JoAnne Sekowsky's work was written specially for the Women's Aglow Fellowship (and refers throughout to the soldier as "she") and was so successful that a spiritual warfare prayer diary was produced to accompany it. These writers are clearly at ease with the concept of warfare and, indeed, convinced of the actuality of being in the thick of battle.[84] There do seem to be one or two dimensions of their exegesis that differ, however. To take the most interesting example, Sekowsky's exegesis of Paul was the only one that I saw which went into considerable detail about the role of Roman soldiers as part of an occupational army: as peacekeepers and ambassadors of Roman culture. She tells her readers:

> This week try to seriously visualize yourself as a soldier in an occupational army. You are a citizen of Heaven and your Commander in Chief has sent you

[82] I have encountered other materials which pick up the Scripture phrases but do not exegete them concertedly. A good example of these would be Mab Graff Hoover, *Lord, Please Zip Up My Armor* (Grand Rapids, MI: Zondervan, 1986). This is a book written for working mothers to help them, as the blurb says, "grapple with the necessity and the benefit of putting on the armor of God to protect them from the glancing blows of the enemy in the workplace" because, as the editor says in the preface, "Working women need armor for their minds to keep them from compromising values . . . and they need armor for their hearts to resist the temptation to put job responsibilities ahead of family responsibilities" (p. 10). The book itself, however, contains barely so much as a breastplate. The author clearly finds the concept of protection important, but the traditional military language totally irrelevant.

[83] Van Burkalow, "Call for Battle," 17.

[84] It is perhaps odd that Corrie ten Boom should be so enthusiastic. She was incarcerated in a Nazi concentration camp for much of the war. This, however, seems to have increased her view that Satanic forces exist in the world which need to be *fought*. It did not lead her to question militancy in all forms.

to the place where you presently live. See how many ways you can reflect the culture of your "native" land. Remember you are in this country to "heavenize" its culture, to maintain peace, to fight off any rebellious attacks of the defeated enemy and to keep him from resuming any kind of leadership.[85]

This is a considerably more irenic view of soldiery than found in many of the other writers who manage to make even defensive warfare sound pretty aggressive.

Possibilities and Problems

The metaphor of warfare is clearly one which can operate on many levels. It can be used to describe Christian life in terms of participation in actual cosmic warfare. In this context it is perhaps not even appropriate to speak of it as a figurative, particularly if—like John White (*Fight*)—one sees other forms of earthly warfare as mere shadows of the real cosmic battle. At another level, the metaphor can be used in a more clearly figurative way to represent the warring impulses in human beings; especially in Christians. "Interior warfare" of the kind described by Paul in Romans 7 does not necessarily presume any belief in principalities and powers. It does presume a particular view of will and desire which more often than not is associated with a somewhat dualist anthropology which sets physical and spiritual in opposition. Again, however, the connection is not a necessary one; one could still put a high value on the body yet retain a view of sin/desire as something within one which needs battling. In this context of war against the baser aspect of self, the metaphor can be employed pedagogically in two related ways. Firstly, it can be used to teach the individual Christian how to battle his or her own sins so as to become more spiritually mature. Secondly, the churches can use it to try to shape the believers into better church members, emphasizing such corporately useful virtues as obedience and submission.

The dangers and the advantages of the metaphor are relatively straightforward. At the most general level, on the negative side, militaristic imagery may breed militaristic attitudes. An allied criticism is that the metaphor calls for types of behaviour that can lead churches and nations into deep trouble. Unquestioning obedience and blind following of leaders, combined with a sense of being part of the one true army (or nation) with a divinely sanctioned mission, has the potential to lead to pogroms, witch-hunting, and holocaust. The dangers of unthinking obedience are well explored by Dorothee Soelle in *Beyond Mere Obedience*. She and others have argued convincingly

[85] Sekowsky, *Spiritual Warfare*, 9.

that one cannot compartmentalize one's mind in such a way that utter obedience to authority holds sway in one's religious life, but questioning caution reigns in one's social and political life. Either one develops a kind of intellectual schizophrenia, or the attitude spills over imperceptibly from one area to the next.[86]

A further problem lies in the area of the application of the metaphor. How is one to determine what constitutes obedience in a given situation? Some reflection is required by either the individual Christian or his or her advisor. Authors such as Trumbull make much of the concept of utter quiescence and allowing Christ to act through one; however, this image of human divine cooperation seems to ignore the mental filtering process—albeit largely subconscious—which determines how Christ is channeled through one (or how his will is interpreted). Particularly at the level of most strenuous warfare against what is deemed to be evil, there has to be some adequate mechanism for determining whether it is indeed Christ working through one, or perhaps the promptings of selfish desire or evil forces.

The metaphor may also cause problems for the individual Christian if it is employed in such a way that it appears to promise "victory" in all matters to those who sit in right relation to God. There is the danger of becoming hooked on the idea of success and power, and unable to accept reverses. The evangelical orthodox writer Peter Gillquist comments on just this phenomenon:

> Too often our message of "victory in Jesus" is like the half-time highlights on ABC's Monday night football. The network replays only the touchdowns and the long gainers. Rarely do we see the plays that lost yardage, the broken patterns, dropped passes, or injuries. In like manner, are not we evangelicals sometimes guilty of reporting primarily our spiritual highs, implying that they are the norm, and that spiritual lows just don't occur?
>
> The "victorious Christian life" gospel is at best only half true. . . . To gain victory, you must have battles, some of which will end in defeat. And whoever heard of winning battles without casualties?[87]

This, however, is not a flaw in the metaphor itself, but rather a flaw built into a particular use of it. Real warfare gives one no reason to believe that victory can always be gained by the worthy. A convincing use of the metaphor needs to include a convincing interpretation of the meaning of defeat in the battle.

---

[86] Soelle, *Beyond Mere Obedience* (New York: Pilgrim, 1982) 9–10.

[87] Gillquist, "Spiritual Warfare: Bearing the Bruises of Battle," *Christianity Today* 24 (August 1980) 24.

Another drawback to the metaphor is its tendency to run away with the writer and to distort the life matter which it has been evoked to illuminate. There is an aridity to thinking of all of the Christian life in terms of military practice. Spontaneity and delicacy of insight or feeling is missing. To describe conversion in terms of "enlistment" may not be inaccurate in New Testament terms, but it barely conveys the elements of penitence, relief, elation and new vision. Likewise, earth in many ways may be like a bootcamp, a moral and spiritual testing ground; but, it is also a place of beauty for which the Bible exhorts people to be grateful. Just as the writers on stewardship are inclined to overlook the dimension of testing, so the writers on warfare are inclined to pass over the elements of joie de vivre and gratitude for existence. One image speaks to the aspects of life that the other overlooks.

On the positive side, there are certain things to recommend the metaphor. The perception that human life is, at least in part, a battle between good and evil or altruism and selfishness has some cogency. This is evident on a day-to-day level and very clear when one becomes involved in the spheres of politics or business. For those in the front line of efforts to bring about justice and equity, the conflict is very real. Also, one may agree with Arthur Wallis when he says that discipline, hardship and suffering are inevitably a part of the spiritual experience just as they are part of military training. He may also have a point when he says that the "lack of them today is one reason why so much of our Christianity is anaemic, when it ought to be robust and strong."[88] Even without any desire to see a return or uprise of triumphalist imperialist forms of western Christianity, one may note that many forms of western Christianity are rather insipid and their adherents lacking in moral endurance and persistence. The negative side of modern philosophies which recommend "being kind to yourself" and "allowing yourself to accept your emotions" etc. can sometimes be an inability to accept that one is *not* just perfect the way one is; that one (and the people around one) would benefit from making the effort to change certain behaviours. For some, the metaphor of warfare is not helpful in such a process; gentle dehabituation seems a more appropriate description of what is required. But for others there does seem to be an unavoidable element of real violence in the process—a feeling of having to wrestle with and banish particular personal demons.[89]

It could be argued that this kind of personality is maladjusted and self-recriminative and needs reeducation to gentler modes of self-treatment, not

[88] Wallis, *Into Battle*, 9.

[89] Read, e.g., Augustine's descriptions of his old habits and desires and his struggle to combat them. Augustine, *The Confessions* (trans. Rex Warner; New York: New American Library, 1963) VIII and IX.

pandering to with metaphors which only play up to and compound its tendency to think in stark irreconcilable polarities. Conversely, one may argue that the metaphor of warfare provides the *only* key to success for such a personality.

The problem with which this metaphor presents us is a difficult one; on the one hand it seems to provide an illumination of certain aspects of life, and to provide a necessary basis for dealing with particular difficulties within and around one. On the other hand, it has an unpleasant potential for encouraging behaviour quite out of keeping with a religion that exhorts its followers to love one another and to love their enemies. Although non-Christian writers are for the most part outside the scope of this dissertation, it is interesting to take note of relevant discussion about the desirability or undesirability of warrior imagery among feminist writers such as Carol Christ and Karen McCarthy Brown. In an essay in *Women's Spirit Bonding*, Brown speaks of her spiritual marriage to a Youruba Ogou; a masculine warrior deity. She speaks of the importance of transforming the available war energies, saying: "Ogou awakens the spirit of assertion, personal power, and individuality needed to negotiate with the modern world."[90] She maintains that the gods of war will be necessary as long as anger and war continue to exist. It is interesting to consider in this context Penn-Lewis's comments about the importance of fighting suffering and not accepting it necessarily as a divinely imposed cross. Such an insight is very much in keeping with the rationale that leads Karen Brown and other feminist writers to sanction the use of warrior imagery for women. War of resistance rather than war of aggression is suggested.

Carol Christ, writing in the same volume as Brown, expresses strong opposition to this view. She rejects any form of warrior spirituality:

Some feminists have appropriated the image of warrior reflected in figures like the Amazon or Maxine Hong Kingston's Woman Warrior. While respecting my sisters who make this choice, I must ally myself with the long tradition of feminist peace activism. . . .[91]

She feels it is utterly unsafe to retain any warlike aspects in our theology; especially in our picture of the divine:

[90] Brown, "Why Women Need the War God," in Janet Kalven and Mary I. Buckley, eds., *Women's Spirit Bonding* (New York: Pilgrim, 1984) 195.
[91] Christ, "Feminist Liberation Theology and Yahweh as Holy Warrior: An Analysis of Symbol," in Kalven and Buckley, *Women's Spirit Bonding*, 210.

As Clifford Geertz has shown, symbols act to produce powerful, pervasive and long-lasting moods and motivations in the peoples influenced by them. In a world threatened by total nuclear annihilation, we cannot afford a warlike image of God.[92]

What we see here, as we saw in the discussion of women and stewardship, is a crystallization of the issue of whether there is any such thing as safe or productive use of a symbol with dangerous dimensions. In the case of the symbolism of Christian life as warfare, the stakes are perhaps the highest of all.

[92] Ibid., 205.

7

Running the Good Race

If one were looking for a metaphor which retained the strong points of the warfare metaphor but avoided its main dangers, perhaps that of life as athletic training and contest might come to mind. Discipline, excellence and victory are again of paramount importance, while violence is at least less integral. The two metaphors are intimately related (as clearly shown by the ease with which writers switch to and fro between the two) and yet different in their presuppositions and implications.[1]

---

[1] Behind both metaphors lies the concept of life as *agon*, as a heroic contest in which the virtuous person battles his or her way toward victory in the arena of the world. *Agon* originally meant "a place of assembly," then "place of contest," and next "contest." It later came to apply to all forms of conflict, the line between sport and war being blurred (sport perhaps being to a large degree ritualized aggression in the first place). It came early to be used of the conflict of the hero of virtue, and the idea of the *agon* of the virtuous was to become a common theme in Hellenistic Jewish texts, notably the *Testament of Job*, where, it has been observed, the Hellenistic type of the struggling hero of virtue and the Jewish type of the martyr fighting unto death seem to come together in the picture of the divine warrior Job. In this context, the struggle is more fight than sport one might say. By contrast, in the writings of Philo, the ascetic achievements of the heroes of virtue are dwelt upon in a manner more akin to the Greek tradition, *Agrig.* 112, 119. For a discussion of *agon*, see Ethelbert Stauffer, "ἀγών," *TDNT* 1 (1964) 134–40, from which these points are drawn. See also Deborah Steiner's chapter on athletic metaphor in idem, *The Crown of Song: Metaphor in Pindar* (New York: Oxford University Press, 1986) 111–21. An interesting examination of the imagery of combat sport in biblical and patristic writings is to be found in Michael B. Poliakoff, *Combat Sports in the Ancient World: Competition, Violence, and Culture* (New Haven: Yale University Press, 1987) 134–47.

The Renewed Popularity of Athletic Metaphor

The history of the use of athletic imagery is most interesting. For Paul and other early Christian writers who lived in the hellenistic world, the metaphors had great vividness and persuasion. Running and boxing, training and competing for the victor's crown suggested themselves to them as clear analogies for the Christian life as a whole. So, for example, we find Paul writing to the Corinthians:

> Do you not know that in a race all the runners compete, but only one receives the prize? So run that you may obtain it. Every athlete exercises self control in all things. They do it to receive a perishable wreath, but we an imperishable. (1 Cor 9:26)

Or we find the writer of the Epistle to the Hebrews likening sin to the garments that hold back a runner and saying: "Let us also lay aside every weight, and sin which clings so closely, and let us run with perseverance the race that is set before us" (Heb 12.1).[2]

However, the demise of widescale competitive athletics in the ancient world rendered ineffective or dormant the metaphorical usages to which the phenomenon had given rise.[3] One rarely encounters extended treatment of the athletic metaphors in European or American literature prior to the rise of sport as a national pastime in the late nineteenth century. Even then, it is only since the rise of the personal fitness craze in the early 1970s that

---

[2] Some other biblical passages of relevance are: Acts 20:24 (finishing the course with joy); Gal 2:2 (running); 5:7 (running well); Phil 3:12–14 (pressing toward the mark); 1 Tim 6:12 (fight the good fight—*agōnizou ton kalon agōna*); 2 Tim 2:5 (striving for mastery according to the rules); 4:7–8 ("I have fought the good fight, finished the course, I have kept the faith. Henceforth there is laid up for me the crown of righteousness, which the Lord, the righteous judge, will award to me on that Day.").

[3] Poliakoff (*Combat Sports*, 144), speaking of the boxing metaphor, observes the steady process of its detachment from its roots: "In early Christian writings, the metaphor moves steadily farther from its base in actual athletic activities. In I Corinthians 9:24–27, Paul gives an image of personal struggle that develops quite readily from the training and competition of ancient athletes: 'I box not like a shadow-boxer' . . . 'I bruise my body and bring it into subjugation': he is an athlete of the Holy Spirit observing his regimen. Quite different is the metaphorical language of . . . John Chrysostom, who praised a woman for the victory she won by patiently bearing illness. By this, he said, she has taught others to enter the wrestling ground. Her victory, said the bishop, was all the more amazing because she did not win it in the center of the city, as athletes do, but from her sick bed. The ultimate step in this process of abstraction of the spiritual lessons from sport is the creation of the metaphorical wrestler from a figure who originally had nothing to do with sport. The appearance of Job as a wrestler in Christian writings stands as the most intriguing example of this process."

detailed use of the metaphors has become a fixture in popular theological and devotional writing.[4] For many women, athletic metaphors have only come to have any real significance since they began, in recent years, to participate in sports and exercise programs on a large scale. *Running the Good Race* by Anita Bryant and Bob Green is a striking example of an unexpected awakening to the depths of a hitherto uncompelling metaphor as a result of newfound interest in physical training.[5] In it we learn that Anita Bryant kept a "jog log" in which, among other things, she compares the benefits of jogging to those of salvation: both free, both open to old and young, neither requiring special facilities etc., etc.[6] Her husband Bob reminisces:

> As Anita perceived parallels between the jogging discipline she thought she hated, and the spiritual discipline she knew she loved, she began to pitch me some challenging questions.
> How does a lazy Christian get off the starting line? Is it *too late* for me to run?
> How can we help our children develop mental, spiritual, and physical muscle tone?[7]

The athletic metaphor has also received an extra boost as a result of recent attempts by Christian writers to show that mind and body are intimately connected, and that the health of the latter contributes to the health of the former. Careful treatment and training of the body as part of the regime of the

---

[4] A survey of popular Christian periodicals shows that the Olympic Games meetings of the previous two decades breathed temporary life back into the metaphors in the form of such articles as: Maurice Allen, "The Christian's Own Olympics: An Illuminating Article on the Eve of the Tokyo Olympics," *Eternity* (October 1964) 11–13, 30–31. However, most of the pieces on life as a race written prior to the 70s are almost entirely devoid of detailed parallels drawn from experience of the sport; see, e.g., the highly theoretical exegesis of Heb 12:1 produced by Bernard Ramm, "How to Run the Race of Life," *Eternity* (September 1962) 26–28.

[5] Bryant and Green, *Running the Good Race* (Old Tappan, NJ: Revell, 1976).

[6] Ibid., 17.

[7] Ibid., ii. Carol Flake (*Redemptorama: Culture, Politics and the New Evangelism* [Garden City, NY: Anchor Press, Doubleday & Company, 1984]) devotes a chapter to the importance of athletics and spiritual athleticism to the evangelical male in America from the 50s to the present. She writes, "If the model fundamentalist woman of the Falwell era was a positive-thinking housewife in a negligee at the altar of masculinity, the ideal evangelical man was a tireless athlete who exerted his competitive spirit for God, country, and business. While the aspiring Total Woman studied to weaken her will, the total Christian male practiced getting tough for Jesus. It was time for tough love for one's family and tough luck for one's competitors. The paradigm for the Christian life was no longer the pilgrimage but the game, played by the rules of St. Paul [1 Cor. 9.24] and Vince Lombardi ... 'Winning isn't everything; it's the only thing'" (p. 93). Curiously, in an otherwise thorough study, she overlooks the evangelical women writers whose interest has been caught by the athletic ideal.

spiritual life is a concern of many contemporary religious writers.[8]

Writers have drawn on various sports to illuminate the Christian life. Billy Graham, for example, has a liking for team sports, such as football, as sources of metaphor.[9] He and others may have a preference for these because of their ability to speak to the communal dimension of the Christian life: being a team player is the key concept. It is sports ecclesiology, and of course the use of the metaphor of the "team" has much in common with the old metaphor of the *militia christi*.[10]

Nevertheless, the predominant image continues to be that of the more lonely figure of the individual athlete, especially that of the long-distance runner. The reasons for this appear to be threefold: first, it is the imagery primarily favoured in the New Testament; second, life is a long-distance affair and the choice of metaphor must needs reflect this; third, although most of the writers stress the importance of involvement in the Christian community, their primary preoccupation tends to remain the progress of the individual Christian.

The appositeness of the image of the marathon runner is perhaps the key factor that contributes to its popularity. Many writers speak from first hand experience in the matter. Peter Gillquist recounts his first day of practice for the high school cross-country team which began with the coach telling the

---

[8] A clear account of the theological bases for this view can be found in Margaret R. Miles, *Fullness of Life: Historical Foundations for a New Asceticism* (Philadelphia: Westminster, 1981) 155–63. For an example of a work which sets out to put physical training into a theological framework and to make it part of the religious life, see LeRoy Lawrence Hamilton, *Jogging with God* (Bryn Mawr, PA: Dorrance & Company, 1985). Hamilton is a retired minister of the United Methodist Church (and previously of the African Methodist Episcopal Church) who at one time also taught physical education.

[9] Graham, "The Game of Life," *Decision* 23 (May 1982) 1–2.

[10] Some of the most interesting excursions into team sports metaphor take place in the context of religious occasions within the world of team sport itself. Consider the following invocation given at the pregame dinner of the 1976 World Hockey Association All-Star game: "Heavenly Father, Divine Goalie, we come before You this evening to seek Your blessing . . . Keep us free from actions that would put us in the Sin Bin of hell . . . Help us to stay within the blue line of your commandments and the red line of Your grace. Protect us from being injured by the puck of pride. May we be ever delivered from the high stick of dishonesty. May the wings of Your angels play at the right and left wings of our teammates. May You always be the divine Center of our team, and when our summons comes for eternal retirement to the heavenly grandstand, may we find You ready to give us the everlasting bonus of a permanent seat in your coliseum. Finally, grant us the courage to skate without tripping, to run without icing, and to score the goal that really counts—the one that makes each of us a winner, a champion, and All-Star in the hectic Hockey Game of Life. Amen." Quoted by D. Stanley Eitzen and George E. Sage, *Sociology of American Sport* (Dubuque, IA: Brown, 1978) 130.

boys that if they started they must finish: it is finishing that counts. He recalls the pleasure of the early stages, and its rapid evaporation:

> The first mile was almost euphoric. The cool, fresh autumn air was a natural boost to my dogged determination to run a good race. But after a mile and a half or so, the joy began to fade. By two miles, whatever pleasure there had been in all of this was totally gone. From then on it was sheer drudgery.[11]

He carries on despite cramp and exhaustion and manages to finish:

> I can barely remember crossing the finishing line. I was told I came in fifth or sixth, but even that was not of first importance. Every ounce of energy I knew had gone into finishing. I could not believe I had made it.
>
> Over the years, I have thought back to that experience as being an incredible picture of what it is to live the Christian life. In fact, the Scriptures more than once use a race as a metaphor of our life with Christ. And it is not a mere sprint, mind you—it is a marathon.[12]

The Theological Framework

The athletic metaphor generally operates with a more sketchy theology than the others at which we have looked so far. Like the others it tries to elucidate the nature of development in the Christian life, but it manages to operate with a less explicit doctrine of God and God's work. The Father is a shadowy figure; a kind of divine wreath giver and race sponsor.[13] Jesus and the Holy Spirit are far more to the fore. One or other of them is cast as the "coach" demanded by the metaphor. For Women's Aglow Fellowship writer Glenyce Coffin, it is the Holy Spirit that is the coach:

> We . . . have received the Holy Spirit to be our Comforter and strengthener— our Coach. The Lord will not thrust us into the race without help. . . .
>
> Our Coach is never one for standing off to the side, letting us try to figure out how to run the race by ourself. Instead He works right alongside us, and His coaching is intensely practical.[14]

[11] Gillquist, "The Christian Life: A Marathon We Mean to Win?," *Christianity Today* 23 (October 1981) 22. Gillquist was at this time editor of Christian books for Thomas Nelson Publishers, and presiding bishop of the Evangelical Orthodox Church (p. 23).

[12] Ibid., 23.

[13] In the context of the team sports metaphor, Billy Graham ("Game of Life," 2) has the Father as the one who wrote the "rule book" for the game, and as the divine scorekeeper.

[14] Coffin, *Run to Win: Training for the Overcoming Life* (Lynnwood, WA: Women's Aglow Fellowship International, 1984) 10.

For Ken Radke, it is Jesus who is the Coach. In such a context one would expect a soteriology with a strongly exemplarist tone; a Jesus/coach who lays out the strategy and points the trainee to his own victorious example. For the most part, this does turn out to be the case, but Radke also tries to find room in the metaphor to express the atoning aspect of Christ's work. The metaphor is strained to bursting point:

> He is the best coach a person could desire. He has set the example for us with His sinless life. He has called us from the ranks of the spectators and made us participants in the spiritual run. He has entered us in the race of faith and even paid the entrance fee for us with His own blood and righteousness. What coach has ever done this for his runners?[15]

Of the two interpretations of who is the runner's "coach," that of Glenyce Coffin seems closer to mainstream traditional understandings of the work of the revealed or economic Trinity.

Understanding the Christian Life as Athletic Contest

The Main Points at Issue

As with the other metaphors at which we have looked, salvation is already assumed; the race can begin only when salvation has been accepted: "Let us be very clear on this: you cannot even qualify for the Christian life unless you place your faith in Christ."[16] It is the process of sanctification that the metaphor seeks to illuminate:

> It is a race to spiritual maturity, a race characterized by a struggle between our sinful nature . . . and the Holy Spirit, who is continuously conforming us to the image of Jesus.[17]

The goal, the victory, is therefore a state of being which is pleasing to God; a growing more Christ-like. As usual, there is some tension between passive acceptance of imputed righteousness and personal endeavour in the subsequent process of sanctification; however, as the last quotation indicates, it is felt to be the Holy Spirit who plays the major role in the process of sanctification.

---

[15] Ken Radke, *The Race Set Before Us* (Nashville: Nelson, 1982) 125–26.
[16] Gillquist, "Marathon," 23.
[17] Coffin, *Run to Win*, 6.

In such a context, "winning" obviously takes on a primary reference to victory over self as opposed to over other people: "We are the only participant in our particular run, for our race is really against our own sinful nature."[18] Many writers emphasize that competitiveness is not the point. Walter Scragg, for example, writes:

> Here is a race that all may win. You may be the victor. You can share the crown. All who finish, win this race. . . .
> No one is first, second, or last as we press toward the prize that God has promised to us. This prize is so big that all may share in it. In fact, helping others to share in the prize and to win the race is one way of making sure that we receive it.[19]

It is important to notice the emphasis on this point in this kind of literature by comparison to the related but very different material consisting of testimonies of Christians who are *actual* athletes. In the latter, victory has a definite reference to actual victory over other people (as well as over one's own shortcomings) and victory is used as a kind of mark of divine approval or sign of the superiority of Christianity.[20] In the kind of literature under consideration here, victory over other people is beside the point; it is the directedness, discipline and purposefulness of the athlete which is being evoked:

> Once the desire to enter that race is born within us and we decide to enter it, we begin to focus all our attention and energy on one thing, reaching the goal. Here is where self-discipline—the cutting away of the extra weight or whatever distracts us from our main goal—begins. Our need for self-discipline, for working out our salvation on a daily basis, continues throughout the entire race and ends only when life is finished.[21]

The basic interpretative framework is one of life as the arena of the *agon*, where all things work to test the Christian and to develop his or her personal-

[18] Ibid.

[19] Scragg, *Run this Race: A Daily Devotional and Inspirational Guide for Early-Teens and Near-Teens* (Washington, DC: Review and Herald, 1969) 3–7.

[20] There are, of course, also humble testimonies from athletes. See, e.g., the books of testimonies by Christian baseball players edited by Vincent Bove, *Playing His Game* (South Plainfield, NJ: Bridge, 1984). Then catcher for the Houston Astros, Alan Ashby, writes: "Many people see professional athletes as winners. Athletes often have this image of being great champions. This is often an exaggeration. One does not have to be a professional athlete to be a winner. Winning in life is much more important. . . . Anyone who lives a life with and for Christ is a winner" (p. 1). One cannot, however, miss the irony of the fact that he is only in this book and being listened to because of his success on the field.

[21] Coffin, *Run to Win*, 3.

ity and special gifts. The writers express a faith that God has a purpose in establishing the *agon*; the contest or race is divinely established, and it is to be conducted according to strict rules.[22] The Christian must show willing and commitment, and trust herself or himself to the Coach without reservation. The divine Coach (be it Christ or the Holy Spirit) will provide a training program specifically tailored to the individual Christian. Coffin discusses at length how the Holy Spirit/Coach makes a searching evaluation of each newly committed Christian and devises a training program accordingly.[23] Radke speaks in like vein of the importance of the "individualized program":

> Christ has taken us into His gymnasium and is training us through a disciplined spiritual fitness program personally designed for each individual. He teaches us the importance of hard work as well as the restfulness of faith. He trains us not to look at the other runners, but to keep our eyes focused on Him. He helps us to be consistent in spiritual muscle-building by spending time in His Word and prayer each day.[24]

The Finer Points

Athletic training and performance hold out extensive possibilities for detailed comparison with the spiritual life. Glenyce Coffin and Ken Radke both exploit the possibilities to the full. Coffin lays three things out side by side all through her book: the actual physical training of a woman called Lynn, the spiritual race run by St. Paul, and the lessons to be learned by the reader. She describes, for example, the torpor of the fledgling jogging enthusiast whose newfound energy suddenly fails and leaves her longing to curl up in an overstuffed chair instead of going running, and compares the same backsliding one encounters in the spiritual life of new converts.[25] She compares the importance of a good coach to the importance of the Holy Spirit, and emphasizes the necessity for finding the correct regimen in both the athletic and spiritual lives.[26] Taking her lead from Heb 12:1 ("Let us throw off everything that hinders and the sin that so easily entangles . . .") she likens sin and bad habits to the baggy old jeans and sweatshirts that Lynn had worn

---

[22] 2 Tim 2:5: "An athlete is not crowned unless he competes according to the rules." This point is stressed by most authors. See, e.g., Judson Edwards, *Running the Good Race: Looking to Jesus for Ultimate Victory* (Nashville: Broadman, 1985) 59ff. Edwards is a Baptist pastor from Texas and also runs in short and long distance races.

[23] Coffin, *Run to Win*, 16.

[24] Radke, *Race*, 126.

[25] Coffin, *Run to Win*, 8.

[26] Ibid., 9–11.

when she first began running, and explains how the old nature is to be cast off; the new nature must be put on like a new race uniform: "God has given us a whole closetful of attributes of the Spirit with which to be robed. Our job is to *choose* to wear them."[27] We are to become, in racing terminology, "thinclad"; unhindered in our race to the finish line.

Ken Radke draws many of the same analogies, and finds even more dainty points of similarity. He explores the endurance tests faced by athletes and Christians alike, and considers the way to tackle some of the problems. For example, he compares the effect of heat on the long-distance runner to the effect of sin on the Christian, and says:

> Confession is to the spirit what sweating is to the body. When our bodies overheat, we sweat. The body's heat is carried to the skin through the blood. There the sweat evaporates, cooling the blood. A person who doesn't sweat adequately will overheat. In the same way, our spirits will overheat unless our sin is brought to the surface and released by admitting to God that we are guilty and asking for forgiveness.[28]

Elsewhere, he discusses the paralyzing effect of inappropriate emotions for runners and for religious people. He speaks of the importance of finding stability and perseverance:

> The mature Christian is one who has learned to live life at a relatively steady pace. This sometimes involves ignoring our emotions. Feelings are a poor gauge of one's spiritual life. They change constantly and are affected by such simple things as the amount of sleep we get. No runner would drop out of a race just because he felt fear before the race started. He wouldn't use his feelings to determine his level of conditioning or his likelihood of doing well in the race. Rather he would ignore the fear and run anyway. Likewise, a Christian can ignore negative feelings that would paralyze him and do what must be done.[29]

By way of tips for success in the race of life, Radke speaks of the importance of following the leader:

> The second word of counsel for running the Christian race is to "fix our eyes on Jesus." If a runner watches the ground it can have a hypnotic affect causing

---

[27] Ibid., 21.
[28] Radke, *Race*, 35–36.
[29] Ibid., 56.

him to lose touch with the other runners. If he watches the spectators, he also will fall behind. The best strategy is to keep his eyes fixed on the leader of the race.

For us as Christians, Jesus is the leader who goes before us. He has already completed the course successfully, without sin. Yet He still leads the way for us. Our part is to follow closely, not running impatiently ahead nor falling far behind. If we look to the circumstances or to ourselves, we will surely be defeated. . . .

As we find our own resources and strength failing, we turn our eyes from ourselves to Christ, gaining new strength to run the race.[30]

An Evaluation

One could continue at great length giving examples of the kind of parallels found by the writers. The examples given thus far are, however, sufficient to show the contours of the use of the athletic metaphors. Let us now turn to consider what may be some of their advantages and drawbacks.

In one important respect the picture of life as training and running in a race is an improvement on the picture of life as a military struggle: the element of intentional physical damage perpetrated on another is absent, or at least suppressed. If there is violence, it is a violence done to bodily desire; a focused violence of therapeutic intent; an asceticism in the service of development of the person. Obviously, imagery drawn from the boxing ring or the football field is not so free from the mark of violence. Arguably, in these sports the violence has been ritualized in such a fashion that theoretically no injury should be caused; however, the idea of combat is still very much to the fore. Translated to the metaphorical sphere in the context of religious thinking, these sports permit a viewing of opposing persons in terms of legitimate objects for spiritual tackling or punching. In this respect the resultant metaphors are not free from the problems inherent in the military metaphors.

Thinking of the Christian life as a long-distance race (or as training and racing) has definite advantages. The key parallels are convincing at many levels. Insofar as the physical body can act as a metaphor for the mental and spiritual self, its training for excellence provides a most (if not *the* most) convincing metaphor for the training and development of the mind or the spirit. The problem is that the metaphor may not work for the person who has never participated in serious athletic activity. To understand what is being said via the metaphor about the pitfalls, triumphs, and building of endurance in the

[30] Ibid., 45.

Christian life, it is necessary to have experienced their physical equivalents or perhaps to be a passionate sports fan. You need to have experienced success over such obstacles as lethargy, injury, and a string of defeats to know what it means to forge on despite them. The exhilaration that comes from building up endurance and continuing doggedly on, cannot be imagined into existence; it comes from living long enough or from experiencing the telescoped lifetime of ups and downs that the athletic life provides.

To those with requisite experience or imagination, the metaphor may prove highly compelling and helpful. It speaks most convincingly to the benefits of self-discipline and purposefulness. When a person has learnt that she or he can to some extent shape their own capabilities, they have learnt an elementary lesson in combatting fatalistic thinking. From this they can learn that effort will be repaid in other spheres, such as the religious life. Some of the drawbacks of the metaphor are, however, closely linked to these very same advantages. The metaphor may convey too optimistic a notion of the extent to which one may have control over one's destiny. For some, it may seem to place too much emphasis on personal effort and leave too little room for grace in the proceedings.

Also, the metaphor focuses almost exclusively on the training and perfection of the individual. When the writers try to squeeze altruism and community mindedness into the metaphor they meet with little success. The charm of the biblical image of the runner running forward with eyes only on the leader and ultimately on the prize lies precisely in its evocation of the lonely progress of the individual soul back to its Maker. The grandstand of saints, the cloud of witness, roars encouragement in the background, but the effort of the runner is self-contained; the journey is essentially solitary at a profound level. A life viewed primarily in these terms will be a life lived against a backdrop of community, but with a pronounced sense of the importance of an individual asceticism which may take priority over community concerns.

This individualism is not present in the metaphors drawn from team sports. There the emphasis is on a balance between development of personal skill, and performing for the good of the team. This concept of the religious life has much more in common with the concept of the religious life as membership in the *militia Christi*; order, self-sacrifice, obedience, and team spirit are the key virtues. To the degree that it provides greater balance of personal and social dimensions of life, the team metaphor seems preferable. To the degree that it may discourage individualism and foster dangerously unquestioning obedience, it suffers from the same drawbacks as the concept of life as part of the *militia Christi*. It may encourage an over-simplicatory vision of life. In a different context, William H. Whyte, Jr. speaks of the seductiveness of the football analogy to people in the business world, saying it is satisfying, "It is bounded by two goal lines and is thus finite. There is always a solution. And that is what makes it often so treacherous."[31]

[31] White, "The Language of Business," in Herman A. Estrin, ed., *Technological and Professional Writing* (New York: Harcourt, Brace & World, 1963) 83; cited by Francine Hardaway, "Foul Play: Sports Metaphor as Public Doublespeak," *College English* 38 (1976) 79.

8

Pilgrims and Sojourners

Of all the images, that of journey or pilgrimage is the hardest to present in short compass because every person who speaks of the Christian life as a journey, has in mind a journey of a slightly different kind. Their understandings of the journey are as varied as the stories and examples that have shaped their vision of what it means to travel through this earthly existence in the company of Christ, his people, and indeed all the peoples of this earth of generations past, present and to come:

> Doubtlessly, each of us holds in memory some especially beloved pilgrim or pilgrim band. Perhaps it is Abraham and Sarah encamped for a time by the oaks on the plain of Mamre in their life-journey to inherit God's promise; perhaps it is Ruth speaking to Naomi, "Entreat me not to leave you or to return from following you; for where you go I will go, and where you lodge I will lodge." Or it is William Bradford standing in 1620 on the November beach of Cape Cod and gazing upon the somber wilderness of the mainland, or some other ancestor refugee who established here the family to which we belong. . . . All of us are the descendants of one pilgrim-pioneer band or another, and we are the offspring of their stories.[1]

I started out by trying to differentiate journey and quest from pilgrimage,

---

[1] Richard R. Niebuhr, "Pilgrims and Pioneers," *Parabola* 9 (1984) 8. Thus, to take one example, we find Paul Powell (*Complete Disciple*, 105-6) drawing upon the westward pioneering journey to elaborate the progress of the Christian life. Lakoff and Johnson (*Metaphors*, 42-45), in fact, use the idea of life as a journey to illustrate the way that a basic metaphor for the nature of life is susceptible of very different treatments according to context.

treating the latter as if it was clearly recognizable and was the foundational model, with journeys and quests being, respectively, secular or fairytale deviations. I think that the model that I had in mind was based on a kind of blend of the travelling band of the Epistle to the Hebrews and the arduous lone pilgrimage of Bunyan's Christian and of the hymn "He Who Would Valiant Be." Because it was my own picture, it seemed to me normative. I would come across other pictures such as the following from Richard Peace's *Pilgrimage: A Handbook on Christian Growth*:

> I have long been intrigued by the image of the pilgrim. For me, he has always been a tall gaunt individual: weather-hardened, rugged, possessing only what he could carry in his back pack. I see him on top of a ridge, resting on a wooden staff, looking out across the land with deep, penetrating eyes. . . .
>
> I am not at all sure where this picture comes from. The figure himself, as best I can tell, is an amalgam of various images: a knight from King Arthur's Round Table, the character in old woodcuts from *Pilgrim's Progress*, Charlton Heston in one of his biblical roles, and Saint Francis of Assisi.
>
> The land this pilgrim treads is agrarian in nature—full of cultivated fields, forests, streams, and mountains. The era he lives in is medieval. . . . It is an age in which evil is present, but well-defined, and very concrete. It is an age of great deeds.
>
> For me, this is a very positive, very powerful image. It symbolizes a life which is deeply satisfying—a single-minded pursuit of a significant goal which is undertaken because one is called to do so. It is not an easy life. The journey is long and hard, and fraught with very real dangers which must be overcome. But it is a life lived in touch with elemental realities, and is thus deeply fulfilling.[2]

And I would feel mildly irritated, commenting in my first draft, "Here we see a conscious assimilation of the figure of the pilgrim to that of the archetypal quest-hero; an assimilation which is a feature of many psychological/devotional treatments of the theme of pilgrimage." I have now given up trying to decide what constitutes a "real" pilgrim or pilgrimage.[3]

---

[2] Peace, *Pilgrimage: A Handbook on Christian Growth* (1976; reprinted Grand Rapids, MI: Baker Book House, 1984) 17–18. In 1984 Peace was an associate professor of Evangelism and Media at Gordon-Conwell Theological Seminary.

[3] I was doubly chastened when I discovered that my pilgrims had actually disappeared from Hebrews and even from Exodus. The "strangers and pilgrims" of Heb 11:13 (KJV) have metamorphosed into "strangers and exiles" of the RSV. And "Canaan, the land of their [the patriarchs'] pilgrimage" (Exod 6:4) has reappeared as "Canaan, the land in which they dwelt as sojourners." Thus, the sole biblical references to "pilgrims" and "pilgrimage" which once fed the use of the metaphor by reader, preacher, and exegete have literally disappeared from the most widely used modern Protestant translation of the Bible.

chapter focuses on the Christian life as motion toward. And how and toward what will become apparent only in the concrete instance.

The Current Fortunes of Pilgrims and Journeyers

A Handful of Naysayers

As was the case with the image of warfare, that of pilgrimage or journey has its nay sayers. There are those who worry about its traditional intimate connection with the idea of exile in a foreign land whose "city" has no lasting value by comparison to the "real" city where the pilgrimage will end. They associate it with the kind of old Johanno-Pauline exile/pilgrim theology exemplified by the following passage from Johannes Gerhard's *Practice of Piety*:

Thus I, the object of the world's disdain,
With pilgrim face surround the weary earth;
I only relish what the world counts vain;
Her mirth's my grief; her sullen grief my mirth;
Her light my darkness; and her truth my error;
Her freedom is my gaol; and her delight my terror.[4]

---

[4] Johann Gerhard, *Ger[h]ards Prayers: Or, A Daily Practice of Piety*, 1638; cited by Charles E. Hambricke-Stowe, *The Practice of Piety: Puritan Devotional Disciplines in Seventeenth-Century New England* (Chapel Hill, NC: University of North Carolina Press for the Institute of Early American History and Culture, 1982) 57. The idea of the exiled soul or community of souls has its roots in Greek thinking that predates the New Testament by centuries. It appears to have taken hold in the sixth century BCE in connection with the orphist and dionysian cults, whose adherents believed that each human is a mixture of gross earthly matter and imprisoned fragment of heavenly being. Their rituals were designed to free the latter. Little gold plates found in Cretan and Southern Italian tombs of the fifth century are inscribed with such hopeful messages as: "I have flown out of the sorrowful weary circle, I have reached my goal." The idea of liberating the soul from the body was at the heart of Pythagorus's philosophical ascesis. Plato was to develop a dualistic anthropology which saw the soul as the only part of us connected to the divine realm of the forms and capable of aspiring to their knowledge and which saw the philosopher's task in terms of freeing the soul from its association with the body so far as possible (see, e.g., *Phaedo* 64–67). In the Hellenistic Jewish and Christian contexts, this dualism is to some degree mitigated by the presence of the more positive view of creation from the Hebrew tradition. In Christian works, the body also belongs to the whole person as created by God and is believed to be resurrected in some form together with soul and/or spirit. It is the person, body and soul, who is in exile from their heavenly native land. This is a theme developed in Christian theology from the earliest times. Augustine's *City of God* is the fullest and most well-known treatment. One of the earliest, briefest but most explicit is that of the writer of the Epistle to Diognetus. He writes of Christians, "while living in Greek and barbarian cities, according as each obtained his lot, and following the local customs ... they show forth the wonderful and confessedly strange character of the constitution of their own citizenship. They dwell in their

There is a wariness, especially among American liberals, about theologies which seem to abandon the Hebrew insight of the essential goodness of creation and which postpone all happiness until the next life. This tendency is by no means a recent one. It is rooted in robustly optimistic nineteenth-century theologies with their faith in human potentialities and their renewed appreciation of the goodness of the natural world. The impact of these upon the image of life as "pilgrimage" was well brought out in a polemical essay written by T. R. Glover more than sixty years ago:

> The pilgrim seems to be dropping out of our religious conceptions. There are hymn-books which still keep a place for pilgrim hymns, but they are probably not often sung, except by children. And we are told often enough that the sentiment is false—if the hymn-writer insists that he is "but a stranger here," it is his own fault; earth is not, as he asserts, "a desert drear"; and the reference of all happiness to another world is unsound, and, perhaps, unchristian. On the contrary, R. L. Stevenson is a good deal nearer the mark: The world is so full of a number of things, I'm sure we should all be as happy as kings.[5]

Glover himself was one who saw all the flaws and unregenerateness of creation and was determined to put to rights such once-born fools as Stevenson. If he were alive today, he would have plenty of targets. In the time since he wrote, many more people have become aware of the rootedness of world-fleeing spiritualities in a highly negative view of nature, and of their dangerous ramifications for those groups traditionally associated more closely with the realm of nature than with that of spirit: especially women.[6]

Some also express an opinon that the image of journey or pilgrimage is misleading or inappropriate because for them it carries overtones of a clearly known definite destination and they no longer feel sure of this. For such persons the Holy City, which once drew eager pilgrims on, has the quality of a

---

own fatherlands, but as if sojourners in them; they share all things as citizens, and suffer all things as strangers. Every foreign country is their fatherland, and every fatherland is a foreign country. They marry as all men, they bear children, but they do not expose their offspring. They offer free hospitality, but guard their purity. . . . They pass their time upon the earth, but they have their citizenship in heaven. They obey the appointed laws, and they surpass the laws in their own lives. They love all men and are persecuted by all men. . . . To put it shortly what the soul is in the body that the Christians are in the world" (Epistle to Diognetus, V – VI). The passage points up well the fact that the exiled souls have a *purpose* in the body of the world; they are not simply fleeing from it or waiting for escape as parodiers of exile theologies are often wont to imply.

[5] Glover, *The Pilgrim: Essays on Religion* (London: SCM, 1921) 11.

[6] See, e.g., Rosemary Radford Ruether, "Woman, Body, and Nature: Sexism and the Theology of Creation," in idem, *Sexism and Godtalk: Toward a Feminist Theology* (Boston: Beacon, 1983) 72–92.

kind of mirage rather than an object of trusting faith; it is deeply longed for but epistemologically unsustainable. The City is perhaps illusory, and the nature of its ruler is unsure and even unknowable. It is not surprising that they therefore find the image irrelevant. The conception of life as pilgrimage is only as coercive as the vision of its end.[7] Speaking presumably with such doubters in mind, Edward Farley links the decline of what he calls "pilgrim piety" with the fact that "the twentieth century Christian simply has no clear goal toward which the Christian life leads, the pursuing of which gives point to his religious activities."[8]

We move now from the camp of the disgruntled and unconvinced to that of the unaware or uninterested. Pilgrimage and journey do not feature largely in the Protestant writings of the fifties and sixties that I examined, and are only becoming prevalent again quite recently. Many authors seem only to use the image in passing because it is part of their heritage; they speak of the way of the pilgrim and even perhaps use the old woodcuts from Bunyan's *Pilgrim's Progress*—drawn perhaps by their flavor of a charming and simple world lost.[9] But, except for a very few writers such as Olive Wyon, they do not use it in an extended way.[10] One may speculate about the reasons for this. It may be due to unstated objections of the kind mentioned directly above. Or perhaps the writers were not raised on the *Pilgrim's Progress* as were generations before them, and therefore were consequently less inclined to see life in terms of its kind of journey.[11] A further possibility is that the physical

[7] U. Milo Kaufmann, *The Pilgrim's Progress and Traditions in Puritan Meditation* (New Haven: Yale University Press, 1966) 133.

[8] Farley, *Requiem for a Lost Piety: The Contemporary Search for the Christian Life* (Philadelphia: Westminster, 1966) 90. I myself doubt that it makes sense for one who is so radically unsure of any destination to keep thinking of him or herself as a Christian. It is one thing to say with Paul that we cannot know the specifics of the resurrection; it is quite another to feel devoid of all hope and conviction about the end of religious existence.

[9] The long-lasting impact of seventeenth-century pilgrim theology on American writing is very evident; the perception of America as a pilgrim nation has perhaps reinforced the tendency on the part of American Protestant writers to understand each soul as a pilgrim soul. There is a deep emotional attachment to the metaphor; however, this does not always seem to issue in much more than an annual Thanksgiving sermon.

[10] Wyon, *On the Way: Some Reflections on the Christian Life* (London: SCM, 1958).

[11] I have tried to discover the publishing figures for Bunyan's *Pilgrim's Progress* in England and America over the last hundred years, but with no success. It is my impression, which will have to remain unsubstantiated, that few of the last two generations actually had it read to them at a formative age. Margaret Miles says in the preface of her most recent book (*Practicing Christianity*, ix), "As a child growing up in a fundamentalist Baptist parsonage, my imagination was awakened and stimulated—for better *and* for worse, as I now think—by an illustrated copy of *The Pilgrim's Progress* that was always on my bedside table." In this, she would appear to be one of a dwindling number of those who have had this mixed blessing. Perhaps it is a result of this decline that so many of the treatments of life's journey at present on our shelves are, depend-

phenomenon of pilgrimage and the accompanying idea of the holy quest which still informed the Puritan usage and the art has gone, and with it a strong feel for the metaphor.[12] Medieval pilgrimage was still fresh in the mind of Bunyan and other Puritan divines who drew upon its actual topography to convey their picture of the progress of the Christian life.[13] Not only do few modern Protestants have the experience of pilgrimage to sacred places to constantly reinfuse the metaphor, but except for Anglo-Catholics or high-church Episcopalians they do not generally participate in ritual/meditative practices such as the stations of the cross which imitate the pattern of physical pilgrimage. The closest one normally comes is the spoken or read meditation on the Passion of Jesus. Thus, for many modern Protestants, there is no external ritual phenomenon which might continue to prompt and invigorate their use of the metaphor of "pilgrimage."

But the Road Is Still Full of Travellers

However, pilgrimage or journey has become perhaps the most popular of all ways of interpreting the Christian life in some circles, and shows signs of a rapid return to popularity in others.

Catholics and the Coincidence of the Physical and Spiritual Dimensions

Both physical pilgrimage and spiritual pilgrimage are alive and well in Catholic Christianity, and most Catholic writers situate the metaphor very firmly in this context of physical pilgrimage.[14] It is interesting to consider the

---

ing on one's outlook, blessedly free of its constricting influence, or sadly lacking in resonance.

[12] The medieval period in Europe was the era, perhaps, in which the idea of pilgrimage of both body and soul had its strongest moment. As Weller Embler puts it, "The master metaphor of the Middle Ages is the pilgrimage as a quest for salvation, the literal journey, perhaps, to the holy place, or simply everyman's journey, his going forth toward an unknown destination in search of a mysterious something not revealed to him. The pilgrim knows only that he must seek and continue to seek with single-minded purpose until, if he is devout and faithful, he is vouchsafed the reason for his journey in the beatific vision which is the consummation of all his wandering and questing" (*Metaphor and Meaning* [Deland, FL: Everett/Edwards, 1966] 64). The Protestant reaction against the tawdry excesses of and the incorrect theology underlying physical pilgrimages did not blind such writers as Bunyan to their greater spiritual significance.

[13] For a discussion of this point, and a fascinating study of seventeenth-century "pilgrim" piety in one context, see Hambrick-Stowe, *Practice of Piety*. Kaufmann's *Traditions* also provides an extensive analysis of the currents of Puritan meditation and practice that helped shape Bunyan's text.

[14] Given the centrality of the image of the journey in its various forms in Catholic literature, I have attempted to incorporate a wide selection of Catholic texts. The interesting thing is writings on this topic seem to cross denominational boundaries with ease. Those drawn to the image

ways in which the physical and spiritual phenomena interact in this context. Metaphor and enactment are seen as supporting each other and forming a powerful coincidence. Louis Cameli speaks of physical pilgrimage as a "dynamic sacramental of inner realities and dispositions and experiences of the Christian life," as a kind of physically enacted statement of theology.[15] And A. M. Besnard speaks of the remarkable ability of the physical pilgrimage made on foot to express a person's theology and strengthen it in a way that verbal theology somehow cannot:

> What he [man] is in a mystical sense, pilgrimage allows him also to become through a temporal and physical practice, with a temporal and fleshly literality. What he is before God and what is conveyed by the symbol of the *homo viator*, pilgrimage intends that he become also in the face of dawns and eventides, of plains and mountains, in the reality of the earthly journey: no longer in image or in the poetical sense, but in the flesh and in temporal verity.[16]

However, it must be said that the relationship between metaphorical and physical pilgrimage is not always as straightforward as this might make it sound. What theology the pilgrim has affects her or his understanding of actual pilgrimage. Hence, when there was a marked emphasis in the Church's theology on penance and the importance of penitential works, physical pilgrimage was more apt to be viewed primarily as a penitential act and envisaged as a retracing of the steps of Christ to an obedient death. On the other hand, in today's theological context, there is perhaps more of a sense of the social dimension of the "pilgrimage" of the Christian life and this finds itself repeated in the understanding of or rationale for actual pilgrimage. Victor and Edith Turner comment on this fact:

> [I]n pilgrimages taken after the industrial Revolution . . . the stress has been on the communitas of the pilgrimage center, rather than on the individual's penance on the journey thither.[17]

This is not an accidental change in emphasis. It reflects a change in understanding of the priorities of the Christian life rooted in a changed perception

---

seem to be almost by definition open to the insights of any fellow traveller, regardless of the band to which he or she belongs.

[15] Cameli, "Outer Movements-Inner Significance: The Spirituality of Pilgrimage," *The Priest* 41 (1985) 18. Father Cameli is Professor of Spirituality and director of the spiritual-life program at Saint Mary of the Lake Seminary in Mundelein, Illinois (p. 20).

[16] Besnard, "Le sens chrétien du pèlerinage," *La Vie Spirituelle* 447 (1959) 147.

[17] Turner and Turner, *Image and Pilgrimage in Christian Culture: Anthropological Perspectives* (New York: Columbia University Press, 1978) 38–39.

of precisely what a pilgrimage in Christ's steps means.[18] And conversely, just as one's theology (esp. one's understanding of what it means to speak of life as pilgrimage) shapes one's understanding of ritual pilgrimage, so whatever ritual pilgrimage the author has in mind when writing of life as "pilgrimage" has a marked influence on her or his development of the metaphor. Pilgrimages do not conform themselves easily to one definition: they may be penitential, in gratitude, to obtain particular blessings; they may be viewed as obligatory or supererogatory. Consequently, many differences are to be expected in metaphorical treatments anchored in these differing historical practices. For Catholics, then, physical, ritual pilgrimage continues to inform the metaphorical usage as well as vice versa, but in a highly complex way.[19]

A Journey of Faith Development and Learning

The image of the journey is immensely popular in both Catholic and Protestant pastoral counselling and religious-education circles where it is employed as a framework for understanding the stages of that pilgrimage which culminates in the "developed" more holy self. The stages of faith are expounded, while the theology of sojourn in an alien world and of pilgrimage to some more "real" world which tended to accompany the faith journey in older writings of both the Catholic and Protestant traditions is put aside, at least temporarily. This allows the writer to appropriate her or his tradition's guidance on spiritual development which was couched in terms of progression and voyaging, without necessarily adopting the often dualistic theology that once accompanied it. This tendency to focus on the earthly "journey" has been compounded by the influence of analytical and developmental psychologists who use the imagery of the journey to describe either the individual's quest for wholeness or development through specific moral and emotional stages. Such works have had a definite trickle-down effect on the kind of devotional writers under primary consideration here, leading them to take the journey out of a broader theological context and to focus on the dimension of the learning process.

Nevertheless, by no means all Christian writers have jettisoned the language of pilgrimage, nor lifted it out of the context of a fuller theology

---

[18] See, e.g., Besnard's ("Le sens chrétien," 169) critique of physical and metaphorical pilgrimage understood in terms of a penitential retracing of the stages of the cross on the grounds that this reflects a partial, and therefore incorrect, understanding of Jesus' own pilgrimage.

[19] In trying to resolve the complexities of this nexus of symbol and actuality, one is reminded of the remark by E. A. Morinis ("Pilgrimage: The Human Quest," *Numen* 28 [1981] 282) that "Journeying to the sacred is a physical but also a symbolic, literary and spiritual image. Pilgrimage as event and pilgrimage as metaphor cannot be clearly distinguished."

which explains the place of the human in the cosmos, the relation of human and divine, and the nature of the goal sought. Before we turn to consider more closely the specific details of how the Christian life is envisaged as "journey" or "pilgrimage," we need to look at how these metaphors are still used in a thoroughgoing way which entails the making of broad theological affirmations about the nature of cosmos, God, and humanity.

The Broader Theological Picture

For most writers, the term "pilgrimage" conjures up journey to a particular destination.[20] All theologies of pilgrimage have in mind a double destination. They speak of a pilgrimage which is a pilgrimage of created beings back to their Maker, and simultaneously a journey toward spiritual maturity:

> The *ultimate* goal in both Catholic and Protestant piety is the vision of God, or as Protestant theologians describe it, glorification. . . . However, both pieties agree that the Christian life also reaches toward a goal realizable in the present life. The Catholic traditions call it "saintliness." Protestant piety used to call it "a righteous, godly, and sober life."[21]

The two destinations or goals are complementary. One may be reached in this life, the other may be anticipated in this life but will only finally be reached once the pilgrim "passes the Jordan of a dividing death and finally reaches the Promised Land of a new joy and a holier security."[22] One might perhaps say however, that the overall pilgrimage is to the ultimate destination.

Like pilgrims travelling toward a sacred place, humans are seen as moving toward the heavenly city and toward union with God. The majority of writers who use the metaphor operate with a strong doctrine of the fall and of human sinfulness. The language is that of apostasy, exile, and reunion. Cast out of Eden, humans have a dim recollection of glory, unity and rest, and

---

[20] This is no doubt under the influence of the Epistle to the Hebrews and actual pilgrimages; it should be noted that the Latin term *peregrinatio* originally implied no such finality of destination; the element of "wandering" was the stronger one.

[21] Farley, *Requiem*, 84.

[22] L. J. Baggott, *Pilgrim in the Modern World* (London: Allen and Unwin, 1963) 73. Baggott was an Anglican author. He was Archdeacon Emeritus of Norfolk when he wrote this book.

There are of course those who envisage the end-time as imminent and who therefore expect reunion to come before death. There are also those who view the establishment of the Kingdom as the culmination of the pilgrimage, and who do not think or speak in terms of an otherworldly Holy City. Here, clearly, one's eschatological views determine the final locus demanded by the metaphor.

they long to refind paradise and return to the bosom of the One who created them. Their pilgrimage is a pilgrimage home: a return to the center in the strongest sense.[23] This note is sounded most strongly by Catholic writers. Catherine de Hueck Doherty writes that the first real pilgrimage began in human hearts when the doors to Eden were closed: "[Adam and Eve] were the first pilgrims of the Absolute because they had known the Absolute."[24] Their journey, and that of their descendants, follows the route of recollection; it is a journey toward reunion with the dimly remembered God. Though the created world may be good, it is nevertheless a place of exile to the extent that it cannot be the locus of the total unity and final peace that the soul seeks. Michael Marshall, the Anglican Bishop of Woolwich, writes: "The Old Testament blood in a Christian's veins should always remind him that here we have no abiding city, but rather we are aliens in a foreign land whose commonwealth is in heaven."[25]

A few writers begin with a similar conviction that the pilgrimage is from separated, imperfect creaturehood toward union with God, but do not couch it in terms of a return of the exiled fallen toward the perfection of unity. For example, Cowley father Christopher Bryant interprets the fall story as a myth designed to show that humans are simply not what their Creator intends them to be. He says we should understand our present condition not as an attempt to climb back toward a once-held perfection, but as a halfway stage on a journey toward a yet unheld perfection, to which the creator is drawing us:

Following this interpretation . . . we should have a powerful incentive to work out our salvation, confident that the Creator having guided us thus far would continue to shepherd us along the road which leads, not back to Eden, but on to the Divine City. We get an idea of what human nature is meant to be not by looking back to the dream figure of Adam in Eden, but to another man, Jesus Christ.[26]

[23] On the idea of the return to the center, see Mircea Eliade, *The Myth of the Eternal Return, or Cosmos and History* (Bollingen Series 46; rev. ed.; 1965; reprinted Princeton: Princeton/Bollingen Paperback, 1971) 17–21.

[24] Doherty, *Strannik: the Call to Pilgrimage for Western Man* (Notre Dame, IN: Ave Maria, 1978) 10. Doherty was a Russian refugee who came to Canada in 1920, rebuilt her fortunes, and founded the Madonna House Apostolate. She has written a number of works on Eastern spirituality for Western audiences.

[25] Marshall, *Pilgrimage and Promise* (London: Collins, 1981) 38.

[26] Bryant, *The Heart in Pilgrimage: Christian Guidelines for the Human Journey* (New York: Seabury, 1980) 20. The Cowley Fathers, or the Society of St. John the Evangelist, are an Anglican monastic community.

In a similar key, but sounding an even more pronounced note of felix culpa, Barbara Wolf writes:

> [T]he promise of Christ is not that we shall be wafted back to some primitive state of inexperience. Christianity offers us the prospect of something called *Sion*, not the forever lost Garden of Eden.[27]

For writers such as Wolf and Bryant, the note of exile is almost absent. The pilgrimage is to a God not yet fully known; the journey is to a perfect selfhood never attained in any previous state or time.

However, whether the pilgrimage is construed as journey back or journey forward, the ultimate destination is constant: reconciliation with and union with God. There is also agreement that the pilgrim is being constantly called forth by a dynamic God. God is not simply a static being which awaits the return of its creatures who are navigating their way home purely by means of some dim platonic remembrance of perfection once known.[28] God as Father also actively calls and guides the individual pilgrim: "He leaps the mountains to come to us, running to meet us with arms open to embrace us."[29] God "goes before" pilgrim Christians as he went before the people of Israel in the wilderness; he is as involved now as he was then:

> The underlying notion of the pilgrimage journey is not, therefore, the mere going forth of a person or of a people, but the presence of God presiding over a movement of liberation to a land of promise.[30]

As we shall see later, the divinely led journeys of Abraham and the Israelite people are the foundational types which lead writers to develop the metaphor of pilgrimage in a variety of ways.

If the Father is constantly going before, and calling Christians, the Holy Spirit works with and within pilgrims to set them upon the path and to keep them there:

> The Spirit seeks to breathe life and a pure intention into every sincere effort to turn to God. It is the Holy Spirit in man who awakens him to the values of

---

[27] Wolf, *Journey in Faith: An Inquirer's Program* (New York: Seabury, 1982) 130–31.

[28] Although sometimes writers use language which rather suggests this static model, e.g., Donald Joy (in idem, ed., *Moral Development Foundations: Judeo-Christian Alternatives to Piaget/Kohlberg* [Nashville: Abingdon, 1983] 21) speaks of the imago in the human responding to the "homing signal" of the creator.

[29] Lucy Bregman, *Through the Landscape of Faith* (Philadelphia: Westminster, 1986) 14. Bregman teaches in the Department of Religion Temple University. She describes herself as an evangelical Christian with a biblically structured piety (p. 11).

[30] Jeffrey G. Sobosan, C.S.C., "Pilgrimage Theology: A Scriptural Basis," *The Bible Today* (December 1973) 1401.

truth, goodness and beauty; it is he who awakens and directs the thirst which only union with God can satisfy; it is he who sets man upon the pilgrimage to the City of God where alone perfect wholeness and peace can be found.[31]

It opens them up to the truths of Scripture, and heightens their sensitivity to the signposts of truth, goodness and beauty in the world. As Baggott puts it:

> The pilgrim learns, as he journeys on, that there is no circumstance in life that does not contain the elements of a Divine purpose, and holds within it the call to an ascent in the scale of being.[32]

But the Christian pilgrim does not simply follow signs in the natural world in a journey toward a discovery of greater meaning and final unity with Beauty and Truth, nor respond just to the memory and calling of the Father. She or he also walks in the steps of Christ, the forerunner (*prodromos*) and pathfinder (*archēgos*) of Hebrews; the ultimate pilgrim whose whole life was a journey toward the Father.[33] While Christ is the end of the Christian journey, he is simultaneously the Way, and the one who travelled the Way:

> Far from being an immobile and totally self-contained endpoint, Jesus is more of a pilgrim than anyone else. He never stands still; he runs along the paths of God to such an extent that he himself becomes identified with the Way (cf. John 14.6), and in his turn he calls men and women to follow him along the road without even taking the time to look back (Luke 9.62). . . . By revealing, through his Son, the depths of his heart, the pilgrim God invites his people to a final and even more radical uprooting, in order to welcome them to their true home.[34]

Christ is also a companion along the pilgrim way. He walks constantly at the pilgrim's side.

Having looked at the theological framework of the metaphor, at the picture of the nature and the relations of human and divine conveyed with its aid, let us turn now to look at what it means to speak of the Christian life as "pilgrimage" or "journey."

---

[31] Bryant, *Heart in Pilgrimage*, 23.

[32] Baggott, *Pilgrim*, 75.

[33] For *archēgos* see Heb 2:10, 12:2; and for *prodromos* see Heb 6:20.

[34] Brother John of Taizé, *The Pilgrim God: A Biblical Journey* (Washington, DC: Pastoral, 1985) 220. Augustine reflected thus on John 14.6: "Although he is our native country, He made himself also the Way to that country" (*Christian Doctrine* 11; see also 34). The theme of the Christian on the road of the Way runs throughout the prologue of this work by Augustine.

Life as Pilgrimage or Journey

The journey has always been a useful way to visualize the human life because of the ease with which space can be used as an analogue for time.[35] The metaphor can be used in a variety of ways which accord with different points of departure and arrival: a journey from birth to death, from ignorance to knowledge,[36] from perdition to salvation, from Athens to Jerusalem, from Egypt to Canaan. It can range from what Janis Stout terms "the allegorical, sunset-directed Journey of Life, a familiar even hackneyed trope,"[37] to a highly structured journey with a particular religious or philosophical goal which need not necessarily fit in with the physical stages of life. Its stages can be biological, epistemological, moral and/or spiritual. Or they can be a kind of hybrid, as in the case of faith development writers such as James Fowler who conflate the epistemological, moral and spiritual categories with the biological category so that the journeys of the lifecycle and the spirit coalesce wholly or partially.

The Place of Beginning

Depending upon one's perception, the pilgrimage of the Christian life may begin at the moment of conversion/awakening or in the dark moments which precede it. In the light of the gospel, it becomes clear that one's journey began well before the moment of conversion: "How many of those who seem to be wandering aimlessly will one day discover that their wandering was in fact obedience to a secret call spoken in their heart by the pilgrim God, a call so intimate that it was not yet recognized as such, even by the person concerned?"[38] Something in us prompts us to set out upon a search

---

[35] Janis P. Stout, *The Journey Narrative in American Literature: Patterns and Departures* (Westport, CT: Greenwood, 1983) 13. This is a very common observation. However, one might wish to note the interesting observation of Murray Krieger that there is no special reason why we should see space as a mode of describing time rather than vice versa, no justification for seeing the temporal as primary. "If," he writes, "as we conceive it, the temporal shares with the spatial the state of being a constructed reality, then we cannot easily find a point of privilege to justify a claim about which serves as a metaphor for which" ("A Waking Dream: The Symbolic Alternative to Allegory," in Bloomfield, *Allegory*, 17).

[36] Perhaps this is the most common. "Since the earliest times, the act of *travelling*, of proceeding from one place to another, has been seen as a natural metaphor for *learning*, for the acquisition of experience and knowledge" (Bishop C. Hunt, Jr., "Travel Metaphors and the Problem of Knowledge," *Modern Language Studies* 6 [1976] 44). The very word "educate" as many point out, has the idea of "leading out" at its heart. On the fact and the implications of this see, e.g., Thomas H. Groome, *Christian Religious Education* (San Francisco: Harper & Row, 1980) 5–17.

[37] Stout, *Journey*, 6.

[38] Brother John of Taizé, *Pilgrim God*, 21–22.

for meaning and true existence. Richard Peace speaks of this phase as the "Quest phase" of the Christian pilgrimage.[39] Depending upon the author's theology, this early movement is seen to a greater or lesser degree as due to the prompting of God.

For some this search for meaning, this feeling of being drawn to find what is condensed in such terms as Truth or Beauty, lasts a lifetime. There is no fixed or final moment of "conversion" as such. Or, after conversion, fixed meaning slips away again and a journey of an open ended kind recommences. On the periphery of every tradition walk men and women whose glimpse of the divine has been inconclusive at some level—those drawn on by the *fascinans* of the divine, yet unwilling to equate this with what the churches have to offer and therefore disinclined to join in the pilgrimage according to the map given them by the Church. A good example of this extra-ecclesial pursuit of the ineffable, or perhaps of the way back to the lost paradise, can be found in Philip Zaleski's "Living in the Rift." Zaleski speaks of the experience of being raised in the Catholic church and retaining the desire to find a way back to the promised lost paradise long after a faith in the church's ability to provide the way back there has dissipated:

> We visit a church and feel a vague regret; there lies our childhood. But we are adults; the gifts of our youth, although we may pass them along to our children in turn, are no longer available to us. Rejoining an old tradition, like slipping into a pair of old shoes, can too easily lead us down dead-end trails. We seek a teaching that will confound our habits, our ordinary way of life—the way that got us into this impasse. We need to see with new eyes.[40]

There are also those who have never been drawn into the sphere of Christianity or any other particular tradition, but are constantly seeking. For these people and for post-Christians alike, the abundance of alternatives is bewildering; the pilgrimage has no fixed trail, and could easily dissipate into a dazed wandering. Zaleski writes:

> [N]ew traditions . . . call to us daily. . . . How to choose what teaching to follow? The abundant options available to us seem to cancel each other out. We are paralyzed by our very freedom. Certain that a path to Paradise exists, able to unfold a sacred map—the Bible, the Dhammapada, the Upanishads—and trace out the route, we are yet unable, in everyday life, to figure out where to plant our feet. Lost in the Neverland, we peer around for a signpost pointing us home.[41]

[39] Peace, *Pilgrimage*, 41–42.
[40] Zaleski, "Living in the Rift," *Parabola* 10 (1985) 11.
[41] Ibid.

Some people actually *like* the idea of never reaching a destination. The journey or the road becomes the goal in itself for them. This outlook has been called particularly American, bred into the bone with stories of the pioneer trails with their constant westering movement. It is a religious version of Whitman's song of the open road; an affirmation of his call to "know the universe itself as a road, as many roads, as roads for travelling souls."[42] This kind of paeon to the open road, or glorification of constant seeking is seen by writers like Peace as purposeless self-indulgence. He says sternly that

> Certain people even make Quest into a life-style. They spend their time going from one exciting option to another—always seeking, never finding; never *willing* to find (or so it seems).[43]

But even for those who, in Peace's language, come to "encounter Christ," a certain openness to continual enquiry will continue to characterize the Christian pilgrimage:

> While the Quest phase of pilgrimage has a definite conclusion to it (i.e., you come to the point where you want to encounter Jesus), the basic *attitude* which characterizes this phase ought to carry over to the whole of the pilgrimage. This is, of course, the attitude of inquiry; i.e., the willingness to go on examining one's beliefs. In other words, the search for truth does not end with the discovery that Jesus is Lord of the Universe. In fact, it only really begins at that point. Now the focus shifts to the ongoing discovery of the wide-ranging implications of this foundational truth. This same attitude of critical inquiry which leads us to Jesus will go on unlocking new understandings and new

---

[42] Walt Whitman, *Complete Poetry and Selected Prose* (ed. James E. Miller, Jr.; Boston: Houghton Mifflin, 1959) 113. Cited by Stout, *Journey,* 18. The first chapter of Stout's book provides a most interesting discussion of the way that historical patterns of westerly journey have shaped the American imagination and contributed to a glorification of the road or the journey itself.

[43] Peace, *Pilgrimage* 41. What we appear to have here is a conflict between two images of journey—one open-ended and the other perhaps circular. Bishop Hunt writes, "In simple logic, there are two patterns or geometrical designs to choose from. You can have a circular journey, a *round*-trip. . . . Epistemologically this pattern implies that the world is *knowable,* is, in fact, substantially known already, and only waits for the individual traveller to discover it for himself in the course of his own odyssey. Alternatively, you can, in the simplest terms, go from *one* place to *another*. . . . In geometrical terms this represents a straight line. . . . Since . . . the individual traveller ends up at a place *different* from where he started, the linear journey suggests a different concept of knowledge: namely that *new truth* exists 'out there' for the traveler to discover" ("Travel Metaphors," 45). Hunt (p. 47) comments on the way that, from the time of Tennyson, the open-ended journey supplants the circular journey in literature: "Knowledge, like the horizon itself, recedes indefinitely before the traveller. Its pursuit may be heroic, but the goal will never be reached."

depths throughout our life. Inquiry is, after all, a characteristic of the pilgrim. Resting upon what you have found is the attitude of the settler.[44]

It is an interesting question the extent to which the pilgrimage remains open-ended after conversion and the extent to which one may legitimately express a desire that the journey itself not end. Miguel de Unamuno said that the traditional notion of the final beatific vision smacked to him of tedium; he argued that it overlooks the fact that our "highest pleasure consists in acquiring and intensifying consciousness. Not the pleasure of knowing, exactly, but rather that of learning,"[45] and that it sits ill with the human predilection for living in hope rather than certainty. He wrote: "And the soul, my soul at least, longs for something else, not absorption, not quietude, not peace, not appeasement, it longs ever to approach and never to arrive."[46]

The quest for meaning may last a lifetime, or even an eternity. However, to return to the realms of the earthly Christian life, the related but more structured pilgrimage toward holiness begins with conversion or reawakening. It is then that the person consciously sets out toward saintliness and the resurrection life. As Gérard Defois has pointed out, "Christian conversion is often preached on the model of the Prodigal Son parable, which is articulated around a double physical movement: 'I will *rise* and *go* to my Father'."[47] The metaphor of pilgrimage picks up and emphasizes this same get up and go pattern. It stresses the breaking away from the everyday and from what has come to be seen as one's old nature and existence to move toward new forms of being. This first stage of the journey or pilgrimage is often expounded with reference to Abraham's journeying forth in response to God's call. Abraham is felt to be par excellence the "man of faith" precisely because his life is fundamentally a long pilgrimage, a journey with God.[48] As Abraham responded to the call and promise of the living God and set out in the direction of the promise, so must the individual Christian set out on the way. The leaving of the old nature and sinfulness is also frequently illumined by means of discussion of the type of the Israelites leaving of Egypt and setting out on their journey toward the Promised Land. This last way of construing the starting point of the journey goes back to the earliest patristic explanations of

[44] Peace, *Pilgrimage*, 57.

[45] De Unamuno, *Tragic Sense of Life* (1921; reprinted, New York: Dover Publications, 1954) 229.

[46] Ibid., 256.

[47] Defois, "The Place of Pilgrimage in French Pastoral Activity," *Lumen Vitae* 39 (1984) 412. Defois is a dioscesan priest who lectures at the Catholic Institute in Paris.

[48] Brother John, *Pilgrim God*, 13.

the meaning of baptism in the light of the type of the crossing of the Red Sea and departure from Egypt.[49]

From another angle, those with a knowledge of psychology or of faith development or with interest in the journey undergone by the person under analysis, are inclined to draw connections between this moment of metanoia and setting out, and the point at which, to take the Jungian example, self begins its journey to find Self and the process of individuation is begun. The problem that can arise with this is that the latter process is not normally found occurring in people younger than their mid-thirties, while the experience of conversion is certainly found in younger persons. The different stages do not always mesh tidily.

On the Way: Different Modes of Visualizing the Journey

The manner in which the actual journey toward greater understanding and a more godly existence is envisaged differs widely. It may be presented as a journey inward to the centre, or a journey outward across the terrain of world and time. The journey may be horizontal, it may be vertical, it may be spiraling.[50] Lucy Bregman has given an interesting analysis of these configurations in her *Through the Landscape of Faith*. The journey inward may be couched in the psychological language of quest for self or in the language of purgation, illumination and union. The journey outward may be seen, amongst other things, as a tracing of the footsteps of the pilgrim Christ, or as an individual Exodus and wandering toward the promised land. There are numerous possibilities. Despite these differences in configuration, those journeys which relate to the shape of the lay Christian life are all journeys of testing, learning, and growth toward greater saintliness. They take account of the key moments of Christian experience: despair, conversion or awakening, the first flush of enthusiasm, falling back, the maturation in faith. Let us look at some of the most prevalent modes of envisaging the pilgrimage or journey of the Christian toward spiritual maturity.

Mystics Meet Psychologists

In most Catholic and some Anglican texts, the terminology of purgation, illumination and union is apt to appear. However, in this literature on the Christian life geared to the laity, the "mystic way" rarely appears in a thoroughgoing form, presumably because its ground is the contemplative life,

---

[49] On this point see, e.g., Jean Daniélou, *From Shadows to Reality: Studies in the Biblical Typology of the Fathers* (Westminster, MD: Newman, 1960) 175–202.

[50] On the journey as ascent, see also Miles, *Practicing Christianity*, 63–79.

whereas the average lay life is the active life.[51] Nevertheless, in a rather diluted form it is used by some of the Catholic and Anglican writers as the framework for a more general "life pilgrimage." Writers such as Alan Jones and Christopher Bryant use the language of purgation, illumination and union and employ these categories in a highly general way. Many of those drawn to this kind of conception of the pilgrimage in interior terms are also drawn to Jungian psychology with its idea of an inner quest for individuation, for self's finding of Self. Consequently, they discuss their pilgrimage in hybrid terms, jumping from one to another, seeking to blend the insights of the two different modes of interpretation. Thus, for example, Christopher Bryant draws clear connections between the older traditional stages and what he sees as their counterparts in the journey inward of the Jungian analysand. To give one example, he links purgation with the idea of dialogue with one's shadow and goes on to say:

> We grow into the peace of oneness with God as we respond to his pressure to face up to the unruly elements within and, with God's help, enable them to become allies, instead of enemies, in the journey to the City of God.[52]

In the process of this hybridization something often happens to the older mystic way. Its goal shifts subtly from forgetful union to personal wholeness. For example, Alan Jones has been speaking of how the Christian pilgrim goes on a journey into the hiddenness and darkness of God, enters the wasteland and so on. Then he says:

> Depth psychology has done much to illuminate the path back to a full humanity. In the language of the Christian pilgrimage, we are on our way to "being" in all its fullness of glory. Depth psychology uses the ambiguous words "self and Self" to describe this pilgrimage.[53]

In works by Christian authors, the secular psychological maps of the development of the self or the journey of the psyche are generally viewed as

---

[51] These are, of course, not mutually exclusive. However, by definition, the life of the average layperson is primarily a life in the world—an active life—in which the aspect of prayer and contemplation is a vital element but not perhaps the primary or overriding one.

[52] Bryant, *Heart in Pilgrimage*, 44. For an interesting attempt to draw selectively (correcting sexist and unwholistic biases) from the traditional ways of the mystics and the journeys of the psyche as charted by such men as Jung and Eric Neumann, see Helen Thompson, B.V.M., *Journey Toward Wholeness: A Jungian Model of Adult Spiritual Growth* (New York: Paulist, 1982). For an example of interpretation of biblical journeys in a Jungian mode, see Jean Gill, *Images of Myself: Meditation and Self-Exploration through the Jungian Imagery of the Gospels* (New York: Paulist, 1982) esp. 45–53 on the meaning of the journey of the prodigal son.

[53] Jones, *Journey into Christ* (New York: Seabury, 1977) 42.

helpful secondary explanations of the process of returning to holiness and to God. Particularly since Jung, however, there has been a flow of treatises by non-Christians or post-Christians attempting to demonstrate the deeper, psychological, meaning of Christian pilgrimage texts such as the *Pilgrim's Progress*. The classic of these is probably Mary Esther Harding's *Journey into Self*, an extended explanation of every aspect of Bunyan's text in terms of the individual's voyage toward individuation through participation in the drama of the archetypes.[54]

Speaking in Allegories

Bunyan couched the Christian's pilgrimage in the form of an overtly Christian allegory. His journey, as Bregman points out, has nothing to do with going through biologically conditioned stages of life.[55] It is a journey from perdition toward salvation, in the course of which the Christian is tested and strengthened by encounter with all the evils and trials of this world (including those of his own psyche). Very few writers now use Bunyan's type of allegorical exposition. Moral allegories gave way to social novels as the preferred reading of the religious middle classes by the mid-nineteenth century and today strictly allegorical treatments of the theme of pilgrimage are rare.[56] Modern attempts to recreate Bunyan's genre seem rather flatfooted.[57] His hand is still felt in the language that many of the writers use, but the overtly religious allegorical genre seems to have been supplanted on the one hand by the modern novel, and on the other hand, by manuals which chart the stages of the individual's sanctification or faith development,[58] and by pilgrim

---

[54] Harding, *Journey into Self* (New York: Longmans, Green and Co., 1956). To give one example of her interpretation, "[I]n his song Christian proclaimed that, as a result of his own ordeal, Jesus would now be crowned. What can we make of this statement? Jesus, the historical Jesus, had . . . fought his own battle . . . and won the reward of his own *athlon*. How can it be that Christian's victory could affect the fate of Jesus, and indeed be represented as necessary for his coronation? This passage shows that Bunyan was thinking on two levels. He could quite well recognize that Christ was already triumphant and transcendent in the heavens, and yet—and this is the remarkable part—he also recognized that the Christ image, or central value of the individual psyche, needed to be crowned king in each man's heart" (p. 184).

[55] Bregman, *Landscape*, 48. This may be something of an overstatement of the case.

[56] For an interesting discussion of this development from allegory to social novel, see Barry V. Qualls, *The Secular Pilgrims of Victorian Fiction: The Novel as Book of Life* (Cambridge: Cambridge University Press, 1982) 1–16.

[57] See, e.g., Geoffrey T. Bull, *A New Pilgrim's Progress: John Bunyan's Classic Imagined in a Contemporary Setting* (London: Hodder and Stoughton, 1969). More successful are such article-length offspring of the *Pilgrim's Progress* as David Downing's "Pilgrim's Digress, All This and Heaven Too," *Eternity* (August 1978) 25–27.

[58] See, e.g., Nazarene author Stephen Manley, *Journey into Wholeness* (Kansas City: Beacon Hill, 1983). Manley's concluding chapter (87–92) summarizes selectively the *Pilgrim's Pro-*

psychotherapies: books which use the journey or pilgrimage as a loose organizing principle for a string of exhortations on particular sins and deficiencies.[59]

Personal Exodus

Another mode of visualizing the Christian pilgrimage is to cast it in terms of the types of the Hebrew Bible: notably Exodus. Thus Jean Hofinger speaks of our life as

> a journeying towards God, exodus from the world, a serious and generous effort to attain God, an effort which entails the crossing of the desert, and finally the entry into the promised land of eternal union and intimacy with God.[60]

Exodus and the journey to the promised land has long been used as a type of the Christian life.[61] A classic modern example of this mode of exposition is James Mahoney's *Journey into Fullness*, which is a work on the Christian life spun out of his observation that the "pilgrimage [of Israel to the promised land] affords us an example of our own spiritual journey."[62] Mahoney

---

gress, and ties what he has been saying into its framework. However, his book makes no use of any such allegorical schema until this final point.

[59] See, e.g., Ed Hindson and Walter Byrd, *When the Road Gets Rough* (Old Tappan, NJ: Revell, 1986).

[60] Hofinger, "The Pilgrimage, Symbol of the Christian Life," *Lumen Vitae* 13 (1958) 261. Hofinger was Professor at the Chinese Seminary in Manila.

[61] See, e.g., John Calvin, *Institutes of the Christian Religion* (ed. John T. McNeill and Ford Lewis Battles; LCC 22; Philadelphia: Westminster, 1960) 4.15.9. There the focus is the stage of baptism. In Edward Taylor's "Preparatory Meditations," each stage of the journey is made to speak both of the later work of Christ and of the journey to God of the individual Christian. Of the cloud and pillar in the desert he writes:

> Oh! Pillar strange, made of a Cloude, and Fire.
>   Whose Stoole is Israels Camp, it sits upon.
> Whose Skirts doe Canopy that Camp: Whose Spire
>   Doth kiss the Heavens, leading Israel on.
> Sure't is Christ's Charett drawn by Angells high.
>   The Humane Jacket, typ'te of's Deity.
>
> Then lead me, Lord, through all this Wilderness
>   By this choice shining Pillar Cloud and Fire.
> By Day, and Night I shall not then digress.
>   If thou wilt lead, I shall not lag or tire
>   But as to Cana'n I am journeying
>   I shall thy praise under this Shadow sing. (*Poems*, 186–87)

[62] Mahoney, *Journey into Fullness* (Nashville: Broadman, 1974) ix. Mahoney is described as Director of Special Ministries and Bible Teacher for Richard Hogue Evangelism.

goes on to tie the major stages of faith development to the stages on Israel's way to possession of the land: the Christian is liberated from bondage and drawn into the wilderness for a time of testing. Like the Israelites who murmured and thought of Egypt, the new Christian is oftimes wistful for the old life left behind. In the wilderness the Christian learns obedience and strength. Only then can he or she be led into the promised land of spiritual maturity. The same themes are developed with greater subtlety by Brother John of Taizé in *The Pilgrim God* and Jeffrey Sobosan in his article "Pilgrimage Theology: A Scriptural Basis." Sobosan emphasizes the importance of tying discussion of faith as pilgrimage firmly into a careful reading of the texts of the Hebrew Bible:

> [T]he understanding of these or any images from the past must also be such that in them are seen values expressed in living persons as prototypes. Only in this way can their value keep from being merely admirable abstractions and become incorporated in the life of the Church today.[63]

Following Christ

The Christian pilgrim is not merely retracing the pattern of going forth toward promise which is found in the Old Testament. The pilgrimage is also a retracing of the steps of the one who in his life brought to consummation this pattern. Christian pilgrimage is above all "a pilgrimage toward the Father in Jesus' train," and most writers are careful to bring this out.[64] The understanding of what it actually means to follow in Christ's steps will vary. The question is as broad as the question of what it means to live in imitation of Christ, or what it means to be a true disciple.

The Quest for Knowledge and the Harmony of Truth

Even of the pilgrim who is overtly and committedly Christian, Peggy Slemeck can write: "A pilgrim is one with vision, although incomplete, who is searching for the meaning of life and always moving on."[65] Certain presentations of life as pilgrimage focus mainly on the individual's quest for greater understanding of what it means to be alive and of the ways of God in creation. Sometimes their impulse appears to be a kind of desire of knowledge for knowledge's sake, but more usually these presentations of pilgrimage and journey are inspired by curiosity and the desire to harmonize the different,

---

[63] Sobosan, "Pilgrimage Theology," 1400.

[64] Besnard, "Le sens chrétien," 169.

[65] Slemeck, *A Pilgrim's Way: Biblical Readings and Thoughts for Different Stages of Life* (London: The Mothers' Union, 1983) 1.

apparently conflicting strands of knowledge that one has received. This is a picture of the journey found particularly in the writings of those engaged in dialogue with other religions, whose opportunity to experience the development of another person or people of faith has instilled in them a sense of a multiplicity of paths to knowledge, whose intersection will perhaps never be known in this life. They are apt to express a conviction that God is guiding the footsteps of different people and peoples toward greater understanding via different paths.[66]

Tensions within the Metaphor

As one studies the literature of "pilgrimage" and "journey" one notices that certain issues and problems surface constantly: the dangers of excessive formalism in mapping out life's journey in predictable stages; the relation of the pilgrim to the pilgrim church; the tension between the individual's development and the mandate to care for others and build the kingdom; the issue of whether the metaphor necessarily presupposes a negative view of creation and of human earthly existence.

The majority of the writers, especially those working explicitly with models drawn from faith-development and moral-development theory desire to discuss the pilgrim's journey in terms of fixed stages; however, they also try to affirm the specialness of the individual journey. Thus, after talking about the general phases of Quest, Commitment and Integration which every pilgrim goes through, Peace goes on to say:

> [E]ach pilgrimage is unique. Each person is at a different point, arrived at in his own special way. This is important to bear in mind. Since no two pilgrimages are alike, our only concern can be with our own path. . . .
>
> We get into trouble when we start comparing our path to that of someone else. . . . Each story is unique. Each has its own inner logic. Each is in God's hand. In the end, our only concern is to follow faithfully the way God has marked out uniquely for us.

---

[66] Those who remain within mainstream Christianity, tend, however to emphasize the superiority of the Christian path. Thus, e.g., Catholic theologian Heinz Robert Schlette (*Towards a Theology of Religions* [New York: Herder and Herder, 1966] 104) writes: "The ordinary ways of salvation represented by the religions lead to the one living God, it is true, but, relatively speaking, they are paths through the darkness, while the extraordinary way of special sacred history . . . is one which leads through clear light. And only on this way, which at the same time is itself life and truth, can the secret of history be recognized, which consists in the fact the salvation which is also attainable by the ordinary ways of general sacred history is the redemption brought by Jesus Christ and as such is the salvation mediated by the Church."

The really important thing is not *where* we are in our pilgrimage, but whether we are moving.[67]

Sometimes, the double affirmation of individuality and uniformity sits rather awkwardly. For example, Father Gregory Smith writes:

Each personal journey in faith is unique. No pattern can fully analyze that process; however it would seem reasonable to assume that the content of all six stages should have occurred in some degree in each believer by the end of the earthly life.[68]

The problem is that Christians inherit patterns of living from the tradition and go through phases determined in large part by their age, gender and maturity. But they also affirm a God who acts in ways not confined by these limits, and feel that each of their lives is in some divinely sanctioned way unique. An element of openness and surprise must always be present. When it is absent, there is a fall into depressing determinism or even fatalism, and the pilgrim path also degenerates into a stultifying moral formalism which can kill the gospel. Speaking in the Protestant context, Farley puts the matter well:

If the Christian life means an advance toward a clearly known goal (holiness, etc.) through specific means, how can it ever be life in response to the living Word of God? The implication is that God's living Word is simply synonymous with those goals fixed in and by the past. If that is the case, the Word is not the living presence of Jesus Christ in his Spirit. The Word is a fixed goal and as such is not living, but dead. Protestant piety turns out to be life in a fixed circle of duties and virtues. Incapable of breaking out of that circle, the Protestant Christian is unable to come to grips with new and complex situations of his life.[69]

So, at one level, the tension is between living gospel and moral formalism. At another level, the tension is between the personal pursuit and discovery of truth:

Every act of faith is as varied as the believer himself. . . . We are pathfinders—discoverers of new lands and byways—for God is as unique as he is varied and communicates in many different fashions.[70]

[67] Peace, *Pilgrimage*, 43.
[68] Smith, *Pilgrims in Process* (New York: Alba House, 1978) 39.
[69] Farley, *Requiem*, 87.
[70] Smith, *Pilgrims*, 37.

And it is between pursuit and received wisdom:

> Journeys have to be planned for. Hopefully the Christian Community of beli-
> evers has prepared the formal itinerary for faith's journey.[71]

The Christian walks by the maps drawn by the church as well as in the direction pointed by the compass of the spirit. But there is always the possibility
that she will be called to go into uncharted territory.

This last area of tension brings us into the broader issue of the relation of
the individual pilgrim to the community of the pilgrim church. In Protestant
circles especially, there has been a definite tendency to speak of the pilgrim
as a lone soul returning to the Father. Gerald J. Jud writes:

> All through the centuries important models of the Christian pilgrimage have
> existed. During recent centuries the most prominent model among English-
> speaking Protestants has been that of Christian in John Bunyan's *Pilgrim's
> Progress*. . . . This model emphasized the individual, solitary aspect of pilgrim-
> age, the uniqueness of each person in his relationship to the eternal.[72]

Gustavo Gutiérrez is of the opinion that in fact this kind of unhealthy individualism has characterized far too much of Christian writing on the spiritual
life—Catholic as well as Protestant. He writes:

> The spiritual journey has often been presented as a cultivation of individualistic
> values as a way to personal perfection. The relationship with God seemed to
> obscure the presence of others and encouraged individual Christians to be
> absorbed in their own interiority in order to understand and develop it better.
> For this reason the spiritual life was called *the interior life*, which many under-
> stood as a life lived exclusively within the individual. The important thing in it
> was the deployment of the virtues as potentialities that had to do with the indi-
> vidual and had little or no connection with the outside world. In this outlook
> the important thing is one's intention. . . .
> The community dimensions inherent in all Christian life became formalities;
> they were unable to alter the perspective that turned the journey to God into a
> purely individual venture.[73]

---

[71] Ibid.

[72] Jud, *Pilgrim's Process* (Philadelphia: United Church Press, 1967) 26–27. Here it should be
noted that Jud simply overlooks the story of the journey of Christiana and her family—a tale
marked by the concern of the characters for each other's well being on the path to salvation.

[73] Gutiérrez, *We Drink from Our Own Wells: The Spiritual Journey of a People* (Maryknoll,
NY: Orbis Books, 1984) 14–15.

A substantial number of contemporary writings on the life of faith as pilgrimage exhibit a different but equally marked concern with the fate of the individual as opposed to the fate of the community. It is not so much that they encourage an obsession with one's own immortal salvation; rather, they encourage a potentially narcissistic focus on "personal wholeness" as the primary goal of the pilgrim. Some writers are worried by the new form of individualism manifested in this trend. They see it as indicating a failure to appreciate the corporate nature of the Christian faith. Olive Wyon writes:

> The Christian ideal . . . is not that of a number of "integrated" individuals, concerned about their own spiritual progress, but of growth into Christ, as members of the Body of Christ, in which we all live by the same Life, which flows through the Body, and animates us all.[74]

Wyon is an example of those who feel the need to emphasize the communal aspect of the Christian enterprise, and to stress the place of the ecclesia in the life of the pilgrim. L. J. Baggott is another such:

> [L]et this be clearly understood,—we who know ourselves to be pilgrims cannot go forth into the world as witnesses unless we have first gone into the sanctuary as worshippers. That is why every pilgrim needs the Church and the love of the brethren. The communion of love is indispensable for the understanding of truth, for the highest knowledge of truth is beyond the reach of an isolated mind; it is open only to a society of souls bound together by love. An isolated or self-sufficient pilgrim is a sick being."[75]

This sense of the importance of the institutional church and of its sacraments is, as one might perhaps expect, most strongly manifested in the writings of Catholics and Anglicans. Cardinal Hume's book, *To Be a Pilgrim,* is a good example. After setting the scene with a general discussion of what it means to speak of humans as pilgrims and of God as a pilgrim God, Hume goes on to discuss at length the divinely instituted sacraments which he understands as the gifts that God has given pilgrims to help them on their journey.[76]

In fact, the metaphor lends itself very well to this stress on communality. Most actual pilgrims have never "gone alone." It is only when the pilgrim figure starts to approximate to the hero archetype of myth and literature that he becomes a solitary—usually male—figure.[77] In real life, the traditional

---

[74] Wyon, *On the Way,* 33.

[75] Baggott, *Pilgrim,* 75–6.

[76] Basil Hume, *To Be a Pilgrim: A Spiritual Notebook* (Middlegreen, Slough: St. Paul Publications, 1984).

[77] Monica Furlong (*Travelling In* [1971; reprinted Cambridge: Cowley Publications, 1984] 60) remarks, "Literature abounds in spiritual combats and spiritual journeys, but it is striking that the

pilgrimage has usually been a joint venture. Pilgrims tend to travel in bands. As Besnard puts it: "tout pelerinage est une confluence avec multitude de freres. Tout pèlerinage est une révélation de l'Église."[78] Further, the biblical background to the metaphor nearly always presupposes a group. It is the people of Israel who are led out of Egypt and into the promised land. It is the cultic community of Hebrews that is moving onward toward the heavenly city. The church itself, as the language of Vatican II reminds us, is a pilgrim church. This solidarity of those making their individual pilgrimages is well brought out by Hume:

> The people of God on pilgrimage is made up of an endless variety of types. Each carries a special burden of responsibility—bishops, priests, religious and the laity who seek to sanctify the everyday world in which they live and work.[79]

So, the relation of the individual pilgrim to the pilgrim band is one issue which arises. A linked issue is that of the pilgrim's relation to others outside the immediate Christian community, along the way. As noted earlier, built into much of the older "pilgrim theology" is a marked disparagement of the fallen earthly world and its temporal city, and a tendency to focus on the individual's flight from this. Earthly responsibilities are viewed as important, but care for one's fellow human beings beyond setting them on the same path to eternal salvation is not so much an integral part of the overall pilgrimage, as a kind of unfortunate temporary necessity. There may well be an affirmation that the pilgrim has a duty to help build the kingdom in the world (or at least to replicate the heavenly city as well as possible), but this is not the Christian's ultimate concern; the true Christian always has her or his eyes fixed on the next world. As Gutiérrez points out, in such a context charity becomes one "virtue" for the heaven-bound individual to perfect, rather than the overriding keynote of the Christian life.[80] Individual perfection rather than social justice is to the fore.

Many contemporary writers are more convinced of the primacy of social justice component in the Bible and they try to incorporate it fully into their concept of the spiritual life as expressed within the framework of the metaphor of pilgrimage. Again, this is especially well exemplified in Hume's writing:

---

voyager or combatant is rarely a woman. Woman is, again and again, the inspirer of the journey or the task . . . but she is not the explorer."

[78] Besnard, "Le sens chrétien," 180.

[79] Hume, *To Be a Pilgrim*, 200.

[80] Gutiérrez, *We Drink from Our Own Wells*, 14–15.

The pilgrim's progress today passes through a world of beauty and opportunity. Yet it also winds through valleys of death and cruelty never previously explored. The pilgrim cannot pass by the hungry masses or those who clamour for justice and the recognition of their human dignity. The pilgrim's mind and heart are fixed on far horizons but must never ignore or make light of injustice, pain and deprivation here in the passing world. Each day provides for the pilgrim the tasks that have to be undertaken.[81]

Hume is careful to emphasize that these tasks are not extraneous, saying:

> They do not distract the pilgrim, nor deflect us from our goal. They are themselves the road we must pursue in our search for God and the fulfilment of His will.[82]

Another manner of resolving the dilemma within the framework of the metaphor is to see outward ethical behavior as the result of success in the continuing inner pilgrimage and to continue to maintain the importance of individual development for this reason. Baggott takes this position:

> [F]or in thus realizing himself the pilgrim brings the greatest progress to the social order. The truth of this becomes apparent when we understand that the highest selfhood of the individual can never be a selfish one.[83]

Baggott also thinks that if one envisages one's pilgrimage in terms of Christ's own pilgrimage, there need be no necessary tension between participation in the society of this world, and looking with joy to the resurrected life.

It should be said, though, that the old correlation between pursuit of individual salvation and disparagement of the created world is not strongly present in most contemporary writings. Today, few writers seem to be developing pilgrim theologies which are rooted in the world-disparaging theologies of Hebrews and the Gospel of John in which the world itself, and not merely the old carnal nature, becomes Egypt and wilderness and in which the promised land and the heavenly city are strictly future and postponed to

---

[81] Hume, *To Be a Pilgrim*, 157. Wallis (*Agenda For Biblical People*, 97) writes of the gospel calling us to a "downward pilgrimage" toward identification with the poor and oppressed. The way runs through a solidarity with the suffering world, not in flight from it.

[82] Hume, *To Be a Pilgrim*, 158. The picture of a people ministering to others and to themselves as they travel toward God is perhaps captured better by the terminology of "sojourning" than by the terminology of "pilgrimage." The latter emphasizes journey toward a destination, while the former focuses on the present state and life of those on the journey. As noted earlier, the idea of a ministering community living as sojourners, and moving ahead together in pilgrimage, is prominent in the writings of Wallis. See, e.g., *Agenda for Biblical People*, 101; 139.

[83] Baggott, *Pilgrim*, 33–34.

the next life. Rather, most contemporary pilgrim theologies seem to be much more specific about what it is that pilgrims must up and leave; it is not "the world" *in toto*, but just those aspects of it antithetical to true Christian growth and achievement of the final goal. The leaving of the pilgrim is a figure for bidding farewell to sinfulness and situations that hold back one's development. Consequently there is less of a tendency to confuse flight from evil with flight from the material world in which evil exists. And the Christian pilgrimage becomes more a measured journey toward greater humanity and toward the life of resurrection rather than a kind of running jump toward eternity.

However, it would be true to say that although the element of denial of the world has lessened in contemporary pilgrimage theologies, the metaphors of pilgrimage and journey still appear to have a certain tendency to focus the Christian's thought on the "not yet"; to inculcate a certain dissatisfaction with the present and with the mundane structures of earthly life, and to foster an ideal of detachment from these. In this regard writers such as Sharon Parks have characterized them as masculine metaphors in that they appear to reflect men's tendency to "tell and recognize their story of becoming primarily in terms that celebrate moments of separation and differentiation," as opposed to women's tendency to "tell and recognize their stories in terms of moments of attachment and relation."[84] They emphasize leaving and questing rather than home, relationality and building.[85] This is particularly the case where the journeyer/pilgrim figure has become fused in the mind of the writer with the archetypal hero/dragon-slayer figure who enacts a separation/initiation/return pattern which is fundamentally alien to the traditional experience of women.[86] For this reason, Parks and others have argued that

[84] Parks, "Pilgrimage, Home, and Revelation: Spirituality as Nurture toward a Vision of our Planet as a Dwelling for the Whole Human Family," paper presented to the Ecumenical Institute of Spirituality, Florida, 1987. Here Parks is summarizing the insights of Carol Gilligan, Mary Belenky and colleagues.

[85] These points are also taken up and discussed in Kathryn Allen Rabuzzi, *The Sacred and the Feminine: Toward a Theology of Housework* (New York: Seabury, 1982).

[86] Not all would assent, however, to this categorization of male/questing and female/home and relationality. For example, William C. James ("The Canoe Trip as Religious Quest," *Studies in Religion* 10 [1981]) takes specific issue with Rabuzzi's separation of the "questing" (male) and "nesting" (female) realms, saying, "Throughout this paper I have been quoting, even from nineteenth-century accounts, the testimony of female as well as of male canoeists. . . . Of a dozen poets cited by the author of *The Romance of the Canadian Canoe* as having celebrated the canoe in poetry, one-half are women. . . . The photographs in a recent book, *Canoeing and Kayaking*, show a woman demonstrating the arts of paddling and portaging. There is, I think, something important in these facts, something which ought to make it possible for women to develop the ramifications of this particular quest story, rather than prematurely abandoning it as an exclusively male preserve" (p. 161).

the metaphors are not all-sufficient; they have to be supplemented by imagery of homemaking and abiding. This criticism mirrors another more traditional criticism of the metaphors: namely, that they are unable to pick up on that aspect of the biblical message which encourages us to see creation as good and to care for the earth and build the kingdom. To this extent one might say that the Christian tradition itself contains a warring blend of feminine and masculine ideals (according to stereotype). Only in the language of the writer on the Christian life, the question becomes one of how one can be simultaneously a steward and a pilgrim.

Some writers are also very uncomfortable with the metaphors of pilgrimage and journey for the reason, mentioned earlier, that they appear to make the goal or destination the all important thing, and to either denigrate or instrumentalize the stages and living along the way:

> When we think of a journey, we think of an undertaking that has some length, that requires preparation, that has various stages or landmarks along the way, and always, that has a clearly defined destination. . . . The various stages along the way acquire value insofar as they contribute to the goal, which lies at the journey's end.[87]

The writer in this case, Carol Ochs, finds the instrumentalizing consequences of the metaphor insupportable, and advocates jettisoning the image of the journey—and one would assume that of pilgrimage. It is her view that it would be more appropriate to visualize our spiritual life as a destinationless "walk" where the emphasis is on enjoying the walk and the company of fellow strollers and where the value lies in the experience of the walk itself, and not in some distant goal.[88] Such a change of image would avoid the problems of instrumentalizing charity as a "stage" to be passed through, and of failing to deal with other humans as ends in themselves. In fact, Catherine de Hueck Doherty's notion of the pilgrimage journey is in some ways like this walk. She calls the Christian pilgrimage "strange" in its unhurriedness, and speaks of it as being "formless" in that people stop and start along the way helping people as they go.[89] For her, though, the journey is still most definitely toward a fixed destination.

---

[87] Carol Ochs, *Women and Spirituality* (Totowa, NJ: Rowman and Allanheld, 1983) 117.
[88] Ibid.
[89] Doherty, *Strannik*, 24.

Problems and Possibilities

It seems, then, that the authors themselves have highlighted some of the potential problems with the metaphors of "pilgrimage" and "journey," and some of their strengths. Of the problems discussed in the last section, those relating to the "masculine" aspects of the metaphor are perhaps the most troubling. The metaphors are valuable insofar as they foster a spirit of openness to adventure and change, and responsibility for setting out on one's own path to responsibility and spiritual maturity. They are dangerous insofar as they construe this journey in such a way as to put the stress upon the aspect of "leaving behind" and insofar as they equate spiritual movement with a repudiation of human relationship (esp. of relationship with women, the mother above all) and groundedness in the created world. At this level I am in strong agreement that the metaphor is in serious need of supplementation by another, such as stewardship, which has the structural demand of at least temporary dwelling and cultivation.

As we have seen, in a criticism directly related to the one discussed directly above, there are those who also raise objections to the metaphors on the grounds that these see the whole point of existence as getting from A to B and never mind the in-between. The critics see this preoccupation with the goal as a betrayal of Jesus' emphasis on relationality and social justice and as fostering a highly instrumentalizing view of charity. These criticisms are all part and parcel of the overall objection to the assessment of the earth as a negative environment, a place of exile, that underlay the older pilgrim theology. If one agrees with the general theological outlook underlying the criticism, one will be apt to find these aspects of modern developments of the pilgrimage metaphor troubling. However, should this prevent one from using the metaphors of "pilgrimage" and even "journey" at all? Perhaps not. As we have seen, many authors have jettisoned the dualistic theology while retaining the metaphors. It does not necessarily follow that the valuing of heaven or of the as-yet-unrealized kingdom must lead to a devaluing of the present. A life envisaged as a journey toward heaven and toward the kingdom need not by any means be a life lived in disregard of the present or of the needs of those around one. If God is understood to be travelling, perhaps even evolving, with each individual pilgrim and the whole pilgrim band of the church or of humanity, then the value of the present, in which God is moving with us, is more firmly established. The metaphor of life as "pilgrimage" has a radically different feel if the notion of God as Pilgrim is taken with great seriousness and the final destination becomes the Kingdom of God's intent as opposed to a kind of celestial city frozen in a state of glorious perfection and simply waiting for our arrival.

And in terms of the general discussion of the relation of humanity to the divine and also to our own godliness, I am not sure that it is possible or even entirely desirable to try to get away entirely from the metaphors of pilgrimage and journey. What other ways are there to describe development toward greater being and closer union with God? One can certainly speak in the language of maturation, of organic growth. And one can emphasize the social aspect of the human and speak of mutual nurture and growth. But it seems to me that these ways of speaking have their own shortcomings insofar as they do not reflect the experience of those who have a pronounced feeling of being less than perfect and who exercise a degree of autonomy in setting out to try to change; to chart a course in life in accordance with ideals or a call that they have experienced. Journeying, voyaging, pilgrimaging and so on are the only metaphors that can pick up this aspect of human aspiration and decision. In the case of feminist critiques, I would argue that rather than say that because "traditional" women have not experienced life in these terms of linear pursuit of a goal we should avoid journey language, perhaps both at the actual and metaphorical levels journey should become a greater part of female life, just as homemaking should become more a part of the male life. It may be that women are far more in need of the journey metaphor than men; it could have a corrective capacity, just as that of homemaking or stewardship might have for the overly goal-oriented man.

There is also another reason why Christians are unlikely to move completely away from metaphors of pilgrimage and journey. For those Christians who continue to shape their religion at least in part in the light of the Bible, the metaphors have the added attraction of reflecting faithfully a strong pattern to be found there. The Tanakh in particular, is a record of journeys in response to God's call. The Gospels arrange Jesus' life in the shape of a journey, and Acts and the letters of Paul are theological travelogues to some high degree. The important thing to note is the *diversity* of these journeys because when writers speak of life as "pilgrimage" or "journey" the theological implications will differ tremendously according to which biblical journeys they have in mind. If it is Hebrews one may end up with a journey envisaged as one from one sphere of being to another. If it is Exodus one may have a journey from bondage to liberation. If it is the gospels, the pilgrim following in Christ's steps may be tracing what she sees as Christ's journey toward the establishment of justice which ended in death, or he may be tracing what he sees as a journey toward the Father in obedience. The possibilities are numerous.

"Pilgrimage," and its more secular relation "journey," are likely to endure as guiding life-metaphors for mainstream Christians. They are biblically rooted, deeply embedded in the tradition, and congenial because of the way that their structures can reflect analogically the progress of the spirit. The question that confronts us is one of how they are to be developed. Here, as we have seen, there appear to be a number of dangers, chiefly revolving around the issues of spiritual narcissism and denigration of the Creation. With these in mind, we need to develop the metaphor with a greater eye to its communal dimension and to that aspect of the creator God which leads us to affirm the goodness of the created order. We need also to take seriously the idea of the Pilgrim God who works with us to *create* the destination, as well as to draw us close.

9

The Theological Task in Hand

There are two dimensions to the task of appraising the symbolic heritage of one's part of the Christian tradition. The first is the practical examination of how, exactly, the symbols actually function in the discourse of the tradition and how they may reflect and shape Christian experience. The second dimension is more overtly theological. It is the consideration of what it means to "evaluate" symbols. Some clear criteria need to be established lest one fall prey to the kind of magpie syncretism which is characterized by a gleeful collecting of sparkly symbols from different traditions or from one's own in pursuit of building a new nest of self-realization in which to roost.[1] In relation to discussion of the Christian-life images, we see this in the kind of approach that says: the warrior image helps me develop my sense of independence, I'll weave that in; the stewardship metaphor helps me relate to the earth better, I'll weave that in. The impulse to bring together all that is best and most helpful may well be a sound one, but the telos needs being made explicit.

The methodological question posed at the beginning of the dissertation was: What does it mean to evaluate our inherited images and to propose changes or reprioritizations in our language about the Christian life, and indeed about God? First of all, it should be said that when we evaluate religious ideas we are seeking what is *true*. This word, along with other words

[1] This kind of process can of course happen at the community level, however it is more obvious in individuals. It seems especially common in connection with New Age outgrowths of humanistic psychology with its latent telos of total realization of one's inner potentialities—usually envisaged in Jungian terms.

that imply absolute conviction about a thing's rightness or wrongness, has a bad odor about it for those who are convinced that the world is so complex that none can say for certain what be true. Many religions exist. The jury is out until eternity. Who can say which is "true"? Many cultures exist and disagree upon fundamental moral issues. Who, if anyone, holds the "true" view? Only the force of circumstance demanding action will prompt us to come down firmly on an issue. But the fact that we *will* come down on an issue points to the fact that the notion of truth and value do indeed have meaning for us—if only when they are about to be snatched away from us. Whatever the risks of the dangers of misguided absolutizing and ideological imperialism, I wish to retain the word "true"—to retain it to refer to the quality of authenticity that people respond to in an image which they believe: describes the world with some accuracy, speaks convincingly of their place within it, and calls them forth to be what in their hearts they believe they have been created to be.

To look at the images in terms of the truth that they are seen to hold, is to ask in what way they do speak accurately of the cosmos, of the individual's experience within it, and of the true nature of the human being. One may also ask whether the images have an absolute or instrumental truth or goodness: can they have a practical value of a therapeutic variety even if one disagrees with the broad theological picture that generally accompanies them? If one is going to winnow out some as unhealthy or unhelpful what are the criteria for doing this? And how shall one set about the finding of new ones and assessing their suitability? An additional issue of importance is the rhetorical power of symbols. It is important to consider what it is about certain ways of presenting them which lends them a special effectiveness— for good or ill, depending upon one's perspective.

A number of other questions also need to be raised. These concern the theologian and her or his audience. For whom is the project being carried out? Is it a helpful thing to be trying to get churchgoers to reappraise their symbolism? Is it pointless? Even if people are convinced of the need for change, can new symbols be created to order? Will they have any power, particularly in the context of prayer and worship? Should such issues be any concern of the theologian?

Evaluating the Truthfulness of the Images

All Have an Established Absolute or Dependent Truth Status

One could perhaps preempt certain areas of the evaluative task by responding rather flatly that the images are all in the Bible and that there is no need to question their truth status, justify or condemn them, or employ them selectively. They are all rooted in God's own revelation of the way that things are and should be. God may exceed human understanding, but we have been given firm grounds for speaking of God in such terms as Father, Lord, King, and so on. These are not metaphors, nor analogies. They were verbally or propositionally revealed. Likewise, in relation to God and God's saving work we may speak with accuracy of ourselves as God's stewards, servants, citizens. We are not mistaken. We are not unsure.[2] Some of our language such as that of the race or that of union with the vine may be figurative, but the truthful status even of these is guaranteed by God's having established the figure itself. As Horace Bushnell put it, the Divine Logos who is in the world "weaves into nature types or images that have an inscrutable relationship to mind and thought."[3] God stands potentially expressed everywhere.[4] Thus Timmerman can develop the figure of the True Vine with confidence: "The concept of the spiritual fruit is an analogy: a divine principle *rooted* in physical reality."[5] As to which dimensions of the world may be drawn upon by us or were drawn upon by the writers of the scriptures, it is generally said that these were somehow specially indicated by God. In such a context, the only appropriate response to the symbols is to show how beautifully they

[2] For this kind of approach see, e.g., Carl Henry, *God, Revelation and Authority*, vol. 1: *God Who Speaks and Shows* (Waco, TX: Word Books, 1976). Henry (p. 27) writes: "Judeo-Christian religion centers supremely in the living God self-disclosed in his Word, and this biblically attested Word is communicated intelligibly in meaningful sentences." Gordon Clark's writings provide an example of extreme literalist position on revelation which insists that God revealed what was in God's mind in words that permit us to know it truly. This is vital, he says, to any meaningful notion of revelation. "In philosophy and theology analogy is not of much use. If two known objects are compared, for example, if we say that man is the image of God, it is not immediately evident what the point of similarity is . . . we need a definite, positive, identification of the similarity. Analogy does not give us this information" (*The Philosophy of Gordon Clark* [Philadelphia: Presbyterian and Reformed, 1968] 77). Elsewhere he writes: "The metaphor or the parable has meaning only if there is some similarity that can be stated in non-metaphorical, literal language. . . . It seems obvious that if we have no knowledge of God there would be no basis for choosing the parable 'God loves us' instead of the parable 'God hates us' " (*Religion, Reason, and Revelation* [Philadelphia: Presbyterian and Reformed, 1961] 143). Further on he states: "The Scriptures contain metaphors, figures of speech, and symbolism . . . [b]ut since symbolic language and metaphor depend on literal meaning, the most intelligible and understandable expressions are to be found in *the literal theological statements, such as those in Romans*. And outside the Bible the most accurate and satisfactory expressions of Christianity are the carefully worded creedal statements of the Westminster Confession" (p. 146; emphasis mine).

[3] Bushnell, "Preliminary Dissertation on the Nature of Language as Related to Thought and Spirit," in idem, *God in Christ* (1849; reprinted New York: Garland, 1987) 43.

[4] Ibid., 30.

[5] Timmerman, *Way*, 8.

express the truths of our lives; how they speak to different dimensions of our responses to God and together illuminate the complex whole of the Christian life.

To the religious conservative, there appears to be a basic flaw in seeing these images as "metaphors" or "models" if by these terms one implies a lack of authority or ontological grounding. The very grounds for calling for an evaluation of truthfulness are in error. He or she might agree that the whole structure of the process of *natural* human knowing is metaphorical— the slow creation of a web of similarities, or an endless series of small knowledge explosions caused by inspired collisions of category or realm— but will surely not agree that *Christian* knowing is the same kind of process, a kind of halting circumscription of the spiritual by means of similarities projected onto it from the material world. The concept of the new seeing through the Spirit and through the spectacles of Scripture is supposed to bring one the ability to see the world as it truly is, and to be able to speak of matters religious with an accuracy impossible to even the righteous pagan. Those focusing on the human origins of language and pointing accordingly to the weak epistemological status of all religious concepts are simply proceeding from pagan and misguided assumptions. The response of a John White to the argument that metaphor involves the characterizing of one realm in terms of another and that therefore to say warfare is a metaphor for Christian life drawn from the everyday world, is to say that the whole thing has been put back to front.[6] Christians are truly involved in a cosmic battle against evil, and of this all specific earthly battles are mere reflections, echoes, or perhaps tiny fragments. This is the logic that is applied by Karl Barth when he insists that we do not by some analogy draw the word "Lord" from the human realm and apply it to God; rather, God is in the primal sense "Lord" and earthly uses of the word are derivative of this original use.[7]

These kinds of positions, of which a spectrum exists, assume a portion of

---

[6] White, *Fight*, 216.

[7] "We possess no analogy on the basis of which the nature and being of God as the Lord can be accessible to us. We certainly think we are acquainted with other lords and lordships. But it is not the case that we have only to extend our idea of lord and lordship into the infinite and absolute and we will finally arrive at God the Lord and His lordship. The decisive distinguishing mark of the lordship of God is this fact that He is really the Lord over all things and therefore supremely over ourselves, the Lord over our bodies and souls, the Lord over life and death. No idea that we can have of 'lord' or 'lordship' will ever lead us to this idea, even though we extend it infinitely. . . . Only as we know God's lordship will our own ideas of lordship have content, and within their limits, existence . . . [and] [i]f we know about God as the Lord . . . it is in consequence of God's revelation alone" (Karl Barth, *Church Dogmatics*, vol. 2.1: *The Doctrine of God* (ed. G. W. Bromiley and T. F. Torrance; Edinburgh: T. & T. Clark, 1957) 75–76. Barth continues to make the same point about other terms such as "Creator" and "Reconciler."

the Christian message that is indisputable, clear, literal.[8] Such patently symbolic dimensions as the Bible does have are clearly interpretable with reference to this core. Or more peripheral symbolisms may be interpreted by reference to more foundational ones.[9] Relatively speaking, they are less important, but even these lesser symbols are not to be supplanted or added to by modern equivalents. The broad theological contours of the images that we have been examining belong to the heart of the Gospel. To the most conservative eye, they would in no way be seen as open to alteration or disposal. Each is rooted in a particular, revealed, understanding of God. As God's stewards we respond in gratitude to the Creator. As God's servants our gratitude takes the form of obedient service to the will of the Lord. As pilgrims we are those who are embarked upon a journey toward reconciliation with the loving God who has offered redemption and a new pattern for life in the Son—and so on.

This kind of nexus of response and divine image in which all facets are seen to coexist harmoniously is found also in writings which establish the inevitability of the contours of Christian faith by appeal to their psychological groundings in the human response to the divine. This is brought out well in the writings of James M. Gustafson, who tends to eschew detailed justifications of revelation, offering instead a kind of psychological rationale as a support for the existent composite understanding of God and world. Here is one of the many passages in which he ties each of the dimensions of God's nature into motivating dimensions of the religious life and makes an extended case for the need for each of them:

> The sense of radical dependence is correlated with the experience of and belief in God as Creator. The sense of gratitude is correlated with the experience of God as beneficent, as good in his creation, sustenance, and redemption of the world. The sense of repentance is correlated with the experience of God as moral authority and as judge. The sense of obligation is correlated with the experience of God as the orderer and sustainer of life. The sense of possibility is correlated with the experience of God as one who continues to act creatively and redemptively, as a God of hope. The sense of direction is correlated with the experience of God as the *telos*, the end of all creation. . . .
>
> [I]t is *one* God who is experienced, whose being, presence, activity, and relatedness to man is not separable into discrete aspects of creator, judge, end, and so forth. . . . The texture of experience, the theological articulation of it,

---

[8] The idea of the literal core may not always be linked to theories of propositional or verbal revelation.

[9] As Austin Farrer (*The Glass of Vision* [Westminster: Dacre, 1948] 111) puts it, "within the field of revealed truth, the principal images provide a canon to the lesser images."

and even the morality of the religious community become distorted when useful distinctions become separate aspects or moments, such as those that are made between God the Creator and God the Redeemer, or between moments of his creative activity and moments of his redemptive activity. The schema distorts the human reference as well."[10]

All Images May be Evaluated in the Light of One

Despite all the warnings about limited human vision and the metaphorical "is and is not" quality of all language about God, those who continue to write as Christian theologians generally continue to treat one small portion of the biblical revelation as safe high ground. Sallie McFague may perhaps be taken as a good example of this one hold barred approach. By granting what she views as the root metaphor of Christianity immunity from epistemological scrutiny she guarantees that all her probing and assessing of images will not ultimately lead her to a new position which is not recognizably Christian. The picture of the world as the creation of a loving God who acts to save is taken as a given, even though all the specifics of the tradition are held up for scrutiny.[11] Rudolf Bultmann once remarked, "Perhaps we may say that behind all the objections against demythologizing there lurks a fear that if it were carried to its logical conclusion it would make it impossible for us to speak of an act of God."[12] This does, indeed, seem to be the bottom line. If one does not secure one's enterprise to the mooring of a personal God who acts, and acts specifically in a way revealed preeminently by Christ, one's theological enterprise drifts off into foreign seas. One has entered the tramp and vagrant world of the post-Christian theologian where no fixed center of truth secures the issue of the flux.[13] Liberal and radical theologians are aware of this bottom line. An uneasiness overtakes them as they sail further and further away from the idea of a fixed truth. By according God's action a non-metaphorical status so that it can be the criterion by which they can judge and ultimately validate other metaphors, they retain a toehold in traditional Christianity.

The reasons for establishing this high ground are rarely spelt out with the kind of detail that Bultmann himself offered. What, in effect, seems to happen is that after much discussion of the relativity of all viewpoints, theologians vote with the heart and land foursquare back in the court of their lifelong

---

[10] Gustafson, *Can Ethics Be Christian?* (1975; reprinted Phoenix Books, n.d.) 92–93.

[11] See, e.g., McFague, *Models*, 30; 44.

[12] Bultmann, "Bultmann Replies to His Critics," in Hans Werner Bartsch, ed., *Kerygma and Myth: A Theological Debate* (rev. ed.; New York: Harper and Row, 1961) 196.

[13] To paraphrase William James's description of the pragmatists view of truth (*Pragmatism*, 117).

faith with the assertion that in the life of Jesus, a profound truth about God is revealed. This truth tends to get smaller and smaller as the theologian goes along, dwindling to an assertion that what the parables reveal is a divinity who relativizes all structures of this world and thus reveals a particular kind of revolutionizing love. This is the kind of process we see, for example, in the works of Sallie McFague. Thus, in *Metaphorical Theology*, in addition to judging models by their fit with our experience, McFague suggests judging models according to how they fit or do not fit with "the surprising rule of God as we have it in the parables and the parable of Jesus,"[14] according to the "root-metaphor of Christianity," which she defines variously as the kingdom of God,[15] or Jesus as exemplar of this.[16] Insofar as she phrases the question like this, McFague continues to speak to those for whom Christ is the central lens for the interpretation of reality. However, there is a problem with this. She also wants to say that Jesus realigns rather than initiates our understanding of God,[17] that he does so in the manner of a parable, and that other religions may also provide metaphoric insight into the divine. In her most recent book she describes Christian faith as basically a claim that there is a power in the universe on the side of life and its fulfillment and that we have some clues for fleshing out this claim in the life, death, and appearances of Jesus of Nazareth.[18] It is never made clear in any of her works why someone should look to Christ rather than somewhere else for illumination. Nor is it made clear why anyone should really wish to retain the language of traditional theism to express themselves. There is much discussion of the revealing dimension of religious metaphor, but a discomfort with pushing its truth claims far.

One of the unfortunate ironies of doing metaphorical and narrative theology is that you often end up being boxed into systematic discussions of precisely the kind that made you feel a blessed escape when you first lit upon the possibilities of symbol. Those drawn toward these forms of theology are usually attracted by the non-systematic, tentative dimension of symbol and metaphor. They find this to be somehow truer to the nature of religious experience, and indeed truer to the complex way in which they believe God to reveal Godself. But when they try to develop a case for the primacy of this delicate mode of discourse, they are obliged to adopt a mode of discourse that runs flat counter to it. Horace Bushnell's writings provide a very good

---

[14] McFague, *Metaphorical Theology*, 22.

[15] Ibid., 109.

[16] Ibid., 111.

[17] Ibid., 50.

[18] McFague, *Models*, x.

example of this kind of tension. He developed a theory of words and symbols as the pots or husks of spiritual truths which, by virtue of their material origins, necessarily falsify to some degree these truths that they convey. Language, he believed, could provide only hints or images of the truth; descriptions are therefore not determinate propositions that clearly lay out the reality of a thing—rather, they are symbols that attempt to throw light on a truth by means of a particularly appropriate choice of type. It was his conviction that, because of this, the disclosure of truth is effected most efficiently by a constant multiplication of contradictory signs which play off one another and in the pattern of their conflict shed crossing lights on the field of knowledge. Dogmatic theology is theology which rests on a misguided use of words as highly determinative and reflective of the truths that they convey. It is prone to confuse divine matters with the physical mechanistic figures that underlie the terminology employed to describe them. The model of competing definitions is the one that works best for theology. The poet understands the use of competing definitions perhaps best of all, and it is to poetry that the theologian should look as model:

> [I]f we are ever to have any sufficient or tolerably comprehensive theology, it can never be matured, save through the medium of an esthetic elevation in the sensibilities of our souls, which only the possible union of the life to God can produce. For the scriptures offer us the great truths of religion, not in propositions, and articles of systematic divinity. They only throw out in bold and living figures, often contrary or antagonistic in their forms, the truths to be communicated. Language is itself an instrument, wholly incapable of anything more adequate. Therefore, what we want, in the receiving of light from the Scripture, is a living, ingenuous, patient, pure sensibility—a heart so quickened by the Spirit of God, as to be delicately perceptive of God's meaning in the readings and symbols he gives us.[19]

All the same, Bushnell acknowledged the human need or desire to systematize, and wrote hefty systematic treatments of his own perspective on language and the nature of religious truth.

Even so, his systematizations have a different quality, for Bushnell had an option of which few liberal theologians today appear willing to avail themselves. He appealed without trepidation to divine inspiration and to the idea that the Logos had woven types into the world to assist us. If unable or unwilling to appeal confidently to such sources of understanding, the

---

[19] Bushnell, "A Discourse on Dogma and Spirit; or The True Reviving of Religion," in idem, *God in Christ*, 308. The foregoing overview of his description of the nature of language is drawn from this discourse, and from the "Preliminary Dissertation."

theologian is obliged to step onto the treadmill of fruitless attempts to establish the truth claims of language of the noumenal in terms convincing to those who deal only in the phenomenal. Yet, one might reasonably argue that if you are going to continue to speak of the validity of the root metaphor of God's salvific action and to judge all the subsidiary metaphors in its light, you might just as well appeal to some insight from this God salvifically acting. God may only be said to be acting from the point of view of the eye of faith, and the one who speaks from the perspective of an awareness of such a God must surely be aware in some sense of communication with God.

Why Retain the High Ground of Theistic Action?

Maurice Wiles has commented that in the religiously diverse environment of the contemporary world, many individuals and communities seem to want to call simultaneously for an absoluteness of commitment and a recognition of the limitation of their own perspectives.[20] This is precisely the dynamic we encounter in dealing with the limited nature but absolute claims of religious language. If one is going to take the middle ground and continue to evaluate the symbols of Christianity in the light of a general notion of God's saving purpose as made particularly clear in Christ, while at the same time wishing to emphasize the relative perspective of one's views, one has to make a strong case for staying put. It is curious how often writers continue to devote great energy to the evaluating of symbols of a tradition without explaining why they continue on in that tradition at all, given their view of the relative status of their understanding of God.[21] One has to be honest about the subjective dimension that makes one stay. We are forced by the recognition of the epistemological, cultural and historical limits of our claims to ask the

---

[20] Wiles, *Faith and the Mystery of God* (Philadelphia: Fortress, 1982) 4.

[21] Here one might note that the theologian may be in a nice bind. If he or she has been trained academically in the history of Christianity alone, declaring its insufficiency and moving on will most likely lead to a necessary career change—or it will lead to writing generalist books picking up aspects of other traditions which the writer has been drawn to in private reading. This last option is surely that of the tenured person or emeritus/a. A discussion in a Harvard Divinity School theology colloquium in the Spring semester 1989 bore in upon me the extent to which one's circumstances can make it a hard choice to maintain intellectual honesty. Two comments registered in my memory particularly: one to the effect that if a World Council of Churches Dialogue participant became too self-evidently Buddhist or Muslim as a result of their various dialogues, they would probably do themselves out of a job. In some situations one's livelihood depends on being "one thing or the other." The other comment came from a person who freely admitted that she had no intention of revealing her actual theological views on some points to the church where she works because this would make them suspicious of her and she would then not be able to do anything good there. The temptation for the theologian to be persuaded by this kind of logic is great.

question of whether Christian ideas may be worth retaining because they may
be said to be at least as true, if not more so, than other interpretations. It
seems as though there are two ways to go. Either one can set about empirical
evaluations of the symbols and take leave when they prove unsatisfactory
according to criteria established on some presumably extra-paradigmatic
basis. Or, if one still finds oneself resistant to relinquishing in one's heart the
absolute claim that one's mind has reluctantly let go, one must make some
sense of this fact—clarify the reasons for continuing to take the tradition with
ultimate seriousness, despite a recognition of its limited perspective.[22] The
question is one of how the relative may be said to have absolute
importance—at least for oneself. One possible response is to say that history
or fate has placed one in a given tradition, and this tradition affords its own
limited but nonetheless revelatory glimpse of the true nature of things. H.
Richard Niebuhr's explanation of his sense of loyalty to the cause of Christ
and his theory of the possibility of a vision of the absolute through partial
means, offers one of the clearest statements of the latter option.[23]

It is very hard to be clear in one's mind why one may be espousing a position of fatedness or loyalty. Individual persons will have to ask themselves
whether they take this position because of a real feeling that Jesus has a profound and undeniable significance or whether they may be taking it because
they are unwilling to uproot from the familiar and to run the risk of upsetting
the living and the loved dead by rejecting the symbol that is or was the center
of their lives. For many people, the rejection of Jesus as the cornerstone of
their religious life feels like a betrayal of their parents and those others they
respected, of whose lives Christ was the center. Loyalty to and love of others

[22] One could, of course, continue without clarifying this issue. Humans can live with a high
level of ambiguity in their thoughts about life's meaning. Ambiguity is not necessarily bad. It
is, perhaps, not in human nature to be able to make rapid and sharp transitions between different
ways of thinking about the world. Ambiguity is the mark of the overlap of ways of thinking that
each have their own cogency. Only as the new way becomes clearer does it become possible and
necessary to reconstrue the old.

[23] See, e.g., Niebuhr, *The Meaning of Revelation* (1941; reprinted Macmillan Paperback, 1960)
13–14; 16; and *Responsible Self*, 42–44. Niebuhr is particularly interesting because he (*Revelation*, 60) is one of the few theologians who openly assert that going off and trying to participate
in other community's truths will probably lead you to desert your own. It is interesting to compare this with Wilfred Cantwell Smith's works which focus on attempting to know the "other"
as fully as possible but which are marked by the author's insistence that all this knowing and
resultant becoming will stop short at a certain point. People will "wittingly choose to maintain"
their distinctions (*Religious Diversity: Essays by Wilfred Cantwell Smith* [New York: Harper and
Row, 1976] 114). Similarly, his proposed world theology will "not displace but subsume its
erstwhile sectional parts" (*Towards a World Theology: Faith and the Comparative Study of Religion*; [Philadelphia: Westminster, 1981] 130). This begs the question of why one would "wittingly" remain a Christian, having appreciated the truths of other people's faiths.

may prompt a decision of continued loyalty to Christ—if only in the realm of public declaration—and may turn a person from exploring other avenues that their intellect suggests to them. These issues are highly complex and painful. It is perhaps hard to be sure of the way that Christ continues to operate in one's life. Even the one who has moved to a different realm of religious understanding may be aware of Jesus standing behind their shoulder at certain moments. Is it because he is simply a figure who has been a part of our cultural lives so long that he cannot be exorcised? Is he a fictive figure who has become embedded to a point where no total escape is possible, or does he continue to abide because in some sense he is truly risen and walking alongside us? The answer can perhaps never be final. And perhaps that is why so few can depart from their tradition without a backward look.

Proceeding to Evaluate from the Standpoint of God's Salvific Love

If one is comfortable with judging the images in part according to the trueness to a particular aspect of the Christian message which one has accorded immunity for reasons of conviction or passion, then one will assess them in this light, looking to see whether they reflect it accurately and whether they lead people to shape their experience in accordance with this. Just what one thinks is the core of the gospel will, of course, incline one to judge certain images much more highly than others. As we saw, stewardship presents itself to writers such as John Hall as the most authentic construction of Christian, indeed human, existence.[24] For such persons, the other images serve simply to qualify the one which appears central to them. Pilgrimage helps to remind the steward of the temporariness and uncertainty of her tenure; warfare reminds her that dimensions of existence remain within and without her which resist easy nurture and turning toward the good; the image of athletic endeavour reminds her of the importance of developing endurance and direction in her life as God's steward.

However, this method of prioritizing and making one image central, then drawing upon the others has its dangers, one of which being that the guiding principle for prioritizing and selection can become utterly vague. We might, for example, affirm that at the heart of the Gospel is the perception of God's salvific love, but why and how would this lead us to say, for example, that spiritual belligerence is bad? Or that low self-esteem is a bad result of servant language? Or that nurture of one's talents is good? The idea of salvific love has to be developed in some definite way to make clear what the end is that God desires for God's creatures and how, in the short term confines of

---

[24] Hall, *Steward*; and idem, "Mission as a Function."

our daily lives, that good is to be brought about. Self-evidently judgments are being made upon the basis of a definite notion of the telos of human life and on the basis of principles according to which, when the needs of individuals and societies clash, prioritization can occur. As stated in the Preface, the evaluative comments made in the earlier chapters are rooted in the assumption that the world was created by force/spirit/being that intends and supports the development of all beings to the fullest extent of their potential, and this potential is understood in terms which owe much, on the one hand, to liberal humanism and which on the other hand derive from the biblical pictures of Christ and his followers.[25] One can only understand potential and the notion of the good in terms of one's own experience. I understand the fullest form of human life to be one in which one's freedom, dignity, compassion, and wisdom, and ability to live amicably and justly with others are brought to fruition.

I believe one needs to guard against slipping into the kind of language of "self-realization" found in the humanistic psychologies of this century. Isaac Franck has spoken trenchantly of the moral vacuousness of the concept of self-realization as it is presented in humanistic psychologies which assert that humans have a propensity toward self-actualization, then proceed to elevate this descriptive concept to a moral mandate: realize thyself.[26] No attempt is usually made, in such contexts, to clarify why certain propensities should be worthy of development and others not. Aristotle clearly set out the development of the rational as his telos. Bradley elevated the social self as the telos of development.[27] One may disagree with their choice of criterion for their teleology but it is at least explicit. Further, writers such as Abraham Maslow never tackle the issue of whether the world is such that it supports harmoniously the existence of millions all seeking personal realization.[28] There is no acknowledgement that self-realization always needs to be

---

[25] Although this thesis is short on discussion of specific biblical texts, their importance in providing a picture of Jesus is assumed. "To experience the impact of Jesus is, for the Christian . . . to recognize the particularities of Jesus, [even] if not in detail (for we do not know enough of them) . . . he was no universal or timeless symbol, but one who had *these* characteristics rather than *those*; not clay on which the imagination can work at will, but of specific shape and pattern. It was such a one who was 'of God' " (J. L. Houlden, *Connections: The Integration of Theology and Faith* [London: SCM, 1986] 182).

[26] Franck, "Self-Realization as Ethical Norm: A Critique," *The Philosophical Forum* 9 (Fall 1971) 2.

[27] Aristotle, *Nicomachean Ethics* (ed. Martin Ostwald; Indianapolis: Bobbs-Merrill, 1962) I. 7, 1097b23 – 1098a18, and X. 7, 1177b25 – 1178a5; F. H. Bradley, "My Station and its Duties," in *Ethical Studies* (Oxford: Clarendon, 1927) 160 – 213.

[28] For an extended discussion of these issues, see Don S. Browning, *Religious Thought and the Moral Psychologies* (Philadelphia: Fortress, 1987).

balanced by self-restriction. Franck notes that Kurt Goldstein, to whom writers such as Carl Rogers look as a founding figure, never endorsed self-realization as a self-explanatory good. He viewed self-actualization simply as a tendency that could be seen in human beings and did not afford it a normative status. Indeed, he identified it with the child's immature state and said it could only take place without harming others where society was organized to keep its harmful effects in check.[29]

Picking and choosing from the Christian tradition uncritically, or with the intent of taking only what nurtures certain dimensions of one's individual personality, is subject to all these same criticisms. So also is an uncritical use of the part of the stewardship image which sanctions the developing of one's own talents and potentials without concern for others. Don Browning makes the interesting comment that ''what one has in Erikson and Kohut, and even more so in the humanistic psychologies and Jung, are implicit metaphors of harmony and redemption—two of the great foundational metaphors of the Western religious tradition. What is missing in both are metaphors analogous to those of God as governor, that is, metaphors that point to those deep resources and demands stemming from the depth of life which make moral claims and provide moral supports to the life of moral seriousness.''[30]

This, I think, points us very clearly to the way that in one respect the life images of Christianity supplement each other, just as do the images of God which they accompany. Together they provide balance. It is a perfect example of Lakoff and Johnson's theory that when a concept is structured by many metaphors they usually fit together in a coherent fashion and jointly provide a coherent understanding of the concept as a whole.[31] From the sociological perspective one could describe this in terms of our having projected the necessary grounds for the ethical functioning of society. From the traditional believer's point of view, our well-being depends upon our living out our lives as citizens of God the legislator or orderer as well as living our lives as children of a loving parent.[32] There is no logical inconsistency in the existence of these two dimensions in the divine. As Paul Tillich writes, ''They cannot be separated; even the attempt to emphasize the one over and against the other destroys the meaning of both. The Lord who is not the Father is demonic; the Father who is not the Lord is sentimental.[33]

---

[29] Franck, ''Self-Realization,'' 20.

[30] Browning, *Religious Thought*, 237.

[31] Lakoff and Johnson, *Metaphors*, 86.

[32] It is for precisely these reasons that McFague (*Models*, 113; 182) stresses the importance of achieving a similar functional balance in new imagery used for God.

[33] Tillich, *Systematic Theology*, 1. 287. The fact that the images can be seen as complementary should not lead us to forget, however, that they are developed in different ways and can be construed in such ways as to reveal quite contradictory theologies. Real tension may exist between

Stressing the Empirical Dimension

If one is not comfortable with simply accepting the truth of the root metaphor of the tradition, one will have to reopen the question of how one authenticates *any* symbolization of reality, and one will also have to clarify even more carefully the ethical criteria that one is using to evaluate the symbols.

The statement that one encounters again and again in writings on metaphor in all fields, is that metaphor "both reveals and creates similarities" that despite its tentative quality, it does not simply present an arbitrary point of correspondence, but if it is valid will be shown to disclose an actual correspondence, only "creating" it to the degree that it uncovers something not previously recognized.[34] Theologians try to adopt the language of science (esp. physics and linguistics) to explain how it is that their symbols can both create and truly reveal and how, despite the imaginative element, truth claims can reasonably be made for religious constructions of reality.

Ian Barbour was one of the first to put forward what he viewed as a theological version of the "critical realist" view of metaphors and models found in science. Let us look at his argument as an example of the position. In science, says Barbour, the critical realist is the one who understands models to be partial but true insofar as they may actually speak of the world's structures:

> Descriptions of nature are human constructions but nature is such as to bear description in some ways and not others. No theory is an exact account of the world, but some theories agree with observations better than others because the world has an objective form all of its own.[35]

What this means is that

> the critical realist makes only a tentative commitment to the existence of entities something like those portrayed in the model. He says that gas molecules exist, and are in some ways like tiny elastic sphere—or, he would now say, like the wave and particle models of quantum physics.[36]

Barbour wants to argue that religious language is to be seen in the same way.

---

the view of creation expressed in the stewardship literature and that found in many of the theologies of warfare and pilgrimage. The dispositions fostered by each image qua ethical model may fit together much more tidily or complementarily than do the cosmologies and theologies with which they have been allied. We have seen that these tensions are often passed over in Christian life literature, but they remain latent and potentially problematic.

[34] I question this use of the word "create."
[35] Barbour, *Myths, Models and Paradigms*, 37.
[36] Ibid., 47.

Even though the verification processes differ, our religious models do make the claim to say something true about reality just as much as they create new ways of looking at it. The new ways are true ways in some real sense. The fundamental problem with all such claims, lies in how to establish whether the world actually *is* as the religious picture says that it is, in proving that the similarity or structure that the metaphor discloses is *real* in itself as opposed to real only as the products of our own projection are real. Can the images or models be verified or falsified in any meaningful sense? There are numerous problems, as Barbour admits, however he continues to maintain that despite the differences between models in science and religion, the divide is not absolute and the process of verification remains meaningful in the realm of religion:

> [E]ach of the *"subjective"* features of science . . . is *more* evident in the case of religion: 1) the influence of intepretation on data, 2) the resistance of comprehensive theories to falsification, and 3) the absence of rules for choice among paradigms. Each of the corresponding *"objective"* features of science is *less* evident in the case of religion: 1) the presence of common data on which disputants can agree, 2) the cumulative effect of evidence for or against a theory, and 3) the existence of criteria which are not paradigm-dependent.[37]

Barbour may not feel the divide is absolute, but it seems to have widened to a point where it comes perilously close to this. Let us consider briefly, why verification of religious claims is so problematic. What would it mean, to try and verify, say, the perception of life as pilgrimage which incorporates at least the idea that humans were created by a loving God (generally understood as Creator/Father), that they fell or fall from a state of goodness to sinfulness but by God's grace are permitted to journey back to Him?

It would mean, presumably, that you could determine that: (a) the world was created by and is governed by a God whose creatures seek reunion with their creator; (b) humans should be loving like their Creator; (c) they are not; or (d) the work of Jesus in some way permits the journey back toward goodness and God. The impossiblity of proving all these points to the satisfaction of an unconvinced observer is manifest. For one thing every perspective, be it theological or metaphysical, is subject to the criticism that it is the product of a limited subjective vision. Language and its categories themselves arise in the service of particular interests[38] and are correspondingly subject to the

---

[37] Ibid., 144–45.

[38] This point is explored in detail with particular reference to the Italian Humanist tradition in Ernesto Grassi, *Rhetoric as Philosophy* (University Park, PA: Pennsylvania State University Press, 1980). It was from the insights of such writers as Vico and Latini that the linguistic theories of such modern writers as Coleridge and Cassirer (that tend to be cited more often in

restrictions of their particular slant and are indeed to be suspected of serving
some fundamental need. The theistic worldview is no exception. It may be,
the cynic or reductionist might suspect, a useful fiction produced by society
as an underpinning for its self-perpetuation. It is hard to counter such arguments as Durkheim's to the effect that "the god of the clan . . . [is] nothing
else than the clan itself, personified and represented to the imagination."[39]
Much historical evidence speaks on his side. One can perhaps get around
this problem by an evasive manoeuver. Do as Durkheim did and say that this
does not mean that we are not talking about "reality": the "reality" of
society is profoundly real and important, and all religions are true insofar as
they answer to the given conditions of human existence. But let us face the
fact that when people speak of truth they generally do not think that it means
response to our exigencies. Pace James and others, it means that they think
that the religion's picture of things has some ontological basis in the nature of
things.[40]

Unfortunately, the matter is difficult to prove by means of establishing
some kind of empirical "fit" between theological model and the realm of
one's experience. The evidence around one might suggest that humans are
indeed wicked and could do with improvement, but as for a Creator God who
made them, and to whom they are travelling—the world itself, as Hume,
Kant, and their modern day followers demonstrate amply, offers no logically
compelling "evidence" for a divine creator of the kind envisaged by the
tradition, nor for the presence of loving and saving divine activity. The
assumption of such a deity is only reasonable to the degree that the individual
is subjectively convinced that some portion of the universe should be allowed
to speak more loudly than another in the discussion—that, in the words of
John Wisdom's example—the flowers in the deserted garden should attest to
the continued presence of a gardener rather than the weeds attesting to the
gardener's absence.[41] As to the idea that Jesus is the guaranteeing revelation
of God's nature, we are faced with the old conundrum to the effect that he

works on theology) grew. On these connections see, e.g., George Whalley, "Coleridge and
Vico"; Enzo Paci, "Vico and Cassirer"; and Stuart Hampshire, "Vico and the Contemporary
Theory of Language"; all in George Tagliacozzo and Hayden V. White, eds., *Giambattista Vico:
An International Symposium* (Baltimore: Johns Hopkins University Press, 1969).

[39] Durkheim, *Elementary Forms*, 236.

[40] A. O'Hear ("Statements of Religious Belief," *Religious Studies* 14 [1978] 365–66) makes
that point that if you convince a believer of the fact that God is, e.g., a projection of society's
ordering, the believer will now believe in a quite different way from that of his or her unen-
lightened co-religionists. A different religious position will have emerged.

[41] Wisdom, "Gods," *Proceedings of the Aristotelian Society* 45 (1944) 187; reprinted in
Anthony Flew, ed., *Logic and Language*, (1st ser.; Oxford: Blackwell, 1951).

could not be realized as such without a prior idea of what God was. He could offer a partial reinterpretation of God, but the idea of God preceded him. Faith in his gospel cannot be explained with complete rationality, nor conveyed with entire reasonableness, insofar as the reasonableness of the prior beliefs concerning God is not already established—which we have seen it is unlikely to be. A leap of faith into the charmed circle is necessary.

The issue of what constitutes "evidence" in the religious sphere is problematic in a number of other respects. First and foremost, as Ian Barbour himself admits, there is "a tendency for any set of basic beliefs to produce experiences which can be cited in support of those beliefs, which are then self-confirming."[42] We find behind the bush the treasure that we ourselves hid there.[43] If one has been raised with the idea of the world as fallen, but as travelling back in the light of grace to reunion with a loving Creator God, one is likely to see it in that light and to have a very hard time critiquing the position; it will seem manifestly reasonable. Familiarity produces, as William James puts it, the illusion of reality.[44]

Nevertheless, we are not completely trapped in received views. The events and experiences of our daily lives find meaning in the inherited patterns of interpretation, but also strain them. We move between discomfort and ease with our frameworks of interpretation. James speaks of the feeling of peace and ease that comes over the person who feels they have made sense of the universe.[45] Most of us have felt that for at least short periods of time; however, the events of our lives and the opposing interpretations of our companions frequently prove to undermine the newfound ease. We are nudged by these into reappraisals of our understandings. On other occasions it is the

---

[42] Barbour, *Myths, Models, and Paradigms*, 123.

[43] Nietzsche, "Truth and Falsity," 7.

[44] James ("The Sentiment of Rationality," in idem, *The Will to Believe and Other Essays in Popular Philosophy* (1897; reprinted New York: Dover Publications, 1956] 77) writes: "The daily contemplation of phenomena juxtaposed in a certain order begets an acceptance of their connection, as absolute as the repose engendered by theoretic insight into their coherence." It is interesting to consider the parallel insight of Ernst Gombrich (*Art and Illusion* [Princeton: Princeton University Press, 1956]) who has detailed the way that what is understood as "realism" in art is entirely dictated by the traditions of the age. This is an issue which Nelson Goodman has explored in detail in recent years. See, his *Languages of Art* (Indianapolis: Hackett, 1976) where we find such observations as: "Realism is relative, determined by the system of representation standard for a given culture or person at a given time" (p. 37); "Realistic representation . . . depends not upon imitation or illusion or information but upon inculcation" (p. 38); "Representational customs, which govern realism, also tend to generate resemblance. That a picture looks like nature often means only that it looks the way nature is usually painted." (p. 39)

[45] James, "Sentiment," 63.

unexpected brightness of events that prompts a reappraisal of grey pessimism. With regard to the premises of the pilgrimage image, this may mean that over the course of a lifetime, we may shift on many occasions between, for example, optimistic and negative views of human sinfulness or goodness. Our frame of mind and the quality of those around us will affect our vision. And depending on the degree to which we see progression in our lives we are more or less convinced of its journeying quality. To the extent that we are capable of recognizing disparity between framework and experience, empirical fit and scope of interpretation remain meaningful concepts in the verification process.[46]

There is simply no way to verify the first stage of religious conviction as a "true" picture of "reality." Logically, first principles cannot be grounded on prior principles. The *archai* or topics must necessarily precede the introduction of reasoning on their basis. All knowledge commences with the *ingenium*, with the catching sight of similarities and making of them the basis of further discussion. One may see this moment in terms both of discovery and creation of similarity.[47] In the sphere of religion, the language of disclosure rather than discovery may be dominant. Epiphany, rather than creative genius is assumed. Thus the theologian who would justify the symbols at hand from an ontological point of view, even while maintaining their tentative status, insists that there are situations where the divine somehow disclosed itself authentically even though it may disclose itself again in other different situations. Theologians like Ian Ramsey see God's self-disclosure occurring in ways which are continuous with what is believed to be the natural metaphorical process of connection between two events: in this case a

---

[46] The observation of James and others that something about our temperament inclines us to construe matters in particular ways needs also to be taken seriously; however, I would argue that we are not entirely slaves to our own organisms. There is a degree to which people's personalities are molded by the intellectual directions that they take, in addition to the latter being shaped by the former.

[47] Even in the sphere of science, these initial stages continue to resist tidy description: "Throughout the history of philosophy and science scholars have attempted to conceptualize the creative inference process: inductive intuition (Carnap, 1956), abduction (the generation of hypotheses; Pierce, 1903), apodictic judgment (Brentano, 1874), reflective judgment (Kant, 1790). They have tried to describe where rationally justifiable metaphors come from: a 'flash of insight', an 'associative leap', the 'click of comprehension', the 'recognition of similarity', the 'perception of a resemblance', the use of 'intuitive heuristics', and it has been said that inferences and analogies simply 'come to mind'. Haskell . . . put it best: 'Living reason is a Möbius strip where the surface of metaphor turns into the edge of logic'" (Robert R. Hoffman, "Some Implications of Metaphor for Philosophy and Psychology of Science," in Wolf Paprotté and René Dirven, eds., *The Ubiquity of Metaphor: Metaphor in Language and Thought* (Amsterdam: Benjamins, 1985) 362. See also idem, "Metaphor in Science," in Richard P. Honeck and Robert R. Hoffman, eds., *Cognition and Figurative Language* (Hilldsdale NJ: Erlbaum Associates, 1980).

spiritual phenomenon and an appropriate material circumstance. Ramsey introduces a number of categories for judging the acceptableness of models—simplicity, coherence, comprehensiveness, consistency, empirical fit[48]— but says that the actual objective reference of the models is guaranteed because the object declares its objectivity by actively confronting us: "[T]heology...is founded in occasions of insight and disclosure when...the universe declares itself in a particular way around some group of events which thus takes on cosmic significance."[49] What this means, for example, is that "The aptness of messiah and logos models to Jesus is seen in a moment of insight."[50] Truth is located to a high degree in the moment of religious experience, in what is believed to be a divinely guided confluence of religious insight and mode of expression. Any area of life may serve as an appropriate vehicle because all things participate in Being and thus may serve to illustrate its nature.

This kind of initial appeal to "disclosure" is, I believe, inevitable in all religious discourse.[51] Given that there is a certain irreducibility about the initial stages of thought, however, there has to be discussion of their significance. What this means can only be drawn out with reference to their relation to other perceived truths and to their adequacy to the evidence. The theologian who puts a strong premium on the moment of experience has to exercise great care in laying out how one distinguishes real moments of disclosure from misguided ones and needs to consider carefully what evidence if any would lead to its abandonment. Fundamental metaphysical interpretations can never be criticized *in toto*, because we have no place beyond the world wherefrom to judge. Even so, they do draw their convincingness from the way that they fit with experience, and as has been shown some degree of verification does take place.

As far as Ramsey's moments of disclosure go, it remains to decide the question of whether the model at hand in the moment of disclosure has permanent validity, or whether the truth content of the moment of disclosure

---

[48] Ramsey, *Models for Divine Activity*, 62.

[49] Ramsey, *Models and Mystery*, 58.

[50] Ibid., 16. Ramsey explains this kind of process in the following terms, "there are . . . certain situations in which we find ourselves, certain situations of a cosmic character, which in virtue of some feature or other echo, chime in with, are isomorphous with other situations in which we speak, for example, of strong towers, of kingship, of fathers and son, and the two together, because of the common feature, generate insight" (ibid.).

[51] Even in constructive theologies this is acknowledged. In the absence of correspondence modes of establishing the truth of claims about God, "appeal must be made to the intuitive or self-evident plausibility of the 'root-metaphors' on the basis of which the principal metaphysical or theological concepts have been constructed" (Kaufman, *Theological Imagination*, 255).

may be linked with a new analogy in a new time. Did God choose to reveal Godself at a particular time in particular figures because God thought they were especially apt? How does one decide what is to be restated?

Practically Speaking, a Foolish Task?

Some have wondered whether, in trying to inject greater rationality and self-consciousness into the tradition, theologians may not be sawing off the branch upon which they sit—whether the life blood of an active piety may actually be the kind of unreflective naive realism which is simultaneously its bane. In moving to more rationalistic modes of discourse, are theologians moving away from religion in its traditional form and ceasing to be helpful to the traditional reader?

Once one abandons the idea of a picturing, literalized notion of the human-divine relationship, some might argue, one has let go of the average person's notion of what it means to think, say, of God as really Lord and humans as really stewards:

> [T]he noetic quality of religious experience in theistic traditions is closer to the force of ordinary perception than it is to the power of fiction. To experience God or his providential activity is not, from the subject's point of view, to entertain a possible world in which there is a God and he governs events in the world, nor is it to entertain a concept that permits one to externalize certain hopes and fears by projecting them onto another plane. One might suspect that the proper explanation of religious belief and experience would be found along these lines, but it is not the account given by the believer. The experience has a noetic quality for the subject and is taken to reveal something about the world beyond the individual self. In this way, it is similar to the experience of actually skiing down a slope, as contrasted with that of thinking about skiing down a slope.[52]

The example of the ski slope is perhaps a little odd, but the distinction he draws needs to be taken seriously. William James writes in the *Varieties* of the "habitual" and "chronic" sense that many believers have of God's presence. He takes a number of examples from Starbuck's manuscript collection, saying of the first that "probably thousands of unpretending Christians would write an almost identical account."[53] The passages speak of the people's overwhelming sense of divine presence and guidance. James comments:

---

[52] Proudfoot, *Religious Experience*, 215.
[53] James, *Varieties*, 72.

Such is the human ontological imagination, and such is the convincingness of what it brings to birth. Unpicturable beings are realized, and realized with an intensity almost like that of an hallucination. They determine our vital attitude as decisively as the vital attitude of lovers is determined by the habitual sense, by which each is haunted, of the other being in the world. . . .

[T]hese feelings of reality . . . are as convincing to those who have them as any direct sensible experience can be, and they are, as a rule, much more convincing than results established by mere logic ever are. . . . [I]f you do have them, and have them at all strongly, the probability is that you cannot help regarding them as genuine perceptions of truth, as revelations of a kind of reality which no adverse argument, however answerable by you in words, can expel from your belief.[54]

In this kind of awareness, images of God as Father, for example, may be realized to have their bounds, but they are lived with as if they were as truly informative as descriptions of visible things. We need to look carefully at these kind of claims and decide how to respond. Are these characterizations of the way that "real" believers think really accurate, and if they are, what does this mean for the theologian?

First of all, I think one must acknowledge that for the vast majority of practicing Christians, the biblical language of God does indeed have a less provisional or tensive quality than the epistemologically fastidious and those with supposedly broader or deeper insight might wish. Even the triple decker cosmos that Bultmann declared dead is clearly alive in some quarters; as Jaspers remarked, "Surely you do not think that the vivid images of an upper and a lower region, of nearness and distance, have become obsolete . . . that they have lost all meaning?"[55] But what does this mean for the theologian whose works may be read by such people.

Faith development theories present an interesting angle on the issue. James Fowler says straightforwardly that most people remain (he is careful not to use language like "get stuck") at stages where they are unable to "see beyond" their symbols, to see the universal in the particular.[56] They retain a mythic/literal mode of understanding religious symbols. Now, Fowler and others are extremely careful to disavow any claims that one stage is "better" than another, or that everyone goes through them the same way. I do not want to debate this issue. What should give the theologian pause for thought is the remembrance that he or she writes as a very peculiar case—as the product of a seminary education which has served to speed up artificially the

[54] Ibid., 73.

[55] Karl Jaspers, "The Issues Clarified," in Bartsch, *Kerygma*, 86.

[56] On these points, see James W. Fowler, *Stages of Faith: The Psychology of Human Development and the Quest for Meaning* (San Francisco: Harper & Row, 1981) esp. 135–83.

process of developing from a mythic/literal perspective to a symbolic understanding of religion—and that she or he is now trying to set others out on this journey.

Two things should concern us here. Firstly, is it "better" to be a non-naive believer? If setting out to rouse people from unreflective naive faith, the theologian must surely have a conviction that it is better. Why might it be better? Various kinds of arguments might be presented. One might be that God created us with reasoning minds and must therefore clearly intend us to use them: faith necessarily seeks understanding and this process has no limits. Another might be that uninformed literalistic believers behave in ways that jeopardize our world; they must be reeducated. A third might be that a more self-conscious faith will make one happier or more moral. The second and third reasons are essentially pragmatic, even though the grounds of both may be truly biblical in that God desires the best for all God's creation.

The first contention has no adequate rebuttal except appeal to the corruption of the reason whose existence is being appealed to as a mandate for enquiry. With regard to the third, some might dispute the contention that greater knowledge will bring greater happiness or morality. Is it a loving and responsible thing to try and move all people "beyond" mythic or literal understandings to what may be potentially a more arid form of faith? Or indeed no faith? It is a noticeable fact that seminary makes most people miserable as they suffer the dissection of their naive faith and then struggle to attain the position Ricouer has called a second naïveté. Most lay people do not have the years and the teachers and the libraries that are necessary to piece together an avowedly more sophisticated or developed understanding of the symbols of their tradition. The matter is a sensitive one. On the one hand theologians write as if the mature, reasoning person is mandated to consider the status of their symbols and to come to a thorough understanding of their function. On the other hand, they must surely be aware that this kind of activity is for a lucky (?) elite who have the wherewithal to engage in the higher levels of (academic) gnosis of our day. Given this situation, should they encourage the clergy to try to bring all their flocks to this more reasonable form of faith? Or should they run the risk of being patronizing, addressing only their peers, on the assumption that as Max Weber, for example implies, the masses need simpler brands of faith?[57] It is a thorny question. Many modern writers tend to assume that what is good is good for all. It is undemocratic and deeply patronizing to assume that people have differing intellects, talents and capacities, and to set out to teach them accordingly, so

[57] Weber, *The Sociology of Religion* (rev. Johannes Winckelmann; 4th ed.; Boston: Beacon, 1964) 102–4; 125–27; 244.

one must instead set out to direct the same message to the world *in toto*. There is a bracing honesty to this, and yet it may be one that overlooks the reality (to which the churches have always adapted their teachings) of people's differing temperaments, intellectual capacities, and needs.

One might draw another conclusion from the fact that millions of Christians persist with thought patterns that liberal theologians view as inadequate. Does it mean that because the former are in the majority, they have the last word, and the theologian should shut up? One does sometimes feel that this is where discussions like Proudfoot's may be going. Nobody loves a liberal theologian: she or he is neither fish, flesh nor fowl—juggling metaphysical and epistemological categories culled from secular philosophies with biblical and traditional concepts from his or her religious heritage, trying to satisfy two audiences whose demands and needs are usually very unlike if not flatly opposed. How can you conceivably make a case for the truth status of symbols that will satisfy both a Nelson Goodman and a middle-of-the-road parishioner or congregant?

It would be fascinating to find a survey of who are the readers of liberal and radical theologies. One suspects that they are a relatively small group of people who sustain an uneasy blend of traditional piety and free thought, remaining gripped by the idea that reason and the religion of their youth (still dear to their hearts) will one day be revealed to be compatible, that respectable grounds will be found for belief in God. Whoever they are, they do not seem to fit the same bill as the people described by Proudfoot. Perhaps to the statement that no one loves a liberal theologian, one should add the statement that few love liberal Christians in general. They seem wishy washy. They are neither "properly religious" nor "properly philosophical." Categorizers hate them. It is this kind of categorizer that would, I think, have the theologian shut up. Religion should be clear cut. True religion is the religion of the simple peasant. Tolstoy, Graham Greene, Ignazio Silone—how used we are to sentimental appreciations of simple literalistic piety—usually of peasants.[58] The theologian should take her hands off. She is a tiresome citified sophisticate who would lead the faithful astray. Even her good intentions are suspect.

But numbers are not everything, and complexity should not be ruled out of court simply because it is troublesome. The theologian and the pastor have to make an initial decision about to whom they will address their teaching. They must ask themselves initially, Is it better to allow people to hold whatever faith they have without complicating it, lest by tinkering with it you

---

[58] Weber (*Sociology*, 83) comments "that the peasant has become the distinctive prototype of the pious man who is pleasing to god is a thoroughly modern phenomenon."

destroy it? Or should one speak for the world to hear and do as it will?

If one decides to speak as one will, the question becomes in part a practical one of who will hear and respond and whether one's proposals are likely to bear fruit. One of the biggest questions concerning proposals for reinterpretation of our symbols, and for additions to them concerns the *feasibility* of this. We are up against a number of obstacles. One of these is what Santayana spoke of as loyalty to our sources of being. Piety, says Kenneth Burke, building on Santayana's work, is precisely this loyalty. Reorganization of one's orientations from the past has an *impious* aspect.[59] People are aware that any new way of construing the character of events is an attempt to "convert" them in a real way.[60] We are deeply resistant to change, especially when it relates to patterns of interpretation and behaviour of long-standing. Franz Boas observed that in modern societies there is an undoubted tendency to eliminate traditional elements and to think with increasing logic about one's surroundings.[61] He noted that "in our civilization ... many actions are performed merely as means to a rational end. They do not enter sufficiently deeply into our minds to establish connections that would give them emotional values; hence our readiness to change."[62] "We recognize, however," he says:

> that we cannot remodel, without serious emotional resistance, any of the fundamental lines of thought and action which are determined by our early education, and which form the subconscious basis of all our activities.[63]

At the more sophisticated level of explanation which our modern psychological theories provide, we are the products to a high degree of early experiences which shaped our psyches for better or worse. At the level of common sense, this means what every parent and teacher knows, that what you teach children well will stay with them all their lives.

From the point of view of suggesting new images for God and of relating to God, this surely means that the images will take a long time to take root. They will be met with resistance by those whose lives are deeply informed by a cluster of other images which they believe to be exhaustive, and they will be hard even for those for whom they are meaningful to actually absorb into their prayers. Some, such as Maurice Wiles, have gone so far as to suggest

[59] Burke, *Permanence and Change*, 80.

[60] Ibid., 86–87. Burke (p. 154) makes the interesting comment that evangelization may be seen as motivated by guilt at having changed one's allegiances.

[61] Boas, *Mind of Primitive Man*, 206.

[62] Ibid., 240.

[63] Ibid.

that because of these obstacles we should not even try to introduce new images:

> The primary source for the evocative language of worship cannot be found in the present; it is given in images that have established themselves over a long period of time and have come to fulfil a symbolic role within the life of the worshipping community. So worship has, and must have, a strongly traditional and conservative character about it.[64]

Wiles, despite his generally liberal brand of Christianity, takes our need for symbolic resonance as the dictating concern. "Imagery," he says,

> cannot be conjured up at will. We may call for it, but will it, any more than the spirits from the vasty deep, come when we do call? But we do not need to call, for it is there in the tradition. It is not always perfectly suited to our needs; but whatever its shortcomings on that score, there is always a substantial compensation in its traditional character.[65]

> [T]he dynamic character of human existence makes it inevitable that many a hymn or prayer will embody a theology or speak an idiom that few Christians today can conscientiously adopt as a natural expression of their own beliefs. That must be accepted as a necessary concomitant of the irreplacable role played by ancient tradition in the evocative function of worship. And once we do accept that, the way is open to enjoy that tradition as a whole, free from scrupulosity, as a powerful though imperfect medium of the grace of God.[66]

A very large dog is being wagged here by a small tail. Surely one generation's desire for ease of prayer cannot be used as an argument against adding to the traditional language?[67] We may have the awkwardness as well as the exhilaration of seeking new language, but the coming generations that grow up with them in their liturgies and books will be able to find in them the kind of consolation that comes from the familiar.[68]

---

[64] Wiles, *Faith and the Mystery*, 93.

[65] Ibid., 126.

[66] Ibid., 98.

[67] Wiles' stance brings to mind Durkheim's (*Elementary Forms*, 403) characterization of persons who continue to participate in the cult even when rejecting certain dogmas because they feel that if they began to pick and choose, they would fall into total confusion. Here it is well to remember the caution of Cupitt (*Crisis*, 120), quoted earlier, to the effect that choosing to stick with the traditional imagery of lord and servant etc., strongly suggests a conviction, however well masked, that these do speak most truly about the nature of God and world.

[68] A similar argument is put forward in a slightly different context by Regina Coll, "Challenging and Reclaiming Symbols," *Religious Education* 80 (1985) 379. She argues (p. 379) that we should stick with old symbols and rehabilitate them—it is easier because people have made a psychic investment in them, "[T]hey speak to memories and elicit an emotional response. They

A related but somewhat different argument against the establishment of new symbols arises from a different quarter. There are those who believe that each of the key ideas of Christianity is paralleled in other religions in some form; religions are repositories of *Völkergedanken* or universally occurring archetypes which, to use the language of the archmythologarch Joseph Campbell, "are biologically grounded and at once the motivating powers and connoted references of the historically conditioned metaphorical figures of mythology throughout the world."[69] Likewise, the key images that we have been studying may not be within our control to structure entirely to our liking because their contours are universal, and reflect perhaps archetypes of the collective human unconscious.[70] If this is the case, one may try all one wants to eradicate the image of the Christian soldier or the more belligerent questing pilgrim: they will not disappear since they are mythic crystallizations of a vital archtype; "the symbols of mythology are not manufactured; they cannot be ordered, invented, or permanently suppressed. They are spontaneous productions of the psyche, and each bears within it, undamaged, the germ power of its source."[71]

These kind of theories are notoriously difficult to substantiate. The central problem is that of whether the recurrent themes in a given culture or cultures are really biologically rooted or whether they are simply the product of "recurrent reactions of the human psyche to situations and stimuli of the same general order."[72] If they are the product of culture, they will gradually shift as a result of our efforts to change the culture around us, or in this case

---

provide a context . . . for the incorporation of newer insights." They can, she argues using Mary as an example, still have their meanings radically changed to suit the situation (pp. 379–81). This seems reasonable up to a point. We saw earlier, how authors do indeed use such images as the journey in radically different ways to put across different ideas. However, if the imagery should become strained to bursting point, it is surely time to consider new avenues.

[69] Campbell, *The Inner Reaches of Outer Space: Metaphor as Myth and Religion* (New York: Van Der Marck Editions, 1986) 19.

[70] References to this concept in Jung's work are too numerous to bear citation. A relatively clear account of the ideas is found in his essay on the "child archetype" in C. G. Jung and C. Kerényi, *Essays on a Science of Mythology: The Myth of the Divine Child and the Divine Maiden* (Bollingen Series 22; rev. ed.; New York: Harper & Row, 1963). One of the difficulties with the theory is that Jung oscillates between use of the term "archetype" to refer to an "organ" or "structure" of the psyche and to refer to inherited symbols such as that of the hero figure. For an overview of the strands of this area of his thought by a sympathetic follower, see Jolande Jacobi, *Complex/Archetype/Symbol in the Psychology of C.G. Jung* (1959; reprinted Princeton/Bollingen Paperbacks, 1971).

[71] Joseph Campbell, *The Hero with a Thousand Faces* (Bollingen Series 17; 2d ed.; 1968; reprinted Princeton/Bollingen Paperbacks, 1972) 4.

[72] Clyde Kluckhohn, "Recurrent Themes in Myths and Mythmaking," *Daedalus* 88 (1959) 268.

to change its religious dimension. Even so, the process of change will be slow.

Let us turn now from the problem of obstructions to that of difficulties of source. We are faced by another problem: that of fertile sources of new imagery for the Christian life. Boas spoke of how the actions that we carry out in our society today are frequently just means to ends and do not engender deep emotional attachment. There may also be another reason that many actions do not engender attachment. They are not simple. Not basic. Journeying, warring and competing, caring for the land, serving—these are all images drawn from the simplest functions. "The most pleasing metaphors," says Thomas Fitzosborne, "are those which are derived from the more frequent occurrences of art or nature, or the civil transactions and customs of mankind."[73] If a metaphor is going to be sustained and embracing it needs to be drawn from an activity which is both workaday and rich in potential parallels with the religious life, few new ones suggest themselves. I do not believe we will add many substantially new ones to those in existence— only perhaps those drawn from women's experiences of bearing, nurturing and raising children (a domain previously overlooked for the most part). It is easier to multiply names for God than to come up with new images for the religious life. There is even a problem with updating existent images. I remember reading and attempting to grade a student paper which told the tale of a pilgrim's progress by airplane. The gadgetry somehow intruded. It distracted from the progress. Susanne K. Langer wrote of the charged economy of the good symbol, giving as her example the ship "the image of precarious security in all-surrounding danger, of progress toward a goal, of adventure between two points of rest, with the near, if dormant, connotation of safe imprisonment in the hold, as in the womb."[74] It was her view that

> Human life in our age is so changed and diversified that people cannot share a few, historic, "charged" symbols that have about the same wealth of meaning for everybody. This loss of old universal symbols endangers our safe unconscious orientation. The new forms of our new order have not yet acquired that rich, confused, historic accretion of meanings that makes many familiar things "charged" symbols to which we seem to respond instinctively. For some future generation, an aeroplane may be a more powerful symbol than a ship. . . . Poetic simile, not spontaneous metaphor, is its status as yet.[75]

[73] Fitzosborne, *The Letters of Thomas Fitzosborne on Several Subjects* (7th ed.; London: Dodsley, 1769) 109–10.

[74] Langer, *Philosophy in a New Key: A Study in the Symbolism of Reason, Rite, and Art* (Cambridge: Harvard University Press, 1942) 285.

[75] Ibid., 287–88.

This is perhaps why the airborne pilgrim failed to move me. Again, however, it is only by beginning new traditions of symbolization that one opens up the possibility for change.

10

Concluding Thoughts

This thesis has looked in detail at particular images and at the way that they are employed by the kinds of writers who have, perhaps, the greatest influence on lay Christians in North America and Great Britain. The studies of the individual metaphors disclosed, I hope, the diversity of ways that each can be and has been developed, and the ways that each can operate quite differently depending upon the author's interests and political persuasions. It is important for those working in the area of "metaphorical theology," and for others discussing symbol in theology to acknowledge this openness of metaphors to divergent treatments. Too many variables enter in to allow one to issue flat statements about the perennial acceptableness or unacceptableness of a given metaphor. Even where one would expect the logical constraints of the metaphor to shape the resultant theological discourse in a predictable manner, we have seen that this need not be so. The writer may twist the metaphor to fit his or her needs: witness John Timmerman's altering of the Pruner and the Vine image to allow him to inject greater room for human agency.

What becomes clear as one looks at the material is that servanthood, stewardship, warfare and pilgrimage appear more foundational than the other images. They offer a fuller picture of the nature of the theological cosmos, being perhaps more closely linked to or rooted in the basic mythic narratives of the tradition. They also tend to offer the possibility of more extensive discussion of all facets of the religious life.

As noted throughout, moral guidance of a specific variety does not arise automatically from the metaphors. They speak to disposition, and perhaps to the virtues, but it is for the individual writer—drawing on the various sources of Christian ethical reflection—to develop their exact ethical implications. Again, it is important for those whose theological interest is focused upon metaphor and image to recognize this limit. No more than narratives and stories, do metaphors give rise to clear moral mandates. The "ought" comes no more easily from the "is" than in any other mode of theological discourse.

The great strength of the kind of metaphorical popular theologies examined in this thesis, is their use of the cornerstone of traditional image in the edifice of their theology. The moment the reader opens their pages he or she is in the realm of the familiar and consoling. Because of this fact, some of the works which develop the images uncritically may compound escapist tendencies and feed tendencies toward Christian triumphalism. But others use the starting point of the familiar and the pleasing elaboration of likenesses between the spiritual and physical (metaphorical) domain to develop new and more complex lines of thought and to lead their readers gently down new avenues of Christian reflection. Even for the trained theologian, this approach is a refreshing change.

Reading the materials one becomes personally aware of the strong call of traditional images. Even those of which one intellectually disapproves to some degree have the quality of old acquaintances—they have been with one since childhood and call forth an echo from the deepest levels of memory. One may be more drawn to them than to potentially appropriate but less familiar imagery. I found this particularly with the imagery of the Christian soldier. For these reasons, and for those other reasons discussed in this last chapter, it is hard to be optimistic about the chances of bringing about rapid change in the area of symbolization of the Christian life.

Don Cupitt has asked whether the demand for a new body of fundamental images may not really be a demand for a new religion.[1] I am inclined to think that it is. Studying the key images of the Christian life makes one aware of the degree to which they *are* the religion; there is no separate truth which can be repackaged in more acceptable raiment. To evaluate the theological import of the images and to propose changes and additions is to evaluate Christianity itself. If one's criteria for evaluation are drawn primarily from the secular sphere (no matter how much the values of that sphere may be traced back to a Christian heritage), if they are not primarily informed by the biblical pictures of *Christ*, they are not first and foremost Christian in the way that I understand that term. I have no wish to call others Christian or non-Christian on these grounds, but I think that my own standpoint of evaluation might well be said to be that of a person on the way to a

---

[1] Cupitt, *Crisis*, 121.

form of faith which departs significantly from most forms of Christianity that I have encountered. This recognition is the cause of anxiety at one level. At another it is not. Justin Martyr wrote that Christ is the Reason of which every race of humans partakes.[2] In ways that we cannot understand, Christ holds together all forms and products of human reason (and worthy human action). If one tries to live honestly, pursuing forms of thought and action that one sees as right, one cannot depart from this Christ. The study of one's inherited tradition, and the proposal of change where need is seen, is a necessary part of the search for the authentic, for the firm foundations of a life to be lived lovingly and well.

> Finally, brothers and sisters, whatever is true, whatever is honorable, whatever is just, whatever is pure, whatever is lovely, whatever is gracious, if there is any excellence, if there is anything worthy of praise, think about these things. (Phil 4:8)[3]

---

[2] "The First Apology of Justin," *Early Christian Fathers* (ed. Cyril R. Richardson; LCC 1; New York: Macmillan, 1970) 272.

[3] RSV with "brethren" amended to "brothers and sisters."